Prevention

FIBER UP
SLIM DOWN
COOKBOOK

Prevention.

FIBER UP
SLIM DOWN
COOKBOOK

A FOUR-WEEK PLAN TO CUT CRAVINGS
AND LOSE WEIGHT

By the Editors of America's
Leading Healthy Lifestyle Magazine

RODALE

Direct and trade editions are both being published in 2008.

Rodale books may be purchased for business or promotional use or for special sales. For information, please write to: Special Markets Department, Rodale Inc., 733 Third Avenue, New York, NY 10017

Prevention is a registered trademark of Rodale Inc.

Printed in the United States of America
Rodale Inc. makes every effort to use acid-free ∞, recycled paper ♲.

Interior photographs © Photo Alto, pages vi, ix, and x
Photographs by Mitch Mandell/Rodale Images
Book design by Carol Angstadt

Library of Congress Cataloging-in-Publication Data

Prevention fiber up slim down cookbook : a four-week plan to cut cravings and lose weight / by the Editors of America's Leading Healthy Lifestyle Magazine.
    p.   cm.
Includes index.
ISBN-13 978–1–59486–800–9   hardcover
ISBN-10 1–59486–800–X   hardcover
ISBN-13 978–1–59486–801–6   paperback
ISBN-10 1–59486–801–8   paperback
    1. High-fiber diet—Recipes. 2. Reducing diets—Recipes. I. Prevention (Emmaus, Pa.)   II. Title: Fiber up slim down cookbook.
RM237.6.P74   2008
641.5'63—dc22   2008005503

Distributed to the trade by Macmillan

2   4   6   8   10   9   7   5   3   1   hardcover
2   4   6   8   10   9   7   5   3   paperback

RODALE
LIVE YOUR WHOLE LIFE™

We inspire and enable people to improve their lives and the world around them
For more of our products visit **rodalestore.com** or call 800-848-4735

CONTENTS

INTRODUCTION

Welcome to *Fiber Up Slim Down Cookbook*! You're about to embark on a wonderful new journey to a new, slimmer, and healthier you. And I think you'll be delighted to find that path is also going to involve a lot of great-tasting food. But before we get started, let's talk a bit about fiber. I know, I know, that probably sounds like your cue to close this book, but don't. If you do, you'll be missing out on one of the easiest and healthiest ways to get slim—and stay that way for life.

You probably know that fiber can be filling. But did you know that it can actually dampen your cravings for fattening foods, or that it may help block absorption of calories? But that's not all. Research shows that getting the right amount of dietary fiber can have profound health benefits as well. Plenty of studies, for example, tie fiber to a reduced risk of heart disease, type 2 diabetes, high blood pressure, and breast and colon cancers.

If you've been told by your doctor to eat more fiber to lose weight or otherwise improve your health, you've probably made the common mistake of overdoing it. You jump on board with the best intentions and start working in fiber-packed foods—and even supplements—at every opportunity. And if you're like most people, you probably ended up with a lot of gastrointestinal issues and the very firm belief that a high-fiber diet is boring and flavorless. This cookbook is going to change your thinking. It's based on a plan that gradually increases your fiber intake meal by meal, so you can follow doctor's orders without throwing your digestive system into a tailspin.

Here's how it works. For the next 4 weeks, you'll focus on boosting the fiber content at a different mealtime each week. Naturally, we'll start with breakfast in week one since it's such an easy meal to make over, and the benefits of a healthy serving of fiber are most noticeable throughout the day. The next week we'll concentrate on snacks—yes, you read that right. Snacks are actually an important feature of this diet because the right amount of fiber can play a major role in keeping your appetite in check. Week three is devoted to salads, sandwiches, and soups, many of which are portable and perfect for lunchtime meals. We save dinner for the last week because it's one of the most challenging meals for most of us to change, especially if you're cooking for family members, like to eat out, or find yourself relying on takeout too often due to a busy schedule. However, after 3 weeks of gradually fiber-izing your meals, I predict you'll be much better prepared to serve a healthy meal at the end of the day.

Of course, each week you'll also find dozens of delicious new recipes and plenty of tips to help make the transition even easier. And you'll get the incredible health and weight loss benefits of fiber without having to count calories, carbohydrates, or glycemic index (GI) values. At the end of 4 weeks, your body will be completely adjusted to your new high-fiber lifestyle, and you can follow our delicious high-fiber menu plan to keep losing up to 2 pounds a week.

As we all know, for any weight loss plan to work, the food has to taste great. Why else would you want to stay on it? And when it comes to delicious recipes, this is where *Prevention* shines. Each recipe was carefully developed and tested to put flavor first. You'll find dozens of tasty new favorites like Curried Beef with Pineapple, Coconut, and Brown Basmati Rice (page 204) or Tuscan-Style Stuffed Peppers (page 207) that features a delicious fiber-rich mix of brown rice and golden raisins.

And if you're feeding a household, you'll be glad to know there's no need to cook separate meals. This book is full of delicious family-friendly foods like Roasted Sweet and Russet Potato Salad (page 156) and Mom's Turkey Meatloaf with a ketchup glaze (page 200). Best of all, we've found plenty of great ways to sneak some fiber into snacks and sweet treats, too. You won't believe how we were even able to get fiber into desserts like Ginger–Sweet Potato Cheesecake. (Hint: It's in the crust; see the recipe on page 287!) Look for that recipe in the bonus chapter we created for those special occasions when you want to enjoy your success. Once you have the power of fiber on your side, there are sure to be plenty of good things to celebrate.

Here's to the new you!

L. Vaccariello

Liz Vaccariello

CHAPTER 1

GET READY TO LOSE

As any good diet expert will tell you, the basic rule of weight loss is blissfully straight-forward. To lose weight, the calories going out must be greater than the calories coming in. In other words, eat less + move more = a lower number on the scale. Sure sounds simple.

Unfortunately, the reality is not quite so easy. Ask anyone who has tried to lose weight by eating less—less sugar, less bread, less fatty cuts of meat, less pork rinds, less cola, less wine, less of anything—and they'll tell you about another weight-loss formula that goes something like this: thinking about eating less of (fill in the blank) = craving more of (fill in the blank) + overeating more of (fill in the blank) = a higher number on the scale.

Fortunately, there's a better way—a much better way—to approach any weight-loss challenge. Basically, if you eat *more* of the *slimming* foods, it's pretty easy to automatically eat *less* of the *fattening* foods. Now that type of rule *is* as simple as it sounds.

You probably already have a good picture of what fattening foods look like, but let's review them here, just in case: processed junk foods that are high in sodium and sugar, foods that contain the sweetener high fructose corn syrup, fried and fatty foods, and foods that contain trans fats, among others. That's a long list, and the thought of cutting back on any or all of them might seem overwhelming. So for the moment, forget about all of those foods for now. All of them.

Instead, let's talk about the slimming foods, because these are the foods you'll have the pleasure of focusing on during the next 4 weeks with *Prevention Fiber Up Slim Down Cookbook*. The dishes you'll find here were all carefully created to make sure they contain a very important slimming feature, and it's called fiber. In fact, by the end of this 4-week plan, you'll find that by *doubling* or *tripling* your consumption of this weight-loss wonder nutrient, you'll feel so satisfied, so full, and so content that you won't want the ice cream, cheese puffs, or doughnuts. You'll lose weight without trying.

Here's how it works. Because people tend to eat the same weight in food every day, and high-fiber, low-calorie foods like fruits and veggies weigh the same as high-calorie foods like cake and cookies, focusing on fiber will help you fill up on fewer calories. Losing weight this way is practically automatic. Plus, the strategy is relatively easy to follow because rather than focusing on foods you *can't* eat, you need only pay attention to what you must eat. By meeting a daily quota for a range of delicious, fiber-rich foods, you'll feel satisfied after your meals, have fewer cravings, and be able to enjoy every pound that you lose.

LOSE WEIGHT *WITHOUT* TRYING

New York City internist Keith Berkowitz, MD, has successfully used fiber to help his patients at the Center for Balanced Health lose weight and get healthy. He has counseled many patients who tried low-carb diets but whose weight loss stalled. "The diets should have been working, but they weren't," Dr. Berkowitz says. "When I suggested they increase their fiber

> **FIBER FACT**
>
> Women who eat fewer than 13 grams of fiber a day are five times as likely to be overweight as women who eat more fiber.

by consuming more low-calorie vegetables such as greens and broccoli, along with avocado—which is unusually high in fiber—they started losing and were able to reach their weight-loss goals." The fiber, he says, helped to improve digestion and fix underlying metabolic problems. In addition to weight loss, his patients experienced additional benefits.

Their cholesterol, blood pressure, blood sugar, and other heart disease risk factors improved. They felt more energetic, too. They felt less hungry—so much less hungry that they left food on their dinner plates. They couldn't finish their meals. They complained of feeling stuffed, yet the pounds were peeling off. Dr. Berkowitz was so impressed with the results that he went on to create high-fiber muffins and other foods and market them under the NexGen label.

Another weight-loss expert, Tracy Olgeaty Gensler, RD, MS, of Chevy Chase, Maryland, has also been recommending fiber to her clients. "When people eat more fiber-rich fruits, vegetables, and whole grains, they are able to fill up on fewer calories," she says. "Also, they don't tend to reach for sweets to fill them up."

Over the years, many dieters have reported similar experiences. When they eat more fiber, their hunger and cravings diminish, and they naturally find they can eat less. More important, they also claim to have more energy, better moods, and improved overall health.

PROVEN RESULTS

Dr. Berkowitz, Gensler, and hundreds of other health practitioners have been promoting fiber-rich diets because it appears these foods slow digestion, triggering a lasting sense of fullness. You don't have to take the health experts at their word, though. Many well-controlled medical studies have proven this fact as well.

During the early part of the millennium, three researchers from the Energy Metabolism Lab at Tufts University in Boston were curious. They wondered whether fiber really did live up to its reputation—whether it calmed hunger and cravings. After all, there were some people in the scientific community at that time who still doubted fiber's benefits.

So the Tufts researchers did some digging. They uncovered every study available about the connections between fiber consumption and weight regulation, and they added up the collective data. What they later published in the journal *Nutrition Reviews* has been quoted or cited in almost every academic article written about fiber since. The researchers determined that dieters who consumed more fiber did indeed feel more satisfied after meals, and they tended to feel less hungry for longer periods of time than people who consumed less fiber.

There's more. The Tufts researchers found that study participants who ate 14 additional grams of fiber a day—roughly double what they had been eating—automatically consumed 10 percent fewer daily calories, without trying. They weren't dieting. They weren't following a calorie-controlled menu plan. They weren't watching their portions. They weren't really trying to lose weight. The extra fiber filled them up, so they ate less automatically.

So, what does 10 percent add up to in real weight loss? Let's crunch the numbers. For someone eating 2,000 calories a day, that totals 200 fewer daily calories. Eat 200 fewer calories a day and you can expect to lose a third of a pound a week, or a pound every 3 weeks. That may not seem dramatic, especially when some diets promise you can drop 10 pounds in 1 week. But it's painless, and, perhaps for the first time in your weight-loss career, you'll feel satisfied after every meal.

> **FIBER FACT**
>
> Obesity is rare in populations that consume a lot of fiber. But it's prevalent in the United States, where most people consume only a half or a third of the fiber that experts recommend they eat.

More important, fiber helps you stick with other nutritional changes that enable weight loss. If you combine a high-fiber diet with reasonable amounts of exercise and portion control, as the menu plan in Chapter 9 recommends, you can expect to lose up to 2 pounds a week.

HOW FIBER WORKS

How does fiber enable you to automatically eat less? Physiologically, fiber works its magic in many different ways. To see how, let's take a quick tour of the digestive process, starting with the mouth.

Mouth. Many low-fiber foods speed through the mouth with little to no chewing. You can send ice cream and pudding, for example, from spoon to stomach within seconds. If you chug a supersize cola, you can set yourself back 400 or more calories in minutes and still feel hungry. Not so with most fiber-rich foods. Broccoli, carrots, pumpkin seeds, apples, corn on the cob—these and other high-fiber foods require lots of chewing, which in turn slows the pace of eating and draws out the length of a meal. End result: You eat less. Slower eating provides extra time for a complex set of signals in the digestive tract to reach the brain and flip off your appetite switch. The extra chewing also creates more saliva and gastric juice. These fluids mix with food in your stomach, expanding its volume and weighing it down, triggering fullness.

A Short History of Fiber

Fiber, of course, isn't new. It's a natural part of virtually all plant life, so it's been around since the very first plants poked their way through prehistoric soil. But until the mid-1900s, most food scientists considered it nutritional garbage. After all, it was the stuff in plant foods that the body didn't use. Scientists considered this substance so meaningless, in fact, that they didn't bother to give it a name. Food manufacturers thought it was so worthless that they routinely *removed* it from the grains they used to produce the flour used to make pastas, breads, crackers, and other foods.

Conventional wisdom gradually changed in the 1950s as health experts realized that this seemingly worthless plant material might actually be very worthwhile, and they gave it a name: *fiber.* Since then, hundreds of studies have revealed that diets rich in high-fiber foods prevent and reverse your risk for just about every health condition, particularly the ones associated with excess weight.

Stomach. After chewing and chewing, your high-fiber meal lands in your stomach. Here, certain types of fiber mix with water, forming a thick and heavy gel. The heaviness tugs downward on the stomach, signaling nerves to send the "I'm full" signal to the brain. The gel also slows down food as it leaves the stomach and, obviously, the longer food stays in the stomach, the longer you feel satisfied after eating.

Small intestine. As slow-moving, high-fiber foods eventually leave the stomach and move into the small intestine, the body gets ready to send another series of "I'm full" messages to the brain through a chemical known as CCK (cholecystokinin). Foods high in fiber, particularly beans, seem to trigger CCK to rise sooner than do foods low in fiber, flipping off your hunger switch earlier in a meal.

And as if that weren't good enough, as high-fiber foods move through your small intestine, the fiber actually represents calories that don't get absorbed into the bloodstream. In some studies, high-fiber diets have been shown to cancel out up to 180 calories a day. That's enough to add up to an 18-pound weight loss over a year's time.

Bloodstream. Even though fiber is not absorbed into the blood, its presence in the digestive tract helps slow down the pace at which sugar enters the bloodstream. And when smaller, more manageable doses of sugar enter the bloodstream, the pancreas does not have to make as much insulin, a hormone needed to shuttle sugar into hungry muscle cells. Lower insulin levels, coupled with consistent blood sugar levels, add up to less hunger, fat storage, cravings, and fatigue.

> **FIBER FACT**
>
> High-fiber foods clean your teeth as you chew. As a result, people who consume more fiber tend to have less gum disease.

For all of these reasons and more, calorie for calorie, high-fiber foods induce more weight loss than low-fiber foods. This is why, for example, refined white bread is more fattening than whole grain bread even though both types of bread contain roughly the same number of calories per slice. You feel more satisfied after eating the fiber-rich whole grain bread than after eating the white, so you stop eating sooner and eat less later during the day. It's the fiber that makes the difference.

Now for the best fiber news yet. Adding more of it to your diet need not prevent you from ever leaving your kitchen again, and it need not relegate you to a lifetime of eating foods you don't particularly like. You can easily double or triple your consumption of this weight-loss wonder nutrient by choosing delicious and convenient high-fiber options such as bagged salad mix, precut veggies, and steam-in-a-bag products. Going high fiber often involves very simple switches, such as switching from white bread to whole wheat and white rice to brown. You need not give up the foods you love, and you can switch to a high-fiber lifestyle easily and quickly. Turn the page to find out how.

Test Your Fiber Quotient

So now that you know how powerful fiber can be as a weight-loss tool, it's a good idea to see how much fiber you're actually getting before you dive into the rest of this book. Do the following exercise now and again after following the 4-week plan; it will help you to see just how far you've come.

Here's what you need to do: During a typical day, carry a small notebook with you and use it to write down what and how much you eat. Keep track of serving sizes. For instance, don't just write down "breakfast cereal." Write "1 cup of whole grain breakfast cereal."

At the end of the day, count up the number of servings of vegetables, fruit, whole grains, beans, and nuts and seeds. Serving sizes are as follows:

- Vegetables: ½ cup cooked vegetables or 2 cups raw leafy greens
- Fruit: 1 piece of whole fruit or 1 cup berries or cubed melon
- Whole grain breads: half a bagel, 1 slice bread
- Whole grain cereal: 1 cup
- Whole grain pasta, rice, and other cooked grains: ½ cup
- Beans and legumes: ½ cup
- Whole nuts and seeds: ¼ cup
- Peanut butter: 2 tablespoons

Then multiply your vegetable servings by 3, your fruit by 4, your whole grains (refined grains don't count) by 3, beans and legumes by 6, and nuts and seeds by 3. Then add your answers together. Use the sample chart below to help you make these calculations.

Vegetable servings _____ × 3 =_____ grams

Fruit servings _____ × 4 =_____ grams

Whole grain servings _____ × 3 =_____ grams

Bean servings _____ × 6 =_____ grams

Nut servings _____ × 3 =_____ grams

Total: _____ grams

The total is an estimate of the number of grams of fiber you are currently eating. If you'd prefer to keep track of what you eat online, Prevention.com/fiber has a handy tool that tracks the foods you eat and helps you calculate your daily fiber and nutritional intake.

Once you've estimated your fiber intake, don't fret if it's really low, even if it's less than 10. You're hardly alone. In fact, about 96 percent of Americans fall short of the daily 25 to 37 grams of fiber needed to lose weight and boost health. And after all, that's what this plan is all about. No matter your starting point, you can rely on fiber to help you deliciously and conveniently start shedding pounds.

CHAPTER 2

THE FOODS TO CHOOSE

When you think of fiber, what comes to mind? Cardboard? Shoe tread? Grass? Twigs? Rabbit food? You aren't alone. Many people have described fiber using these terms—but it's hardly an accurate list.

In truth, the world of fiber also includes a wealth of sinfully delicious foods. Think dark chocolate. Think guacamole and hummus. Think about corn on the cob and popcorn, about raspberries and baked potatoes, about trail mix and sweet potato chips. The list of high-fiber foods can also include whole grain pancakes, waffles, and bread—even pizza, bean and beef chili, and sloppy joes.

Sounds a lot better, doesn't it? Indeed, fiber can taste as good as it is good for your waistline and your health. And with the plan in this book, you can enjoy an enormous range of flavors with every pound you lose.

To better understand the benefits fiber has to offer, let's begin with a quick overview. Basically, fiber is the tough material in plant foods that forms a protective skeleton to support the plant. You'll find it in the covering that surrounds a chickpea, the skin on an apple, the white pith around an orange, the seeds in a grapefruit or tomato, the firm sections of bok choy leaves, the pulpy interior of an apricot, or the hard covering on a grain of wheat. Our bodies lack the necessary enzymes to break down fiber, so it cannot be absorbed into the bloodstream like other nutrients.

When discussing fiber, it's important to understand that there are two main types, soluble and insoluble, and each has a very specific function in the body. Of course, there's no real need to memorize which foods contain each type of fiber because neither is better than the other. Likewise, there's no magic food that contains an ideal combination. So forget about piling on the wheat bran or hoarding the flax. Those fiber foods are obviously great, but for best results it's generally a good idea to enjoy a wide variety of foods rather than zeroing in on one or two stars. As a side benefit, the variety approach also ensures that you consume a variety of antioxidants, vitamins, and minerals needed for optimal health.

Soluble fiber = slow. If you want to remember the differences between fiber types, it may help to associate the word *soluble* with the word *slow*. That's exactly what it does in the GI tract. It slows everything down.

Soluble fiber got its name because it dissolves in water. In the stomach, fluids mix with soluble fiber in much the same way flour mixes with water to form cake batter or cookie dough. Some types of soluble fiber mix with water to form a particularly thick gel. The gel that these "viscous" fibers create binds to bile acids and other substances present in the digestive tract, slowing or altogether preventing their absorption into the body.

Benefits: Soluble fiber has been shown to slow digestion, slow blood sugar absorption, reduce blood sugar related cravings and fatigue, increase a sense of fullness after eating, reduce cholesterol, and soften stool so it's easier to pass.

Foods that contain soluble fiber: oats, peas, beans, apples, citrus, carrots, and barley

Insoluble fiber = incredible size. If you associate *slow* with *soluble*, think *incredible* with *insoluble*. This type of fiber absorbs water like a black hole absorbs light. As it does so, it puffs up, speeding your body's ability to eliminate it from your system.

Benefits: Insoluble fiber triggers a sense of fullness after eating, keeps you regular, and reduces constipation-related bloating.

Burn Fat Faster with Potatoes

Some amazing new research puts spuds squarely at the center of the latest weight-loss buzz, along with other unfairly maligned carbs like corn and rice. The reason: All these foods contain resistant starch, a unique kind of fiber you'll be hearing a lot more about.

Unlike some types of fiber, resistant starch gets fermented when it reaches the large intestines. This process creates beneficial fatty acids, including one called butyrate, which can block the body's ability to burn its preferred source of fuel, carbohydrates. When the liver is prevented from using carbs as fuel, the body turns to stored body fat instead.

If you think of carbs as fuel for the body, like gas to a car, butyrate essentially prevents some of the gas from getting into the tank, so your cells turn to fat as an alternative fuel source. One study found that replacing just 5.4 percent of total carbohydrate intake with resistant starch created a 20 percent to 30 percent increase in fat burning after a meal.

Foods that contain insoluble fiber: fruit skins, bran, whole wheat flour, nuts, and many vegetables

WHERE TO FIND FIBER

Meat might be chewy, but it doesn't house fiber. Only plant foods—vegetables, fruits, grains, beans and legumes, and nuts and seeds—have it. In the following pages, you'll read about these high-fiber food groups, along with *Prevention*'s recommendation for how often to include each of them in your diet. If you're just beginning to concentrate on fiber, don't allow the number of suggested servings to overwhelm you. Instead, ramp up slowly by making it a goal to reach the suggested amounts in 4 weeks (not tomorrow morning). Go to Prevention.com/fiber, for even more information about the amount of fiber in common grocery store foods.

Your Daily Vegetable Goal: 3+ Servings

Vegetables are your ultimate weight-loss companions. Low in calories and rich in antioxidants and other nutrients, most vegetables provide a vital combination of fiber and water that helps trigger a sense of fullness. Consider three daily servings your absolute minimum, and strive for closer to seven. The following advice will help you reap the most fiber rewards from every bite.

Savor the skin. Forget peeling whenever feasible. For example, raw bell pepper has more fiber than the skinless roasted type. Whole tomatoes have more fiber than stewed, which have been skinned and seeded.

Go whole. Eat vegetables in their most whole form whenever possible. Cup for cup, fresh corn kernels will offer more fiber than an equal amount of corn muffins. Likewise, wheat berries (unprocessed wheat kernels) are better than wheat crackers, and brown rice is better than rice pudding.

Branch out beyond salads. Lettuce and other salad greens are great, but don't rely on them to supply all of your fiber. You'd have to eat 6 pounds of lettuce to get 30 grams of fiber in a day. "When I tell my patients with constipation or irritable bowel syndrome to consume more fiber, they often say, 'I eat lots of salad. I don't understand why I'm still constipated.' I have to explain that salad greens, cucumbers, and tomatoes are mostly water. It takes more than salad to get those fiber grams to add up," explains Katherine Sherif, MD, associate professor of medicine at Drexel University College of Medicine in Philadelphia and director of Drexel's Center for Women's Health.

Eat some of your vegetables raw. Raw vegetables require more chewing than cooked, and this chewing makes for slower eating, so you fill up on fewer calories. In a study from the University of Ulster in Coleraine, Ireland, women ate lunches that included different types of carrots. In one day's lunch, the carrots were raw. In another, they were pureed. In the last, they had carrot juice (which has no fiber). Women felt the most satisfied for a longer period of time when they consumed whole, raw carrots. Blended carrots came in second, even though they had nearly the same amount of fiber. The researchers determined that the crunchiness of the raw carrots helped turn down hunger.

The following veggies are all rich sources of fiber. Unless otherwise noted, the listed grams of fiber refer to a 1-cup serving.

FIBER VALUES OF COMMON VEGETABLES

VEGETABLE	FIBER	VEGETABLE	FIBER
Green peas	8.8 g	Cabbage, cooked	2.8 g
Pumpkin (canned)	7.1 g	Cauliflower	2.5 g
Acorn squash, cooked	6.4 g	Eggplant, cooked	2.5 g
Collard greens, cooked	5.3 g	Broccoli	2.4 g
Potato, medium, baked with skin	5 g	Spaghetti squash, cooked	2.2 g
Turnip greens, cooked	5 g	Carrot, 1 large	2 g
Spinach, cooked	4.3 g	Cherry tomatoes	1.8 g
Mustard greens, cooked	4.2 g	Squash, summer	1.2 g
Corn	4 g	Zucchini	1.2 g
Green beans	3.7 g	Lettuce, romaine	1 g
Swiss chard, cooked	3.7 g	Lettuce, iceberg	0.9 g
Asparagus, cooked	3.6 g	Lettuce, butterhead	0.6 g
Brussels sprouts	3.3 g	Lettuce, green leaf	0.5 g
Bell pepper	3.1 g	Lettuce, red leaf	0.3 g

Your Daily Fruit Goal: 2+ Servings

Like vegetables, fruits are loaded with plenty of fiber and water to weigh down your stomach and trigger a sense of fullness, all of which can make losing weight just a little easier. And it seems eating fruit has been associated with maintaining normal weight. At UCLA, for example, researchers have determined that people of normal weight eat, on average, two servings of fruit—for a total of 12 grams of fiber—a day, but overweight people have just one serving and 9 grams of fiber.

Also, because fruit provides a wealth of antioxidants, it is critical for fighting diseases associated with excess weight. A study done at the University of Navarra in Pamplona, Spain, found that women who lost weight on a diet comprised of 15 percent fruit (compared with a diet with only 5 percent fruit) reduced blood markers for free radical activity, dropping their overall risk of heart disease. The most colorful fruits tend to be richest in antioxidants. Think oranges, watermelon, and lemons.

To get the most fiber from your daily fruit servings, consider the following:

Favor whole fruit over fruit products. Apples, for example, contain more fiber than applesauce. And as with vegetables, don't forget to eat the skin, which is where most of the fiber resides.

Eat fresh or frozen fruit over canned. Most canned varieties have been skinned.

Choose fruit over fruit juice. Some fiber survives the trip through the strainer, but not much. A cup of apple juice, for example, contains 0.2 grams of fiber, whereas the apple offers you 5 grams. Prune juice gives you 2.6 grams, and fresh squeezed orange juice offers 0.5.

Don't pass over the pith. When eating oranges, tangerines, and other citrus fruits, eat the white pith. It contains most of the fiber.

The following fruits are all rich sources of fiber. Unless otherwise noted, the listed grams of fiber refer to a 1-cup serving or one piece of whole fruit.

FIBER VALUES OF COMMON FRUITS

FRUIT	FIBER	FRUIT	FIBER
Prunes	12.4 g	Strawberries, sliced	3.3 g
Avocado, cubed	10.1 g	Banana	3 g
Asian pear, large	9.9 g	Kiwifruit, large	2.7 g
Raspberries	8 g	Peach, large	2.6 g
Blackberries	7.6 g	Papaya, cubed	2.5 g
Pear, medium	5.5 g	Pineapple, diced	2.2 g
Apple, large	5.1 g	Grapefruit, half a fruit	2 g
Orange	4.4 g	Fig, 1 large fresh	1.9 g
Blueberries	3.6 g	Plum	0.9 g

Your Daily Whole Grains Goal: 3+ Servings

Grains come from grasses that produce edible seeds. These seeds—or grains—consist of three basic parts: a hard outer husk (called the bran), a starchy interior (called the endosperm), and an embryo (called the germ). When grains are refined, the tough, fiber-rich bran is removed, essentially stripping the grain of fiber and much of the vitamin E, B_6, magnesium, manganese, zinc, potassium, copper, folate, and protein that whole grains offer. And because there's not much fiber left to slow digestion, when you eat processed grains, your body essentially reacts as if you've just eaten sugar. Blood sugar levels rise rapidly, requiring the pancreas to overproduce insulin. This triggers fatigue, hunger, cravings, and fat storage.

It's easy to get confused when choosing whole grains. To pump up the fiber count, some processors are adding high amounts of processed fiber from wheat bran, corn bran, lentils, or peas to their prepared foods, such as breakfast cereals, bread, and pasta. Although these additives increase the fiber grams per serving, they don't offer the same complete package as true whole grains.

For example, a slice of whole grain bread may contain only 2 grams of fiber per slice, while a bran-enriched slice may contain as much as 8 grams. The whole grain option, however, may contain important disease-fighting phytonutrients that are absent in the supplemented bread. In the end, grains are an important food group because they offer valuable nutrients available only in whole foods *and* they're high in fiber. But remember, that doesn't mean you have to choose a bran product over a whole grain or vice versa. Both are good for you for different reasons.

So eat what you enjoy, and enjoy a variety of different grains and grain products. The following advice can help you get the most from your whole grain choices. Consult the Appendix for a list of recommended brands.

Stock up on whole grain pasta. It used to be that there was just one terrible-tasting whole grain pasta available. But now pasta manufacturers know we want better

---

FIBER FACT

A Canadian study of 34,000 men at McMaster University in Hamilton, Ontario, found that men who ate at least three servings of whole grains a day were 23 percent less likely to suffer tooth-loosening gum inflammation than those averaging less than one. Grains may protect gums by stabilizing blood sugar levels. High blood sugar levels have been linked with tooth decay and gum disease in people with diabetes.

whole grain food choices, so they've found some pretty ingenious ways to add fiber to their noodles. In addition to using whole wheat flour, they are also pumping up the fiber with lentils, chickpeas, and flaxseed. When flavor and texture are largely similar among whole grain versus added-fiber products, it's usually a good idea to go with whole foods over the more processed version. However, in general, these grain blends have a more pleasing texture than the 100 percent whole grain versions of years past, and they even have nutrients like omega-3 fatty acids not usually found in pure wheat pasta.

Sneak oatmeal into everything. Add it to cookies and meat loaf recipes, and eat it hot in the morning. Oats contain a special type of fiber called beta-glucan that has antimicrobial and antioxidant properties. When animals eat beta-glucan, they are less likely to get the flu, herpes, even anthrax. In people, it boosts immunity, speeds wound healing, and may improve the effectiveness of antibiotics. Oats are also rich in avenanthramide, an antioxidant that helps protect the heart.

Switch from white bread to whole grain bread. A slice of white bread contains 0.5 gram of fiber per slice, whereas a slice of whole grain bread generally offers four times that amount. Some power breads with added bran contain 5 grams or more per slice. When choosing bread, look for the words *whole wheat, whole wheat flour,* or another *"whole"* within the first few ingredients on the label. Each slice of bread should offer at least 2 grams of dietary fiber per serving.

Start the day with a high-fiber cereal. A serving of bran cereal offers double or even triple the amount of fiber in supplements. Mix one of these cereals with berries and you can get 15 to 20 grams of fiber—in just one meal. However, keep in mind that not all whole grain cereals are created equal; some offer much more fiber than others. Read labels and make sure there are at least 5 grams of fiber per serving. Cheerios, for example, contains only 3 grams of fiber per cup of cereal, whereas Fiber One offers 14 grams per half as much cereal.

Read labels carefully. Food manufacturers have become quite stealthy at making their products seem like they contain whole grains when they don't. A "multigrain" product, for example, may contain many types of grains, but all of these grains may be refined rather than whole. When purchasing food products made from bulgur, barley, couscous, rye, pumpernickel, and wheat, make sure the list of ingredients specifies "whole" in front of the type of grain. Oats and quinoa are an exception, as they are always whole. Also, look for the Whole Grains Council stamp on foods. If the stamp says "100 percent whole grains," that means all of the grains in the product are whole. If the stamp does not specify "100 percent," then nearly half of the grain may be refined.

The following grains are all rich sources of fiber. Unless otherwise noted, the listed grams of fiber refer to a 1-cup serving.

FIBER VALUES OF WHOLE GRAINS

WHOLE GRAIN	FIBER	WHOLE GRAIN	FIBER
Amaranth	18.1 g	Buckwheat groats, cooked	4.5 g
Whole wheat flour	14.6 g	Oats, cooked	4 g
Cereal, cold	5–14 g, depending on brand	Brown rice, cooked	3.5 g
Barley, cooked	13 g	Wild rice, cooked	3 g
Quinoa	10 g	Whole wheat bread, 1 slice	2.8 g
Pasta, whole grain, 2 ounces	4–9 g, depending on brand	Millet, cooked	2.3 g
Bulgur, cooked	8 g	Pumpernickel bread, 1 slice	1.7 g
Bread, 1 slice	2–5 g, depending on brand	Oat bran bread, 1 slice	1.4 g
Pita, 1 large whole wheat	4.7 g		

Your Weekly Beans/Legumes Goal: 3 Cups

On the menu plan in this book, you'll consume 3 cups of these fiber powerhouses a week, but most people get only 1 cup, at the most, which is a true shame because 1 cup contains as much as 17 grams of fiber. Just think, if you start your day with a cup of high-fiber cereal and include a half cup of beans at lunch and dinner, you'll nearly meet your daily fiber quota with just those foods alone.

Because beans contain both soluble and insoluble fiber, they are particularly effective at keeping a lid on hunger and cravings. They are also an excellent source of vitamins, minerals, and protein. A US Department of Agriculture study placed beans and legumes at the top of a list of flavonoid-rich foods. Flavonoids are a type of antioxidant thought to help fight heart disease and cancer. According to a review of studies done at Michigan State University, diets rich in beans and legumes were linked with a reduced risk of heart disease, diabetes, and several types of cancer. Use the following advice to increase your consumption of beans.

Start with a spread. Smash any type of bean up with some oil and water to make a tasty, high-fiber sandwich spread or dip for veggies, whole grain bread, and crackers. See Smoked Paprika Hummus with Broccoli and Red Pepper Dippers (page 78) and Instant Black Bean Dip (page 79) for inspiration.

Make them your secret ingredient. Chickpeas, black beans, and other beans are easy add-ins for salads. Try slipping some into your favorite soup, or eat them as a side dish or mixed with rice. See Cumin-Toasted Chickpeas (page 72) for inspiration.

Substitute in snacks. Order nachos or burritos with beans, rather than only with cheese. See Bite-Size Bean and Cheese Quesadillas (page 88) and Chipotle Bean Nachos (page 92) for inspiration.

The following types of beans are all rich in fiber. Unless otherwise noted, the fiber grams refer to a 1-cup serving.

> **FIBER FACT**
>
> The soluble fiber in soybean is known to lower cholesterol as effectively as statin drugs. While soybeans and tempeh, a soybean product, contain high amounts of fiber, other soy products, such as tofu and soy milk, do not because most of the fiber is removed during processing.

FIBER VALUES OF BEANS/LEGUMES

BEAN/LEGUME	FIBER	BEAN/LEGUME	FIBER
Navy beans	19.1 g	Chickpeas	12.5 g
Adzuki	16.8 g	Great northern beans	12.4 g
French beans	16.6 g	Chili with beans	11.3 g
Split peas	16.3 g	Kidney beans	11.3 g
Lentils	15.6 g	White beans	11.3 g
Mung beans	15.4 g	Soybeans	10.3 g
Pinto beans	15.4 g	Fava beans	9.2 g
Black beans	15 g	Black-eyed peas	8.9 g
Baked beans	13.9 g	Tempeh, 3 ounces	5 g
Refried beans	13.4 g	Miso, 1 ounce	1.8 g
Lima beans	13.2 g		

Your Weekly Nuts, Seeds, and Peanuts Goal: 4 to 5 Servings

Nuts and seeds provide a delicious and crunchy way to meet your fiber quota, and they are the perfect alternative to fiber-vacant, fattening snack chips. Don't worry about the high amounts of fat they contain. The fat in nuts has been shown to be good for your heart, so a well-measured serving is perfectly appropriate in a healthy eating plan. In studies, people who ate nuts five or more times a week were half as likely to suffer a heart attack as people who ate them less often. Nuts are also a rich source of the antioxidant vitamin E.

The following nuts, seeds, and peanuts (technically a legume) are all rich sources of fiber. For best quality, store all shelled nuts in the refrigerator to prevent rancidity. Unless otherwise noted, a serving equals 1 ounce.

FIBER VALUES OF COMMON LEGUMES

LEGUME	FIBER	LEGUME	FIBER
Almonds, about 23 whole kernels	3.3 g	Peanuts	2.3 g
Pistachios, 49 nuts	2.9 g	Brazil nuts, 6 kernels	2.1 g
Flaxseed, 1 tablespoon	2.8 g	Pumpkin seeds, 85 seeds	1.1 g
Hazelnuts (filberts), about 21 kernels	2.7 g	Sesame seeds, 1 tablespoon	1.1 g
Peanut butter, chunky style, 2 tablespoons	2.6 g	Cashews	0.9 g
Sunflower seeds	2.6 g	Walnuts, 1 tablespoon	0.5 g
Macadamia nuts, 10–12 nuts	2.4 g		

SURPRISING SOURCES OF FIBER

To meet your daily fiber goals, focus on consuming the recommended number of servings of vegetables, fruits, whole grains, beans and legumes, and nuts and seeds from the lists above. After all, those are the plant foods richest in fiber.

However, it's also true that every little bit of fiber helps, and there are actually a number of well-loved foods and beverages that offer small amounts that can help you reach your daily goal, too. Consider the following:

Coffee. For many years, food scientists assumed that coffee contained zero fiber—that is, until researchers in Madrid began to do some coffee experiments. As it turns out, the researchers were able to show that some coffee bean fiber does indeed make its way from bean to grounds to brew. Instant coffee contains the most, about 1.8 grams of soluble dietary fiber per cup. Espresso has 1.5 grams per cup, and filtered coffee has 1.1 grams. Coffee is also a rich source of antioxidant compounds called phenolics, which have been shown to be beneficial in controlling blood sugar, thereby reducing the risk of diabetes, among other diseases.

Chocolate. Chocolate comes from the cocoa plant, and the cocoa plant provides fiber. One ounce of chocolate candy contains just under 2 grams of fiber. A serving of chocolate-coated coffee beans gives you 3 grams. As a side benefit, chocolate may offer some heart protection. In a study done in Madrid, rats that consumed cocoa fiber had lower levels of total and LDL cholesterol.

Spices. Two teaspoons of any spice will get you between 1 and 2 grams of fiber closer to your goal. As a side benefit, some spices, most notably fennel, are known to ease the flatulence and bloating associated with high-fiber diets. Other spices that may ease digestive ills include cardamom, cayenne, cumin, and turmeric, especially when added to bean dishes.

NOT YOUR EVERYDAY CARDBOARD

Now that you've read the lists above, it should be easy to see that making over your diet to include more fiber can be a wonderfully satisfying and easy way to lose weight. After all, high-fiber foods are a delight to the senses, providing every texture that humans crave, including crunchy, chewy, and buttery soft. What's more, they offer a remarkable range of flavors, including many foods that are surprisingly tart, salty, or sweet.

Perhaps most important, learning how to boost your intake of these amazing foods doesn't have to be terribly complicated or time-consuming. In Chapter 3, you'll learn about a convenient step-up plan that will help you slowly ease yourself into high-fiber eating, one delicious meal at a time.

THE FIBER UP SLIM DOWN PLAN

So you're going to lose up to 2 pounds a week, and you're going to do it by filling up on delicious foods you love. You'll improve your health, energy, mood, and more, all with a wealth of mouthwatering foods like corn on the cob, guacamole, and pasta.

Could it possibly get any better? Yes, indeed, it can. This plan is fantastically simple, too. Rather than asking you to count fiber grams or overhaul everything you eat by tomorrow morning, you'll ease into high-fiber eating slowly and conveniently. By making easy food swaps—eating whole grain bread instead of white, for example, or bean dips instead of dairy-based dips—you'll automatically nudge your daily fiber grams into the weight-loss zone.

To get there, let's start by talking about your fiber destination. We need 25 to 37 grams of fiber a day to lose weight and boost health, but 96 percent of us fall short. According to a USDA study, most people get somewhere between 10 and 15 grams. And in fact, the more overweight you are, the less fiber you are probably eating. So to reach the weight-loss zone, you may need to double or triple your fiber intake. That doesn't mean, however, that you have to double or triple it overnight.

This plan will help you conveniently reach the 25-to-37-gram zone in two ways.

Slowly add on the grams. Each week of the plan, you'll up your fiber consumption by roughly 5 grams. By the end of the 4-week plan, that means you'll be consuming up to

20 more grams of fiber than you are today. These mini-increases will help reduce the most common side effects of high-fiber diets, including intestinal gas, abdominal bloating, and cramping. By increasing the fiber grams gradually over a period of a few weeks, you'll give the natural bacteria in your digestive system time to adjust to the change.

The small increases will also afford ample time to make the necessary adjustments to your lifestyle. After all, losing weight and keeping it off requires permanent eating habit changes. And while some people are able to make permanent changes by overhauling their diets over the course of 24 hours, most people best incorporate lasting changes more slowly.

Add fiber to one meal at a time. If someone asked you to eat more fiber all day long tomorrow, you might start to feel a little anxious. After all, you probably eat three to six times a day. It would take a lot of thinking and planning to figure out how to add fiber to each eating occasion.

That's why this plan breaks down the challenge meal by meal. Instead of worrying about getting to 25 to 37 grams by the end of the day, think about getting 5 to 10 grams during each meal and snack. Then, rather than worrying about all of your meals and snacks at once, start by thinking about the most important meal of all—breakfast. Once you master breakfast, focus on the next most important meal—snacks. Then lunch. Then dinner. By the time you're done, you'll have reached the weight-loss zone.

Let's take a look at how the plan works in a little more detail.

Week 1: If you don't currently eat breakfast, you'll start, even if you start with something small. By adding fiber to this morning meal, you'll turn down hunger and cravings for the rest of the day, so it will be easier to make over other meals in coming weeks.

Week 2: You'll add a high-fiber snack midafternoon. This will reduce the overwhelming hunger that often leads to second and third servings at dinner. It will also keep your energy up throughout the afternoon, so you can get more done.

Week 3: Now it's time to focus on lunch. Adding fiber to this meal will help to stabilize energy and mood during the afternoon, so you are less likely to go in search of a vending machine. It will also prevent overeating at dinner.

Week 4: Now you are ready for the meal most people overeat. We've put it last because dinner represents the meal that is hardest to change for most people. Thanks to the previous weeks' high-fiber eating, however, your dinner hour cravings for refined foods will already have subsided.

There you have it: a series of week-by-week, one-meal-at-a-time changes that make switching to the high-fiber lifestyle a completely painless proposition. Now, let's talk about part two of this plan. To lose weight and keep it off, you need to do more than just change the way you eat. You also need to change the way you move.

WALK OFF THE WEIGHT

Exercise goes with dieting as gasoline goes with automobiles. Neither works without the other. Of course, you may be thinking to yourself that this analogy is flawed because you can lose weight *without* exercise but a car can't go without gas. But consider this: If you lose weight without exercise, studies show that the weight you lose primarily comes from loss of muscle and bone. Because muscle is one of the main calorie-burning machines of the human body, this loss of muscle slows metabolism. End result: The only way to continually lose weight by eating less is by continually eating less. That's also why so many people regain the weight they lose.

Exercise, on the other hand, helps to preserve muscle and bone, so you lose the weight you want to lose: fat cell weight. Exercise also synergizes with healthful eating to reduce your risk of diseases associated with overweight, such as cancer, diabetes, and heart disease. Exercise may even help you to make your dietary changes permanent, as some research finds that people who exercise tend to switch over more easily to a healthier way of eating.

Exercise will also counter the gas-producing effect of some high-fiber foods, especially beans. Many obstetricians encourage women recovering from C-sections to get out of bed and pace the hallways, sometimes as soon as hours after surgery. They do this because anesthesia makes the intestines sluggish, causing gas to accumulate postsurgery. Walking and other forms of exercise tone the intestines, encouraging optimal function. Activity also provides gentle pressure, pushing the gas through the intestine and back out.

You can do any form of exercise you enjoy. Many people find walking one of the most convenient forms of exercise. You need no formal equipment other than a pair of sneakers.

FIBER FACT

A high-fiber diet may reduce the absorption of some types of medications, including certain antidepressants and diabetes medicines. It may also improve your health, reducing your need for some prescriptions, such as blood pressure or cholesterol-lowering medicines. Careful monitoring from your doctor will ensure that you are taking the right medicines in the right doses.

Whatever your fitness level, the following advice can help you to start and maintain a walking program to aid your weight-loss efforts.

Incorporate walking gradually. Start with 5 or 10 daily minutes of movement, increasing that time each week by about 5 to 10 minutes a session.

Count your steps. To encourage yourself to walk more often, get a pedometer, an inexpensive device that you wear on your waistband to count your steps. Wear it for a few days to get a baseline, then gradually increase the number of steps you take through lifestyle activities (taking the stairs, walking to your favorite lunch spot rather than driving, parking farther from the mall) and formal walks.

Chart new courses. Change the pace during longer walks. It will keep you motivated. Plus, constantly changing the pace improves calorie burning during your workout.

WHAT TO EXPECT FROM YOUR BODY

As you ease into high-fiber eating, you will experience a slew of side benefits. Your cravings for sugar and processed starch will diminish. Between-meal hunger will subside. Your midafternoon slump will evolve into an afternoon of productivity. Emotional eating will morph into an emotion-powered walk. You'll start reading the paper while sitting in a comfortable chair, rather than on the hopper. Your tight jeans will become your baggy jeans.

All of that said, you may experience a few temporary side effects from high-fiber eating. While bacteria in your digestive tract become acquainted with these new high-fiber foods, you may experience an unusually robust amount of gas and bloating for a few weeks. Your intestines are made of multiple feet of coiled, flexible, balloonlike tubing. When bacteria that line the intestinal wall ferment high-fiber foods, they produce gas. If this air gets stuck, it blows up the balloonlike intestine, making you bloated and uncomfortable.

To make your switch over to high-fiber living as trouble free as possible, keep the following advice in mind.

Follow the week-by-week plan. Don't try to speed your results by making wholesale changes in your eating habits. Stick with the gradual week-by-week increases described in detail in the chapters that follow. This slow step-up plan will allow your gastrointestinal tract to adjust to each small change. Over time, as more healthful types of bacteria flourish and stabilize, gas production and bloating will drop.

Eat food, not supplements. According to Gerard E. Mullin, MD, director of integrative GI nutrition services at Johns Hopkins Hospital in Baltimore, almost none of his patients who get fiber from real food experience GI distress. The GI tract, however, doesn't handle the pure soluble fiber in supplements as easily, he says. It may be that fiber in food comes in a complete package that eases its trip through the GI tract. For example, the oils in flaxseeds help to lubricate the lining of the intestines, allowing stool to slide through with more ease. Stool that stays on the move tends to result in less gas.

Drink more water. Fiber absorbs a lot of water in the GI tract. If it doesn't have enough water to absorb, the large mass of stool it creates can harden, causing constipation and gas. Unless you're the type of person who drinks lots of water, it's a good idea to double your fluid intake over the next 4 weeks. Women need at least 91 ounces of fluid, and men need 125 ounces a day. Assuming that you get some of your fluid from food, that means women need to drink about nine 8-ounce glasses of water daily and men need twelve 8-ouncers. Try to choose water instead of calorie-dense beverages such as cola or fruit juice. Research shows that the brain and GI tract don't notice these liquid calories, so you can still feel hungry after drinking a 400-calorie cola. In one study, dieters who swapped sugary beverages for water lost an extra 3 pounds in a year, on average, compared with those who continued to drink sweet beverages.

> **FIBER FACT**
>
> High-fiber foods that are rich in water, such as fruit, are particularly effective for relieving constipation.

Take an enzyme product. We all get gas when we eat beans and a few other specific high-fiber foods. Some people experience this issue more than others. This doesn't mean you are "bean intolerant." It only means that you do not have enough of the right type of digestive enzymes to break them down. Beans contain starch compounds called oligosaccharides. If digestive enzymes do not break down this starch, it becomes food for friendly bacteria in the intestinal tract. When these bacteria feed on this starch, they get gas . . . and so do you. This problem is easily solved. Just take Beano or another enzyme product when you eat beans and other foods that tend to cause problems. It will provide your GI tract with the enzymes needed to break down this starch.

Cook the gas producers. If specific vegetables such as broccoli and cauliflower cause gas, cook them rather than eating them raw. Cooking makes them easier to digest, says Dr. Mullin.

Add some fennel. This herb naturally helps to curb gas production in the gut, says Dr. Mullin.

DO YOU NEED A FIBER SUPPLEMENT?

In a word, no. Surprised? Many people are, probably because the fiber supplement industry is so good at marketing its products. Here's the real story.

First, as mentioned in the previous chapter, high-fiber foods come in a natural package that includes many other beneficial nutrients. These vitamins, minerals, and antioxidants may be particularly beneficial in fighting diseases caused by overweight. For instance, fruits and veggies are not only rich in fiber, they are also rich in potassium, which helps to drive down blood pressure. This complete package is also important in easing your GI tract into high-fiber eating without triggering uncomfortable side effects. "If you can cut back on processed foods and cook fresh foods more often, you'll automatically increase the amount of fiber you eat. This is much more delicious and easier for your GI tract to tolerate than taking a fiber supplement," says Dr. Mullin.

Second, soluble *and* insoluble fiber are important for weight loss and good health, but most supplements contain only soluble fiber. If you take supplements instead of focusing on getting fiber from real food, you will also get only half of the weight-loss benefits that fiber can provide.

Third, and perhaps most important, most fiber supplements offer less fiber than many high-fiber foods. If you have a fiber supplement in your home, take a look at its nutrition facts panel. Most supplements contain somewhere between 3 and 5 grams of fiber and 25 or so calories. You can easily get that much fiber from food.

"There is this magical food that contains double to triple the amount of fiber of most supplements, and it's called high-fiber breakfast cereal," says Katherine Sherif, MD, associate professor of medicine at Drexel University College of Medicine in Philadelphia and director of Drexel's Center for Women's Health. Add raspberries to the cereal, and you can get up to 16 grams of fiber in just one meal. Most supplements contain less than a third as much.

After all, who wouldn't rather munch on cereal, bite into an apple, or chew on an ear of corn than mix a powder into a glass of water to drink?

Can I overdose on fiber?

If you take fiber supplements, you can consume so much fiber at once that you hinder the absorption of specific minerals such as calcium. This rarely happens, however, when you eat high-fiber foods. Vegetarians who consume lots of fiber tend to have normal vitamin and mineral levels. If you are concerned, however, a daily multivitamin/mineral supplement can't hurt, especially if it contains calcium and iron.

KEEPING THINGS MOVING

One of the most common reasons people resort to fiber supplements is because they face problems with constipation. In most cases, however, the problem lies in the fact that they're not eating enough fiber in the first place. This plan is the perfect remedy!

On the off chance that you find your bowels are still sluggish at the end of this 4-week plan, try altering your morning meal as follows:

1. Have high-fiber cold cereal (see the list of recommended brands in the Appendix) or oatmeal mixed with ground flaxseed. Unlike fiber supplements, flax is oily, so it lubricates your colon. This is important, because in addition to bulk, your colon needs lubrication for the bulk to move. The type of fat in flax is healthy, so don't worry about the oil resting in your arteries. It is rich in alpha linolenic acid, which has been shown to protect the heart and the bones.

2. Drink something hot. Coffee, tea, or even warm water helps to stimulate bowel activity.

3. Drink an extra glass of water. The liquid will also mix with the fiber in your food. Remember, fiber works best when it absorbs water.

[🖱] Log On for More Fiber Tools

At Prevention.com/fiber, you can find everything you need to help you follow the Fiber Up, Slim Down Plan. There you can:

- Find valuable shopping advice to help you choose the best high-fiber foods with our Fiber Up Food Finder
- Meet your daily fiber goals by tracking the foods you eat and receiving a nutritional breakdown of your diet
- Discover new high-fiber recipes
- Get the latest fiber and nutrition news from Nutrition Director Cynthia Sass's daily blog
- See how many calories your body can burn with different types of walking plans

CHAPTER 4

BREAKFAST

Let's start things off easy. The first week of this plan helps you make over one of the most important meals of the day—breakfast. That's because, of the three main meals, it's probably the simplest one to completely overhaul. For example, if your spouse happens to grumble, "Eeww, oatmeal again?" it's easy to send him to the cereal cabinet and tell him to make his own breakfast. And if he doesn't like your high-fiber cereal brand, you need only stock the cabinet with one he likes; let him do his own pouring. Of course, it's not so easy to solve such thorny issues at dinner, which is why that meal will be saved for the last week of the plan. (That said, it's best for everyone in the family to eat more fiber, so hopefully spouses and teenage children alike will find these delicious breakfasts tempting.)

Breakfast is also an easy meal to make over for at least two more reasons. First, high-fiber breakfast foods are just as quick and easy to prepare as low-fiber options. In many cases, you can considerably increase your fiber grams just by switching to a different brand of the very same food. You can make a smoothie or grab a premade bran muffin and eat it during your morning commute. It's even relatively easy to find high-fiber options when dining out for breakfast.

Second, experience shows us that few people jump out of bed with a craving for low-fiber food. Sure, we all have sugar, fat, and salt cravings from time to time, but those urges tend to hold off until noon or later. Most people don't have to wage the same kind of mental battle when talking themselves into a bowl of cereal or a vegetable omelet as they do when talking themselves into veggies with dip versus cheese and crackers.

Not only is breakfast easy to change, it's a change that's easy to maintain. After all, most of us don't have as much time to think about breakfast, so we tend to eat similar things every day, and it becomes a part of a routine, like getting dressed in the morning or brushing teeth. When people get into the pattern of starting the day with a high-fiber breakfast, they tend to stick with it. And according to the latest nutrition research, that's a really good thing.

BREAK THE FAST

When it comes to weight loss, health, memory, alertness, and mood, breakfast is hands-down the most important meal of the day. Consider:

- Researchers at Brown Medical School and the University of Colorado have been studying a group of thousands of people who have lost at least 70 pounds and kept it off for an average of 6 years. Nearly 80 percent of these successful losers say eating breakfast every day helps them control their weight.

- People who skip breakfast are four times as likely to be overweight, compared with people who eat breakfast.

- A New Zealand study of 3,275 children and teens determined that children who skipped breakfast tended to weigh more than children who ate a morning meal, and children who skipped breakfast tended to be low in fiber-rich nutrient intakes of fruits and vegetables and more likely to eat fattening snack foods such as cheese curls. Similar studies done in Italy and the United States have determined that people of every age, race, and sex who eat breakfast tend to weigh less than their peers who do not.

Why is breakfast so important to a slender waistline? When you wake in the morning, you've already gone 9 to 12 hours without food. Your eyes may be open, but if you don't give it some fuel, your metabolism stays asleep. Eating helps to wake up cellular function, kicking up your calorie burn throughout the morning.

Eating also restores blood sugar to normal levels. When you wake, sugar is already low. Your brain in particular needs a fresh supply of sugar (called glucose in the body) each morning. For this reason, breakfast eaters tend to score higher on tests of alertness, concentration, memory, and mood. If you skip breakfast, blood sugar drops further throughout the morning, triggering excessive hunger and cravings. Suddenly, the trail mix or peanut butter and apple that you packed doesn't seem so appetizing. You find yourself staring at the vending machine and yearning for the chocolate bar inside.

THE FIBER CONNECTION

The benefits of breakfast aside, not all breakfasts are created equal. You don't just want to eat breakfast. You want to eat a slimming breakfast. Simply put, a doughnut or refined bagel isn't going to keep you satisfied for hours. Oatmeal, high-fiber cereal, yogurt with fruit, or a veggie omelet will.

Even better, these fiber-rich options have consistently been shown to dial down hunger and cravings *all day long.* That's right. A high-fiber breakfast doesn't just help you eat a more healthful midmorning snack. Numerous studies show that fiber also gives you more mental control at lunch, throughout the afternoon, at dinner, and afterward.

Fiber works by keeping blood sugar stable. As slow-digesting, fiber-rich carbs ease their way into your bloodstream, you get a steady dose of fuel to power you throughout your morning. Insulin levels remain steady, too, which helps to reduce fatigue, hunger, and cravings.

Starting off with stable blood sugar goes a long way toward helping you to make over your meals later in the day. For example, if your levels are steady, you'll be more likely to want a high-fiber snack midmorning than you will be to reach for a doughnut. You'll also have fewer cravings throughout the afternoon. A fiber-packed breakfast can even help you avoid late-night snacking, which is often a consequence of not eating enough of the right foods earlier in the day.

Fiber-rich breakfasts also tend to increase alertness during the morning, versus high-fat or fiber-poor carb breakfasts, finds one study done in Australia. They also boost mood. This is because high-sugar, low-fiber breakfasts—such as sugar-rich cereals, white bread and juice, or Danishes—cause blood sugar to rise quickly and then fall about an hour later. When it falls, you feel hungry, irritable, and moody and have trouble concentrating, so you take a break and reach for more food.

HOW TO OVERCOME YOUR BREAKFAST EXCUSES

It's truly ironic that the one meal most people skip is the one they most need to eat. If you consider yourself to be a veteran breakfast skipper, take note of the following three excuses that may be standing in your way.

Excuse #1: I'm Not Hungry in the Morning

In all likelihood, this is a valid feeling. In fact, the thought of eating may even make you feel nauseous. Your lack of hunger, however, probably stems from what you ate last night.

BEAT THE BLOOD SUGAR BLUES

Being overweight more than doubles your risk of developing type 2 diabetes, the most common blood sugar disorder. It also raises your risk of gestational diabetes, the type that develops during pregnancy. A high-fiber diet can help prevent and reverse these and other blood sugar disorders. A study of thousands of nurses completed at the Harvard School of Public Health in Boston determined that each 10-gram increase in fiber reduced the risk of developing gestational diabetes by 26 percent.

Fiber helps in two ways. First, it slows the entrance of sugar into the bloodstream, keeping blood sugar levels steady and reducing the need for the pancreas to make the hormone insulin. Research shows that a high-fiber meal can reduce postmeal blood sugar levels by up to 28 percent and fasting insulin levels by roughly 11 percent.

Second, when bacteria ferment fiber in the colon, they release acids that enter the bloodstream and sensitize cells to insulin. In one study, 17 overweight or obese people who ate 31 grams of fiber a day—the amount in three servings of high-fiber cereal or two servings of barley—improved insulin sensitivity by 8 percent. When cells are more sensitive to this hormone, they more easily sop up blood sugar.

Your risk of getting type 2 diabetes is particularly high if your diet is both low in fiber and high in high glycemic index (GI) foods. High GI foods digest quickly, raising blood sugar quickly after eating. High GI foods include potatoes, refined foods, white rice, refined cereals, refined pasta, and sugar. Low GI foods do not raise sugar as quickly and are usually packed with fiber. They include legumes, fruit, bran, and cereals.

Overeating at dinner and snacking well into the night will leave you bloated in the morning. In short, this pattern of eating leaves you to wake with a food hangover.

Getting a handle on late-night eating is especially important as it's probably contributing to your weight gain—and is definitely standing in the way of weight loss. To break the cycle, you need to eat breakfast. As you work your way through this 4-week plan, you'll find your late-night cravings naturally diminish because you are eating regular high-fiber meals throughout the day.

FIBER TIP

Some people find that drinking hot water with lemon each morning helps them to work up an appetite for a high-fiber breakfast.

To ease yourself into the breakfast habit, start slowly. If you normally eat your first snack at 11:00 a.m., try to move it an hour earlier and start with a small amount of food, such as a slice of whole grain toast. You may find it easier to drink a smoothie or have a small breakfast bar rather than a traditional breakfast option. As you get used to eating breakfast and start snacking less at night, you'll find it easier to add more food to your breakfast plate. Eventually you'll wake up feeling hungry and looking forward to your morning meal.

You also may find it helpful to take a walk first thing in the morning, especially during the first few weeks of the plan. The exercise will help you to process your food hangover and work up an appetite.

Finally, you simply may not be one of those people who craves carbs or eggs first thing in the morning. If that describes you, there are plenty of nontraditional breakfast options in the recipes that follow. Check out the Sweet Couscous with Pistachios, Peaches, and Figs (page 40), Fruit Sandwich (page 41), and Ricotta and Fig Breakfast Sandwich (page 44).

Excuse #2: I Don't Have Time to Eat Breakfast

In reality, there are many high-fiber breakfast options that take almost no time to prepare and eat. We're talking seconds. If you are rushed in the morning, try these options.

- Keep a bag of high-fiber breakfast cereal in your car or desk, and snack on it during your commute or as you check e-mail in the morning. Other good shelf-stable high-fiber options include whole fruit, nuts and seeds, and high-fiber breakfast bars (consult the Appendix on page 326 for recommended breakfast bar and cereal brands).

- Set out what you need for breakfast the night before, so it's on the counter and ready.

- If you have a supportive partner, ask whether he or she would be willing to make you breakfast for a week or two, until you get in the habit. You can return the favor by cooking dinner.

- Make dozens of high-fiber muffins every other week or so, and freeze them. Just before bed each night, take a muffin out of the freezer to thaw. Then grab it on your way out the door.

Excuse #3: I Want to Eat Breakfast, but I Keep Forgetting

You can overcome this excuse with some planning. First, create a visual reminder for yourself. After dinner, set your bowl and cereal out on the counter so you'll see them in the morning. You also might set an alarm on your watch or cell phone to beep at the time when you should be eating breakfast.

And create a fallback option. If you rush out of the house without breakfast, have

It is if you have a blood sugar disorder. Prediabetes, the precursor to diabetes, is linked to memory and word recognition problems, which can lead to dementia later in life, finds a Tulane University study. Swedish researchers found that prediabetes boosted Alzheimer's and dementia risk by 70 percent. Whole grains, fruits, and veggies rich in fiber can maintain memory by preventing this borderline diabetes.

something stashed in the car or at work, or know of a good place where you can purchase a high-fiber option on the way to work.

Getting in the habit of eating breakfast is like forming any habit. It may take conscious effort in the beginning, but after a while it will become second nature. Eventually, you'll always remember to eat breakfast just as you always remember to put on your underwear.

HIGH-FIBER BREAKFAST EATS

You'll find 23 high-fiber recipes in the following pages that will lend a delicious start to the day. If you are rushed in the morning, as most people are, however, you can fuel up with any of these quick and easy high-fiber options.

High-fiber cold cereal. A long-term study of thousands of men found that those who consumed high-fiber cereal were less likely to gain weight over an 8-year time period, compared with men who ate refined cereal for breakfast. Plus, research shows that eating a cup of high-fiber cereal a day cuts heart attack risk by 30 percent. Breakfast cereals are also fortified with vitamins and minerals, so most act like a multivitamin and mineral supplement.

Choose cereals from the list of recommended brands in the Appendix on page 326. These options all have at least 5 grams of fiber per serving, and some have as many as 14. Add berries, sliced fruit, nuts, or a sprinkle of ground flaxseed to up the fiber even more. If you don't like cereal with milk, try it mixed with nonfat yogurt and topped with a sprinkle of wheat germ or ground flaxseed for extra fiber and crunch. See Yogurt All-Bran Honey Parfait (page 36) and Muesli with Dried Fruit and Almonds (page 38).

Oatmeal. Despite popular belief, all types of oatmeal, including instant, are good sources of fiber, with most offering 5 grams per serving. Manufacturers make instant varieties by heating and flattening the oats with steel rollers. As a result, they cook faster, but they still house the whole grain. Just be careful because some instant varieties are loaded with sugar and other sweeteners. (See the Appendix for a list of recommended hot cereals.) You can up the fiber content even more by adding berries or sliced apples and a sprinkle of ground flaxseed. See Hot Oatmeal with Blueberries, Cherries, and Brown Sugar on page 39.

Frozen whole grain waffles. Many frozen waffle brands are made from refined flour, but there are a few brands that are whole grain. Kashi Go Lean, for example, provides 6 grams of fiber per 2-waffle serving. Top the waffles with berries or sliced fruit and a sprinkle of ground flaxseed for even more fiber. See the Appendix for a list of recommended whole grain waffle brands.

Smoothie. Dump some nonfat yogurt, frozen fruit, and flaxseeds or wheat germ in your blender and press Blend. Pour into a glass and drink on the go.

Whole grain toast with peanut butter. In a study done in Australia, participants who consumed a fiber-rich bread for breakfast ate less at lunch than participants who consumed white bread. Just make sure your bread is really whole grain. See the list on page 330 in the Appendix for recommended brands.

EASY FIBER SWAPS

Getting more fiber at breakfast, whether you eat out or at home, can be as simple as making the following switches and substitutions.

IF YOU NORMALLY EAT ...	SWITCH TO THIS HIGH-FIBER ALTERNATIVE ...
White toast or English muffin	Whole grain toast or muffin
French toast made with white bread and slathered with syrup	French toast made with whole wheat bread and topped with fruit
Pancakes made with refined flour	Pancakes made with whole grain flour and berries or sliced fruit. See Oatmeal Buttermilk and Berry Pancakes (page 56).
Ham and cheese omelet	Vegetable-packed omelet, frittata, or strata. See Ham and Vegetable Omelet Wrap (page 45), Breakfast Strata (page 52), Broccoli Red Pepper Frittata (page 47), Spinach and Spaghetti Frittata (page 49), and Sweet Potato and Pea Frittata (page 50).
Orange juice	Orange
Refined cold cereal	Cereal from recommended list (page 326)

Breakfast Recipes

Orange, Grapefruit, and Kiwi with Toasted Almonds

Start your day with this colorful salad. With 6 grams per serving, this dish offers even more fiber than a slice of whole grain bread.

Prep time: 18 minutes   Cook time: 3 minutes

---

3 medium navel oranges

1 large red grapefruit

3 firm-ripe kiwifruit, peeled, ends trimmed, and cut into half-moon slices

2 tablespoons dried cherries or cranberries

2 tablespoons slivered almonds, toasted

1. With a serrated knife, cut the skin and white pith from the oranges and grapefruit. Working over a bowl, cut in between the membranes, letting the sections drop into the bowl. Squeeze the juice from the membranes over the fruit.

2. Add the kiwi and cherries or cranberries and toss gently to mix. Spoon into 4 bowls and top each with some of the toasted almonds.

MAKES 4 SERVINGS

Per serving: 143 calories, 3 g protein, 31 g carbohydrates, 2 g total fat, 0.5 g saturated fat, 0 mg cholesterol, 6 g dietary fiber, 4 mg sodium

Yogurt All-Bran Honey Parfait

Layers of banana sandwiched between smooth, creamy yogurt and crunchy high-fiber bran flakes make for an easy way to break out of the breakfast cereal rut. A light drizzle of honey adds just the right touch of sweetness.

Prep time: 5 minutes

1 cup nonfat plain yogurt

1 cup All-Bran cereal

1 medium banana, sliced, about 1 cup

2 tablespoons honey

2 strawberries, stemmed

Spoon ¼ cup of the yogurt into the bottom of a parfait glass. Top with ¼ cup of the cereal, ¼ cup of the banana slices, and 1½ teaspoons of the honey. Repeat the sequence, except place a strawberry in the center of the banana slices at the top of the glass and then drizzle with the honey. Repeat with the remaining ingredients in a second parfait glass.

MAKES 2 SERVINGS

Per serving: 253 calories, 10 g protein, 65 g carbohydrates, 2 g total fat, 0.5 g saturated fat, 3 mg cholesterol, 11 g dietary fiber, 144 mg sodium

Mixed Fruit Granola

Studded with dried fruit and crunchy almonds, this flavor-packed cereal is noticeably lighter in calories due to the careful use of oil. For quick on-the-go breakfasts, whip up a batch and store in an airtight container up to 1 week.

Prep time: 15 minutes   Cook time: 50 minutes

3 cups old-fashioned oats

¾ cup All-Bran cereal

½ cup slivered almonds

1 teaspoon ground cinnamon

⅛ teaspoon ground nutmeg

¼ teaspoon salt

½ cup honey

3 tablespoons maple syrup

1 teaspoon almond extract

2 tablespoons canola oil

½ cup dried apricots, sliced

½ cup packed golden raisins

½ cup dried cranberries

1. Preheat the oven to 300°F. Coat a large baking sheet with cooking spray.

2. In a large bowl, combine the oats, cereal, almonds, cinnamon, nutmeg, and salt. In a separate bowl, combine the honey, maple syrup, almond extract, and oil. Pour the honey mixture over the oat mixture and toss well to combine. Spread the mixture onto the prepared baking sheet and spread evenly. Bake, stirring every 10 minutes, until lightly toasted, about 50 to 55 minutes.

3. Remove from the oven and stir in the apricots, raisins, and cranberries. Cool completely.

MAKES 12 SERVINGS

Per serving: 232 calories, 5 g protein, 42 g carbohydrates, 6 g total fat, 0.5 g saturated fat, 0 mg cholesterol, 4 g dietary fiber, 61 mg sodium

Muesli with Dried Fruit and Almonds

Sometimes served after soaking in milk, this version of dry muesli is a simpler version of granola. If you prefer, you can skip toasting the oats altogether and instead simply toast the almonds in a dry skillet. Because wheat germ spoils easily, this dish is best stored in a glass jar in the fridge.

Prep time: 10 minutes   Cook time: 20 minutes

---

4 cups old-fashioned oats

½ cup slivered almonds

½ cup snipped dried apricots

½ cup coarsely chopped dried apples

½ cup dried cherries

¼ cup packed brown sugar

¼ cup toasted or untoasted wheat germ

1. Preheat the oven to 375°F.

2. Spread the oats in a rimmed baking sheet or shallow roasting pan. Bake, stirring occasionally, for 10 minutes. Stir in the almonds and bake for 7 to 10 minutes more, or until lightly browned. Scrape into a large bowl and let cool.

3. Stir in the apricots, apples, cherries, sugar, and wheat germ. Store in an airtight container.

MAKES 10 SERVINGS

Per serving: 225 calories, 8 g protein, 38 g carbohydrates, 5 g total fat, 0.5 g saturated fat, 0 mg cholesterol, 5 g dietary fiber, 57 mg sodium

Hot Oatmeal with Blueberries, Cherries, and Brown Sugar

Dress up the usual bowl of oatmeal with a colorful mix of dried and fresh fruit. A splash of vanilla just before serving highlights the brown sugar and cinnamon flavors.

Prep time: 5 minutes   Cook time: 5 minutes

2 cups water

2 tablespoons brown sugar

⅛ teaspoon salt

1 cup old-fashioned oats

¼ cup dried tart cherries

¼ teaspoon ground cinnamon

½ teaspoon vanilla extract

½ cup fresh blueberries

In a small saucepan over medium-high heat, combine the water, sugar, and salt. Bring to a boil, stir in the oats and cherries, reduce the heat to medium, and simmer, stirring occasionally, until thickened and the oats are cooked, about 5 to 6 minutes. Remove from the heat and stir in the cinnamon, vanilla extract, and blueberries.

MAKES 2 SERVINGS

Per serving: 293 calories, 8 g protein, 59 g carbohydrates, 3 g total fat, 0 g saturated fat, 0 mg cholesterol, 9 g dietary fiber, 151 mg sodium

Sweet Couscous with Pistachios, Peaches, and Figs

Whole wheat couscous is a fitting side dish for just about any dinner, but its mild flavor and delicate texture make it a perfect base for a high-fiber breakfast, too. Consider also how quickly it cooks, and you can have a bowl of sweet couscous in about the same time that it takes to prepare instant oatmeal.

Prep time: 5 minutes   Cook time: 1–2 minutes   Stand time: 5 minutes

¾ cup orange juice

½ cup water

5 Calimyrna figs, quartered

¼ cup dried peaches, sliced

¼ cup sugar

1 cup whole wheat couscous

½ cup fat-free milk

⅓ cup dry-roasted salted (shelled) pistachios

In a medium saucepan over high heat, combine the orange juice, water, figs, peaches, and sugar. Bring to a boil, add the couscous, remove from the heat, cover, and let stand for 5 minutes. Stir in the milk and pistachios; divide among 4 bowls and serve immediately.

MAKES 4 SERVINGS

Per serving: 329 calories, 9 g protein, 66 g carbohydrates, 2 g total fat, 1 g saturated fat, 1 mg cholesterol, 8 g dietary fiber, 17 mg sodium

Fruit Sandwich

Perfect for on-the-go mornings, this easy little breakfast sandwich is a snap to make.

Prep time: 5 minutes   Cook time: 10 minutes

---

2 medium-size firm-ripe pears

⅓ cup light cream cheese

3 tablespoons dark raisins

8 slices whole wheat cinnamon swirl bread, toasted

1. Cut each pear in half. Remove the cores with a melon baller or small spoon. Make a V-shaped cut at the bottom of each to remove the blossom end. Place a pear half cut side down on a cutting board and cut into thin lengthwise slices. Repeat with the other pear halves.

2. In a small bowl, mix the cream cheese and raisins. Spread thinly on each slice of toast. Top four of the bread slices with pear slices and sandwich with the other piece of bread. Cut on the diagonal to serve.

MAKES 4 SERVINGS

Per serving: 255 calories, 9 g protein, 50 g carbohydrates, 4 g total fat, 2 g saturated fat, 10 mg cholesterol, 7 g dietary fiber, 242 mg sodium

Tex-Mex Breakfast Sandwich

Wake up to the flavors of the Southwest! To make sure you're helping this sandwich reach its fiber potential, read the English muffin label to ensure that whole grains are the first ingredient and that each serving offers about 100 calories.

Prep time: 5 minutes   Cook time: 5 minutes

¼ cup egg substitute

2 tablespoons reduced-fat shredded sharp Cheddar cheese

1 multigrain English muffin, toasted

2 thin slices avocado, about ½ ounce

4 teaspoons jarred chunky salsa

Coat a small nonstick skillet with cooking spray and heat over medium-high heat. Stir in the egg substitute and cheese; cook 2 minutes per side. Place the eggs on the bottom half of the English muffin. Top with the avocado slices and salsa, then replace the top of the muffin.

MAKES 1 SERVING

Per serving: 297 calories, 16 g protein, 36 g carbohydrates, 11 g total fat, 5 g saturated fat, 21 mg cholesterol, 5 g dietary fiber, 570 mg sodium

Ricotta and Fig Breakfast Sandwich

This light, fiber-rich, filling sandwich is portable and delicious. Use the very dense, square, sliced European- or German-style bread for this recipe. Each slice is only 70 calories and contains 3 grams of fiber. The bread is often found near the deli section.

Prep time: 5 minutes

8 slices dense European bread

½ cup reduced-fat ricotta cheese

½ cup sliced, stemmed dried figs

½ cup thinly sliced, hulled strawberries

1 tablespoon honey

Spread each slice of bread with 1 tablespoon of the ricotta. On four of the slices, arrange the figs and strawberries and then drizzle with honey. Top each sandwich with the remaining slice of bread and cut in half on the diagonal.

MAKES 4 SERVINGS (4 TRIANGLES PER SERVING)

Per serving: 295 calories, 11 g protein, 53 g carbohydrates, 4 g total fat, 1 g saturated fat, 8 mg cholesterol, 9 g dietary fiber, 310 mg sodium

Ham and Vegetable Omelet Wrap

This garden-fresh breakfast wrap summons a wealth of seasonal flavors, but it's surprisingly easy to make practically any time of year. If you're cooking for one, slip the extra serving into a zippered storage bag (without the salsa) and you're already set for breakfast tomorrow morning!

Prep time: 10 minutes   Cook time: 8 minutes

3 egg whites, lightly beaten

1 egg, lightly beaten

1 teaspoon unsalted butter

⅓ cup chopped onion

1½ ounces deli-sliced ham, such as Healthy Choice, chopped

¼ cup frozen peas

1 small plum tomato, chopped, about ½ cup

⅛ teaspoon ground black pepper

1 multigrain wrap

4 teaspoons jarred black bean and corn salsa

1. In a small bowl, combine the egg whites and egg.

2. Melt the butter in a medium nonstick skillet over medium-high heat. Add the onion and ham; cook, stirring occasionally, until the onion starts to soften, about 2 to 3 minutes. Stir in the peas, tomato, and pepper; cook until the tomato begins to wilt, about 1 to 2 minutes. Add the egg mixture and cook for 2 minutes per side. Warm the wrap according to package directions, then place on a cutting board. Slide the egg onto the wrap, roll up jelly roll–style, then cut in half on an angle. Top each half with 2 teaspoons of the salsa.

MAKES 2 SERVINGS

Per serving: 192 calories, 17 g protein, 21 g carbohydrates, 7 g total fat, 2 g saturated fat, 118 mg cholesterol, 6 g dietary fiber, 530 mg sodium

Broccoli Red Pepper Frittata

Frittatas are Italian-style omelets that usually have the ingredients mixed with the eggs rather than folded inside. Tossing in some leftover brown rice is another good way to add a fiber boost.

Prep time: 15 minutes   Cook time: 15 minutes

1 tablespoon olive oil

1 onion, chopped

1 red bell pepper, diced

2 cloves garlic, minced

2 cups cooked chopped broccoli

1 cup cooked brown rice

4 large eggs

4 egg whites

¾ cup grated Asiago cheese, 2 ounces

½ teaspoon salt

½ teaspoon ground black pepper

1. Heat the oil in a 12" broiler-proof nonstick skillet over medium heat. Add the onion, bell pepper, and garlic, and cook, stirring frequently, until tender, about 3 minutes. Add the broccoli and rice and heat through.

2. In another bowl, whisk together the eggs, egg whites, cheese, salt, and black pepper until blended.

3. Preheat the broiler to high. On top of the stove, spread the vegetable and rice mixture evenly in the bottom of the skillet, add the egg mixture, and spread to the edges of the skillet. As the egg begins to set, use a rubber spatula to lift up the edges of the cooked egg to allow the uncooked portion to flow under. Continue cooking until beginning to set. Reduce heat to low. Cover and cook until the frittata is almost set, about 8 minutes.

4. Transfer the skillet to the broiler and broil until the top just begins to brown, about 3 minutes. Slide the frittata onto a plate. Cut into wedges. Serve warm or at room temperature.

MAKES 6 SERVINGS

Per serving: 185 calories, 11 g protein,
15 g carbohydrates, 9 g total fat, 3 g saturated fat,
149 mg cholesterol, 3 g dietary fiber, 393 mg sodium

Artichoke, Mushroom, and Goat Cheese Omelet

A sophisticated breakfast dish, this open-faced omelet would be welcome for brunch or a light supper. The recipe calls for chopped fresh parsley and chives. You can simply use all parsley, if you prefer.

Prep time: 11 minutes   Cook time: 20 minutes

2 tablespoons olive oil

1 medium onion, halved and thinly sliced

1 package (9 ounces) frozen artichoke hearts, microwaved until tender according to package directions and well drained

2 cups halved and sliced white button mushrooms

Salt

3 large eggs

3 egg whites

2 tablespoons fat-free milk

2 tablespoons chopped fresh flat-leaf parsley

2 tablespoons snipped fresh chives

¼ teaspoon freshly ground black pepper

2 ounces goat cheese, crumbled

1. Set out a 10" ovenproof, nonstick skillet. If the skillet isn't ovenproof, wrap the handle in a double layer of foil.

2. Warm the oil in the skillet over medium heat. Add the onion and cook, stirring often, until tender, about 4 minutes. Add the artichokes and mushrooms and a pinch of salt. Cook, stirring often, until the mushrooms and artichokes are tender and lightly browned, 5 to 7 minutes.

3. Meanwhile, in a medium bowl, whisk the eggs, egg whites, milk, parsley, chives, pepper, and ¼ teaspoon salt. Preheat the broiler.

4. Pour the egg mixture into the skillet. Reduce the heat to low and cook, lifting the edges to allow the uncooked egg to run underneath, for about 3 minutes, until the bottom is set but the top is still runny.

5. Dot the omelet with the goat cheese. Broil 3" to 4" from the heat for 2 to 3 minutes, until the eggs are set and the cheese is heated. Slide onto a warmed plate and cut into wedges to serve.

MAKES 4 SERVINGS

Per serving: 231 calories, 14 g protein,
11 g carbohydrates, 16 g total fat, 5 g saturated fat,
170 mg cholesterol, 5 g dietary fiber, 252 mg sodium

Spinach and Spaghetti Frittata

Here's another variation on the classic Italian omelet that makes good use of leftover pasta. As perfect for brunches and light suppers as it is for breakfast, this delicious combination is sure to become a regular favorite.

Prep time: 10 minutes   **Cook time: 25 minutes**

4 ounces whole grain angel hair pasta, cooked and drained

2 tablespoons olive oil

3 large eggs

3 large egg whites

2 tablespoons fat-free milk

2 tablespoons shredded Parmesan cheese

¼ teaspoon salt

¼ teaspoon ground black pepper

1 package (10 ounces) frozen chopped spinach, thawed and squeezed dry

2 large plum tomatoes, cut crosswise into thin slices

1. Preheat the oven to 375°F. With kitchen shears, cut the pasta into little pieces so it crisps more easily.

2. Warm the oil in a 10" ovenproof, nonstick skillet over medium-high heat. (If the skillet handle is not ovenproof, wrap it in heavy-duty foil.) Add the pasta and spread it out in the pan. Cook, turning often with a spatula and breaking up the clumps, until the pasta starts to crisp, about 8 minutes.

3. Meanwhile, in a medium bowl, whisk the eggs, egg whites, milk, 1 tablespoon of the Parmesan, and the salt and pepper. Add the spinach, whisking to distribute evenly.

4. Pour the egg mixture into the skillet and reduce the heat. Cook for 2 minutes, until it firms up on the bottom; the mixture will be very green. Remove from the heat and arrange the tomatoes on the top. Sprinkle with the remaining 1 tablespoon Parmesan.

5. Transfer to the oven and bake about 10 minutes, until the eggs are set and the frittata puffs slightly. Cut into wedges to serve.

MAKES 4 SERVINGS

Per serving: 277 calories, 14 g protein, 26 g carbohydrates, 12 g total fat, 3 g saturated fat, 161 mg cholesterol, 4 g dietary fiber, 399 mg sodium

Sweet Potato and Pea Frittata

Here the wonderful pairing of sweet potatoes and peas provides a lovely contrast to the salty, smoky bacon.

Prep time: 10 minutes   Cook time: 23 minutes

12 ounces sweet potato, peeled and cut into ½" pieces

4 eggs, lightly beaten

2 egg whites, lightly beaten

¼ cup fat-free milk

¼ teaspoon salt

¼ teaspoon ground black pepper

3 slices reduced-sodium center-cut bacon, chopped

1 sweet onion, chopped, about 1 cup

¼ teaspoon dried thyme

1 cup frozen peas

1. Preheat the oven to 500°F. Place the sweet potato in a medium saucepan with enough cold water to cover by 2". Bring to a boil over high heat and cook for 8 minutes; drain. In a bowl, combine the eggs, egg whites, milk, salt, and pepper.

2. Meanwhile, cook the bacon in an ovenproof 10" nonstick skillet over medium-high heat until starting to crisp, 3 to 4 minutes. (If the skillet handle is not ovenproof, wrap it in heavy-duty foil.) Add the onion and thyme and cook until starting to soften, 2 to 3 minutes. Stir in the peas and cook until thawed, 2 minutes. Add the sweet potato and cook 1 minute longer. Pour in the egg mixture and cook, stirring occasionally, for 2 minutes. Reduce the heat to medium and cook, without stirring, until almost set. Transfer the skillet to the oven and cook until set and browned, about 5 minutes.

MAKES 4 SERVINGS

Per serving: 238 calories, 14 g protein, 30 g carbohydrates, 7 g total fat, 2 g saturated fat, 216 mg cholesterol, 5 g dietary fiber, 380 mg sodium

Breakfast Strata

This comfort food favorite is low-stress to make. Prepare it the night before serving, and all you have to do when you wake up is pop it in the oven.

Prep time: 15 minutes   **Chill time: minimum 2 hours**   **Stand time: 10 minutes**
Cook time: 10 minutes   **Bake time: 55 minutes**

---

2 teaspoons unsalted butter

2 cups chopped onion

1 tablespoon sugar

4 cups broccoli florets

½ teaspoon dried basil

½ teaspoon dried oregano

⅓ cup water

12 slices multigrain bread, halved diagonally

2 ounces reduced-fat Swiss cheese, shredded

½ cup grated Parmesan cheese

5 eggs, lightly beaten

3 egg whites, lightly beaten

2 cups fat-free milk

2 tablespoons Dijon mustard

¼ teaspoon ground black pepper

1. Melt the butter in a medium nonstick skillet over medium-high heat. Add the onion and sugar; cook, stirring occasionally, until the onion browns, 6 to 7 minutes. Add the broccoli, basil, and oregano. Cook, stirring occasionally, until bright green, about 2 to 3 minutes. Pour in the water and cook until evaporated, 1 to 2 minutes longer. Remove from the heat.

2. Coat an 11" × 7" baking dish with cooking spray and arrange one-half of the bread in the bottom with all the triangles facing the same direction. Spread the broccoli mixture over the bread in a single layer, then top with the Swiss and Parmesan cheeses. Arrange the remaining bread in the dish with the triangles facing in the opposite direction. In a bowl, combine the eggs, egg whites, milk, mustard, and pepper. Pour the mixture over the bread; press on the bread to help absorb the milk mixture. Cover and refrigerate for 2 hours or overnight.

3. Preheat the oven to 350°F. Bake the strata uncovered for 55 to 60 minutes, or until puffed, golden, and a knife inserted into the center comes out clean. Let stand for 10 minutes before serving.

MAKES 8 SERVINGS

Per serving: 274 calories, 19 g protein,
32 g carbohydrates, 9 g total fat, 3 g saturated fat,
144 mg cholesterol, 8 g dietary fiber, 480 mg sodium

Bran Cakes with Maple-Mixed Berries

Create your own convenience breakfasts from the freezer. Cool any leftover pancakes to room temperature, then place them in a stack separated by pieces of waxed paper. Pop into a resealable plastic storage bag and freeze. To eat, reheat in a toaster or toaster oven.

Prep time: 12 minutes   Soaking time: 10 minutes   Cook time: 20 minutes

FRUIT

2 cups thinly sliced hulled strawberries

1 cup raspberries (if using frozen, thaw for 20 minutes)

1 cup halved blackberries (if using frozen, thaw for 20 minutes)

3 tablespoons pure maple syrup

PANCAKES

¾ cup All-Bran cereal

1 cup fat-free milk

1 cup whole grain pastry flour

1 teaspoon baking powder

½ teaspoon baking soda

½ teaspoon ground cinnamon

¼ teaspoon salt

1 large egg

2 tablespoons canola oil

2 tablespoons pure maple syrup

1. *To make the fruit:* In a medium bowl, mix the strawberries, raspberries, blackberries, and maple syrup. Let stand while making the pancakes.

2. *To make the pancakes:* In a large bowl, soak the cereal in the milk for 10 minutes, or until softened. Meanwhile, in a medium bowl, stir together the flour, baking powder, baking soda, cinnamon, and salt.

3. With a fork, beat the egg, oil, and maple syrup into the cereal mixture. Stir in the dry ingredients until blended.

4. Coat a pancake griddle or large nonstick pan with cooking spray. Heat over medium heat until a drop of water sizzles when dropped on the surface. For each pancake, spoon 2 tablespoons of batter onto the griddle. Cook for 1 to 2 minutes, or until the undersides are golden brown. Turn and cook about 1 minute more, until the second side is browned. Transfer to a platter; keep warm in a 200°F oven while making the remaining pancakes.

MAKES 4 SERVINGS (3 PANCAKES + ½ CUP FRUIT MIXTURE PER SERVING)

Per serving: 338 calories, 10 g protein, 60 g carbohydrates, 10 g total fat, 1 g saturated fat, 54 mg cholesterol, 11 g dietary fiber, 478 mg sodium

Cornmeal and Corn Griddle Cakes

Perfect for weekend breakfasts, these tasty griddle cakes are a naturally sweet alternative to buckwheat pancakes. In place of syrup, serve with sliced fresh strawberries, fruit butter, or a little honey.

Prep time: 15 minutes   Cook time: 20 minutes

⅔ cup whole grain pastry flour

⅔ cup yellow cornmeal, preferably stone-ground

1 tablespoon sugar

1½ teaspoons baking powder

½ teaspoon baking soda

⅛ teaspoon ground black pepper

1½ cups buttermilk or plain nonfat yogurt

1 large egg

2 egg whites

2 tablespoons canola oil

1 cup drained no-sodium canned corn kernels

1. In a large bowl, stir together the flour, cornmeal, sugar, baking powder, baking soda, and pepper.

2. In a medium bowl, whisk together the buttermilk or yogurt, egg, egg whites, and oil. Stir in the corn. Pour the corn mixture over the dry ingredients and stir to mix.

3. Coat a pancake griddle or large nonstick pan with cooking spray. Heat over medium heat. For each pancake, spoon 3 tablespoons of batter onto the griddle. Cook about 3 minutes, or until the undersides are golden brown. Turn and cook 1 to 2 minutes more, or until the second side is browned. Transfer to a platter; keep warm in a 200°F oven while making the remaining pancakes. Serve hot.

MAKES 4 SERVINGS (4 PANCAKES PER SERVING)

Per serving: 308 calories, 11 g protein,
45 g carbohydrates, 10 g total fat, 2 g saturated fat,
57 mg cholesterol, 4 g dietary fiber, 460 mg sodium

Oatmeal Buttermilk and Berry Pancakes

These oat cakes have such a lovely blending of flavors and pleasing texture from the whole grains.

Prep time: 15 minutes   **Chill time: 30 minutes**   **Cook time: 5 minutes per batch**

1¼ cups quick-cooking oats

½ cup whole wheat flour

3 tablespoons sugar

½ teaspoon baking powder

¼ teaspoon baking soda

⅛ teaspoon salt

1 cup low-fat buttermilk

1 egg

1 egg white

1 tablespoon unsalted butter, melted

1 teaspoon grated fresh lemon peel

1 cup fresh blueberries

½ cup maple syrup

1. In a bowl, combine the oats, flour, sugar, baking powder, baking soda, and salt.

2. In a separate bowl, combine the buttermilk, egg, egg white, butter, and lemon peel. Pour the buttermilk mixture into the oat mixture, stirring until just moistened. Gently fold in the blueberries with a rubber spatula. Refrigerate for 30 minutes.

3. Preheat the oven to 250°F. Coat a large nonstick skillet with cooking spray and heat over medium heat. Spoon four ¼ cupfuls of batter into the skillet and cook until the tops begin to bubble slightly, about 2½ to 3 minutes. Turn the pancakes and cook 2½ to 3 minutes longer, or until golden and cooked through. Transfer to a baking sheet and keep warm in the oven. Repeat with the remaining batter. Divide the maple syrup over the pancakes.

MAKES 12 PANCAKES

Per pancake: 130 calories, 4 g protein,
25 g carbohydrates, 2 g total fat, 1 g saturated fat,
21 mg cholesterol, 2 g dietary fiber, 101 mg sodium

Multigrain French Toast
with Strawberry-Banana Topping

Heating the bananas, berries, and orange juice to create a warm sauce takes just a few minutes but adds immeasurably to the impact of the finished dish.

Prep time: 10 minutes   Cook time: 10 minutes

1 tablespoon unsalted butter

1 medium banana, sliced, about 1 cup

6 strawberries, hulled and sliced

2 tablespoons sugar

⅓ cup orange juice

2 eggs, lightly beaten

¼ cup fat-free milk

½ teaspoon vanilla extract

¼ teaspoon ground cinnamon

4 slices multigrain bread

1. Melt 1 teaspoon of the butter in a medium non-stick skillet over medium-high heat. Add the banana and strawberries and cook until beginning to soften, 2 to 3 minutes. Add the sugar and cook for 1 minute. Stir in the orange juice, bring to a boil, and cook until slightly thickened, 1 minute longer; keep warm.

2. In a shallow bowl, combine the eggs, milk, vanilla extract, and cinnamon. Dip the bread slices into the egg mixture, turning once. Melt the remaining 2 teaspoons butter in a large nonstick skillet over medium-high heat. Add the dipped bread and cook until golden, 2 to 2½ minutes per side.

MAKES 4 SERVINGS (1 SLICE FRENCH TOAST + ⅓ CUP FRUIT MIXTURE PER SERVING)

Per serving: 216 calories, 8 g protein, 32 g carbohydrates, 7 g total fat, 3 g saturated fat, 114 mg cholesterol, 5 g dietary fiber, 178 mg sodium

Banana-Nut Muffins

Serve these delicious, tender muffins warm from the oven. If you happen to have any leftovers, they'll freeze beautifully.

Prep time: 15 minutes   **Soaking time: 10 minutes**   **Bake time: 15–20 minutes**

½ cup organic Grape-Nuts Cereal

¾ cup fat-free milk

1¾ cups whole grain pastry flour

1½ teaspoons baking powder

½ teaspoon baking soda

¼ teaspoon salt

2 large eggs

3 tablespoons sugar

2 tablespoons canola oil

2 ripe medium bananas, mashed to make ⅔ cup

½ cup coarsely chopped walnuts

1. Preheat the oven to 375°F. Line a 12-cup muffin tin with paper liners.

2. In a medium bowl, soak the cereal in the milk for 10 minutes, until softened.

3. In a large bowl, stir together the flour, baking powder, baking soda, and salt. With a fork, beat the eggs, sugar, and oil into the soaked cereal. Stir in the mashed bananas and ¼ cup of the walnuts.

4. Pour the banana mixture into the dry ingredients and stir just until blended. Spoon evenly into the prepared muffin cups, filling each about ¾ full. Sprinkle the remaining ¼ cup walnuts over the top. Bake for 15 to 20 minutes, or until the muffins are browned and firm to the touch. Turn the muffins out onto a wire rack to cool.

MAKES 12

Per muffin: 165 calories, 5 g protein, 23 g carbohydrates, 7 g total fat, 1 g saturated fat, 36 mg cholesterol, 3 g dietary fiber, 199 mg sodium

Spiced Pumpkin-Prune Muffins

These flavorful treats provide a nice mix of warm spices. When preparing the prunes, keep in mind that, due to their slightly sticky texture, it's easier to cut them with kitchen shears than to chop them.

Prep time: 28 minutes   Bake time: 15–17 minutes

---

1 cup whole grain pastry flour

⅓ cup unbleached all-purpose flour

2 teaspoons baking powder

½ teaspoon baking soda

½ teaspoon ground cinnamon

½ teaspoon ground ginger

¼ teaspoon ground allspice

¼ teaspoon salt

¾ cup snipped pitted prunes (pea-size pieces)

2 large eggs

½ cup plain canned pumpkin

½ cup plain nonfat yogurt

¼ cup packed brown sugar

3 tablespoons canola oil

1. Preheat the oven to 375°F. Line a 12-cup muffin tin with paper or foil liners, or mist with cooking spray.

2. In a large bowl, stir together the flours, baking powder, baking soda, cinnamon, ginger, allspice, and salt. Stir in the prunes. In a medium bowl, whisk the eggs, pumpkin, yogurt, sugar, and oil.

3. Pour the pumpkin mixture into the dry ingredients and stir just until blended. Spoon the batter into the prepared muffin cups, filling each nearly to the top. Bake for 15 to 17 minutes, or until the top springs back when lightly touched and a toothpick inserted in the center of a muffin comes out clean. Turn the muffins out onto a wire rack to cool.

MAKES 12

Per muffin: 137 calories, 3 g protein, 22 g carbohydrates, 5 g total fat, 1 g saturated fat, 35 mg cholesterol, 2 g dietary fiber, 188 mg sodium

Raspberry-Oat Muffins

Frozen loose-packed berries (the official term is "individually quick frozen," or IQF) are a great gift to the cook. Convenient, versatile, and easy to use, they are a taste of summer all year long.

Prep time: 25 minutes **Bake time: 20–25 minutes**

1¼ cups whole grain pastry flour

¾ cup + 3 tablespoons old-fashioned oats

1½ teaspoons baking powder

½ teaspoon baking soda

¼ teaspoon salt

1 cup nonfat vanilla yogurt

2 large eggs

¼ cup + 1 tablespoon packed brown sugar

2 tablespoons canola oil

1 cup frozen unsweetened raspberries (unthawed)

1. Preheat the oven to 375°F. Line a 12-cup muffin tin with paper or foil liners.

2. In a large bowl, stir together the flour, ¾ cup of the oats, the baking powder, baking soda, and salt. In a medium bowl, whisk together the yogurt, eggs, ¼ cup of the sugar, and the oil until smooth; fold in the raspberries.

3. Add the yogurt mixture to the dry ingredients and stir gently just to mix. Spoon the batter evenly into the prepared muffin cups, filling each ¾ full. In a small bowl, combine the remaining 3 tablespoons oats and the remaining 1 tablespoon sugar. Sprinkle a heaping teaspoon of the oat topping over each muffin cup.

4. Bake for 20 to 25 minutes, or until the muffins are lightly browned and a toothpick inserted in the center of a muffin comes out clean. Turn the muffins out onto a wire rack to cool. These are best served warm.

MAKES 12

Per muffin: 146 calories, 5 g protein, 24 g carbohydrates, 4 g total fat, 1 g saturated fat, 36 mg cholesterol, 2 g dietary fiber, 179 mg sodium

Currant-Caraway Scones

These tender scones offer a great blend of sweet and savory; both the caraway seeds and currants contribute small amounts of fiber, too. Perfect for breakfast, they're just as delicious as a midafternoon snack with a nice cup of tea.

Prep time: 20 minutes   **Bake time: 14–17 minutes**

2 cups whole grain pastry flour

½ cup unbleached all-purpose flour, plus extra for the board

¼ cup untoasted or toasted wheat germ

2 teaspoons baking powder

½ teaspoon baking soda

1½ teaspoons caraway seeds

¼ teaspoon salt

⅔ cup currants

2 large eggs

⅓ cup sugar

½ cup plain nonfat yogurt

3 tablespoons canola oil

1 teaspoon vanilla extract

1. Preheat the oven to 375°F. Coat 2 baking sheets with cooking spray.

2. In a large bowl, stir together the flours, wheat germ, baking powder, baking soda, caraway seeds, and salt. Stir in the currants. In a small bowl, whisk the eggs, sugar, yogurt, oil, and vanilla extract until well blended. Pour the yogurt mixture over the dry ingredients and stir just until blended.

3. Flour a work surface, a rolling pin, and your hands. Turn the dough onto the floured surface and knead gently 6 to 8 times, or until cohesive (it will be sticky and soft). Pat the dough into a disk. With the rolling pin, roll into a 10" circle. With a floured knife, cut the round into 8 equal wedges, reflouring the knife as needed. Using a metal spatula, transfer the wedges to the baking sheets, spacing them apart.

4. Bake for 14 to 17 minutes, switching the position of the baking sheets halfway through the baking, until the scones are firm, puffed, and lightly golden on top. Transfer to a wire rack to cool.

MAKES 10

Per scone: 211 calories, 6 g protein, 35 g carbohydrates, 6 g total fat, 1 g saturated fat, 43 mg cholesterol, 3 g dietary fiber, 223 mg sodium

CHAPTER 5

SNACKS

Now that you've made over breakfast, you're ready to tackle snacks, the small 200-calorie mini-meals that you eat between your three squares: breakfast, lunch, and dinner. On this plan you'll enjoy one midafternoon snack a day. You have the option of choosing a second snack (in place of an appetizer or dessert after dinner) and having it at a time of day that works best for you.

Because you are now starting the day on the right nutritional foot, you will have an easier time making over your snacking habits than you did just a week ago. Your high-fiber breakfast ensures that blood sugar and insulin levels remain steady throughout the day, so you won't have to battle the cravings you once did for high-fat, high-sugar, and high-salt options. Rather than fantasizing about cupcakes and chocolate chip cookies, you'll feel satisfied with healthier high-fiber options like Bite-Size Bean and Cheese Quesadillas (page 88) or Grown-Up French Bread Pizza (page 95). (Yes, you can eat pizza and still lose weight on this incredible plan!)

As with breakfast, most people tend to have more control over their snack choices than over the other shared meals of the day. Finicky spouses and teenage children generally choose their own snacks, leaving you free to make yours.

Plus, there are plenty of high-fiber snacks—as with their fiber-vacant counterparts— that require little to no prep time. So there's no trade-off in convenience. Easy snacks in this chapter include Instant Black Bean Dip (page 79) and Smoked Paprika Hummus with Broccoli and Red Pepper Dippers (page 78). Simply swap one easy-to-make snack for another and you'll find a snack makeover is an especially easy way to increase your fiber.

WHY SNACK?

When you were a child, did one of your parents scold you for snacking, justifying that "you'll ruin your appetite for dinner"?

Well, moms and dads of ages ago, that's exactly the point. Eating every 3 to 5 hours ensures that you keep your hunger below the overeating danger zone. In this danger zone, your ability to think rationally is overpowered by evolutionary survivalist instincts. Rather than telling yourself something rational like "Dinner will be ready soon; I can wait. I'm trying to lose weight," you find yourself thinking, "I need those cheese curls *and* the corn chips *and* the ice cream *and* the chocolate-covered snack cakes, or I'll keel over and die." Of course that thought makes no rational sense, but by the time you come to your senses, you've already polished off a bag of chips and you're sitting in front of a heaping plate of food.

If you *planned* your snacks, however, you'd rarely feel compelled to participate in this type of speed eating. Eating regularly spaced meals and snacks helps keep your metabolism revved and your stomach full so you don't overeat.

Consider:

• Women who eat three meals and up to three snacks a day spaced no more than 4 hours apart have less body fat than women who eat the same number of calories packed into two or three big meals, find researchers at the University of Michigan.

• In a study completed at the University of Nottingham in the United Kingdom, nine women ate either six regular meals (three meals and three snacks) for 2 weeks or three to nine irregular meals that varied from day to day. The irregular eating reduced calorie burning during the 3 hours after eating, compared with when they ate regularly. It also caused the women to consume more calories in general.

How do regularly spaced snacks help you eat less? Primarily they do so by keeping blood sugar and insulin levels steady. In the University of Nottingham study, when the

---

FIBER TIP

Keep healthy, high-fiber snacks stashed in your desk. When 229 women logged their eating habits and feelings for 4 weeks in a British study, researchers found the women reached for snacks when their work hours stretched beyond 9:00 to 5:00. The treats they most often craved tended to be full of fat and sugar, ingredients that have been shown to release mood-boosting opiates.

participants ate haphazardly, their insulin levels were higher after eating, indicating that their cells were becoming resistant to the effects of the hormone. High insulin levels tend to trigger fat storage, cravings, and hunger.

Dips in blood sugar are what trigger the mental state most of us call the afternoon slump. This midafternoon tiredness, moodiness, and drop in concentration generally makes most people think of one thing: food. The problem is, most people think of foods that are high in fat and sugar or salt. Think snack chips. Think sweet baked goods.

Yet, if you plan your midafternoon snack and consume it before your blood sugar drops, you won't get into this frenzied eating state. You'll be able to enjoy your high-fiber fare without battling sugar cravings. You'll also be more productive during the rest of the afternoon.

Your midafternoon snack is important for another reason. The time period between lunch and dinner is pretty long for most people. If you eat lunch at noon and dinner at 7:00, you're going 7 hours without food. Even if you manage to get through the afternoon without the cheese curls and even if you manage to wait out your urge to eat until dinner, you'll be much more likely to pile your plate high and reach for second, third, or even fourth servings. Obviously, skipping snacks can actually work against the best weight-loss efforts.

That said, it's also important to remember that the best snacks are *planned* and *regular*. If you grab for a snack whenever you feel like it, you will probably *gain* weight rather than *lose* it. Remember the University of Nottingham study mentioned earlier? Study participants gained weight when they ate haphazardly, even though they were snacking.

Your body's caloric needs are closely tied to its other daily rhythms. Your body grows accustomed to having certain meals at certain times. If you skip a meal or snack or go longer than usual between meals or snacks, you'll become too hungry and have more cravings rather than less.

FIBER TIP

One in three people binges when snacks like potato chips and nacho chips are kept in plain sight. If you keep low-fiber snacks in the house, make sure they are in a closed cabinet.

THE FIBER CONNECTION

Now for an apparent contradiction. Many studies have linked snacking with overweight and obesity. Why? Because many people tend to snack on the wrong foods. Snacks that are high in fat and sugar or refined flour, such as a bagel, are calorie dense but nutrient poor.

They contain lots of calories per serving size yet almost nothing in the way of vitamins, minerals, and fiber. If you choose these types of low-fiber foods as snacks, odds are you'll get bigger, not smaller.

For example, when you eat a low-fiber snack such as potato chips, you do little to flip off your brain's hunger switch. In fact, you may do the opposite—flip it on. During digestion, the sugar and starch from food is converted to glucose and absorbed into the bloodstream. Refined snack foods that contain sugar and/or white flour are absorbed quickly, raising blood sugar levels too high. The pancreas overreacts, overproducing insulin and then driving sugar levels down within just an hour. End result: An hour after eating your cookie, you're hungry again.

You'll also eat heartily at your next meal rather than compensating for the snacking by eating slightly less. In a study done in Aberdeen, Scotland, researchers asked study participants to snack twice a day—once midmorning and once midafternoon—from a menu of snack choices. The menu was altered so that all of the snacks were either very high in fat, very high in sugar, or high in protein. The high-fat and high-sugar snacks triggered participants to overconsume calories at subsequent meals, overeating by as much as 500 daily calories.

Snack foods that contain high fructose corn syrup may be even worse than those that contain sugar. This sweetener is metabolized differently than sugar, and some studies suggest that its effect on insulin levels may actually prompt you to eat again sooner. Trans fat, a synthetic fat commonly found in processed snack foods, has also been linked to weight gain.

Eating high-fiber snacks, on the other hand, stabilizes insulin and glucose levels, encouraging you to eat less at subsequent meals. In a study of 23 women done in Australia, those who consumed high-fiber, high-protein snacks midmorning ate 5 percent less at a buffet lunch than those who consumed a high-fat, high-sugar snack bar. They also had lower levels of glucose and insulin throughout the day.

PREVENT HEART DISEASE

Heart disease is the number one killer of both men and women, and being overweight or obese more than doubles your risk of dying from it. By the end of this 4-week plan, you'll be consuming about 30 grams of fiber daily. That's enough to reduce your risk of developing heart disease by 20 to 30 percent and to reduce your risk of dying if you already have heart disease by 10 percent.

Fiber helps prevent and reverse heart disease in a number of ways.

Fiber lowers cholesterol. Heart disease progresses as cholesterol-filled plaque builds up inside the arteries that feed blood to the heart. As more plaque forms, your arteries become hard and narrow, pinching off bloodflow. If a plaque ruptures and forms a clot that completely blocks bloodflow, you have a heart attack.

Fiber drives down LDL, the worst type of cholesterol, by about 10 to 15 percent. That translates to a drop of roughly 13 points, depending on your current LDL level.

Fiber lowers cholesterol in two ways. First, fiber mixes with and removes bile acids from the intestine, preventing their reabsorption into the bloodstream. You need these bile acids to digest fat, and your liver needs cholesterol to make bile acids. To keep bile acid levels optimal, the liver must remove cholesterol from the bloodstream. End result: Blood cholesterol drops.

Second, when beneficial bacteria in the intestines feed on fiber, they create a by-product called propionic acid. This acid inhibits an enzyme that influences the liver's production of cholesterol.

Fiber drops blood pressure. When the heart beats, it pumps blood to the arteries, creating pressure inside the arteries. Your blood pressure rises with each heartbeat and falls when your heart relaxes between beats. Your blood pressure reading comes from two types of pressure. The first, larger, number is the pressure in your arteries as the heart contracts and pumps blood into the arteries. The second, lower, number is the pressure when the heart relaxes. If you're healthy, your arteries are muscular and elastic. They stretch when your heart pumps blood, so each heartbeat creates less pressure. If your arteries are stiff and narrow, blood pressure will rise.

Ideally, your pressure should be less than 120/80 mm Hg (millimeters of mercury). According to the American Heart Association, nearly one in three US adults has high blood pressure, but because there are no symptoms, nearly one-third of these people don't know they have it. In fact, many people have high blood pressure for years without knowing it. Uncontrolled high blood pressure can lead to stroke, heart attack, heart failure, or kidney failure.

High-fiber foods can lower systolic (the top number) blood pressure by 3 to 7 points. That's enough to cut the risk of heart disease–related death by 9 percent. It's also enough to reduce your need for medication, which is probably fantastic news if you are experiencing undesirable drug-induced side effects such as loss of libido. Fiber may lower pressure both by dropping cholesterol levels (which are linked to blood pressure) and by widening arteries. In one study, a meal that contained 19 grams of whole grain fiber widened arteries by 40 percent in people with metabolic syndrome, a disorder that includes obesity, high blood pressure, and high blood sugar.

HOW TO SNACK

To transition to high-fiber snacking, commit to some planning. If you work in an office, stock your desk with nonperishable high-fiber options such as single-serving microwave popcorn bags, nuts and seeds (see Trail Mix on page 97), and whole fruit. If you have access to a refrigerator, make bean dips at home and bring them to the office along with some sliced vegetables or whole grain crackers. You can also make high-fiber muffins (see Snack-Size Sweet Corn Muffins with Pineapple on page 93) to grab and bring with you to work.

With your desk full of high-fiber options, you eliminate just about any excuse you could possibly think of to head to the vending machine, bakery, or co-worker's treat jar.

Here are some great quick and easy high-fiber snack options.

Dried figs. In addition to supplying fiber, they provide 15 percent of the Daily Value for calcium.

Nuts and seeds. Rich in heart-healthy monounsaturated fat and protein, nuts are crunchy, making them a great stand-in for potato chips and other crunchy low-fiber snacks. They are one of the few snacks you'll probably be able to find in a vending machine.

Fruit. Most types of fruit will net you roughly 4 grams of fiber. Stock up on whatever is in season, including apples, pears, oranges, and other easy-to-transport whole fruits.

High-fiber cereal. Cereal isn't just a breakfast food. Scoop some into a plastic bag and carry it with you for a convenient high-fiber snack option.

Frozen soy burger. Just pop it in the toaster and eat it without the bun. You'll get roughly 5 grams of fiber, depending on the brand.

Does watching television increase snack cravings?

You're definitely on to something. In a study done in Auckland, New Zealand, children and teens who watched the most TV tended to snack on foods most often advertised on TV, including colas, fruit drinks, sweets, and fast food.

Getting more fiber during snacks, whether you eat out or at home, can be as simple as making the following switches and substitutions.

IF YOU NORMALLY EAT ...	SWITCH TO THIS HIGH-FIBER ALTERNATIVE ...
Snack chips with cool ranch dip	Vegetables or whole wheat pita dipped in hummus, bean dip, guacamole, or a veggie dip. See Broccoli Dip with Multigrain Chips (page 83), Instant Black Bean Dip (page 79), Roasted Eggplant Dip with Miso (page 80), and Broccoli-Artichoke Dip with Toasted Whole Wheat Pita Chips (page 81)
Canned fruit	Fresh fruit: It has more fiber because it includes the skin and the seeds, whereas the skins have usually been removed during canning.
Bagel	Whole grain toast or muffin or whole grain bread or wrap with hummus, peanut butter, or Caramelized Onion and Lentil Spread (page 84)
Plain nacho chips	Chipotle Bean Nachos (page 92)
Potato chips	Spiced Sweet Potato Chips (page 91)
Chocolate chip muffin	Bran muffin, Banana-Nut Muffin (page 58), cranberry-raisin muffin, or Snack-Size Sweet Corn Muffins with Pineapple (page 93)
Crunchy snack chips (potato chips, pretzels, etc.)	High-fiber breakfast cereal eaten dry, popcorn, nuts, or Trail Mix (page 97)
Applesauce	Apple
Fruit juice	Whole fruit
Pretzels made with refined flour	Whole grain pretzels
Saltines	Rye-Krisp crackers
Sweets	Frozen grapes, frozen banana, dried figs, dried apricots, or dates

Snack Recipes

Cumin-Toasted Chickpeas

Crunchy, nutty chickpeas make for a satisfying snack in large part due to their fiber content. Store in an airtight container for up to 3 days.

Prep time: 5 minutes   Bake time: 30 minutes

---

1 can (15.5 ounces) chickpeas, rinsed and drained

1 tablespoon olive oil

½ teaspoon ground cumin

¼ teaspoon salt

1. Preheat the oven to 450°F. Blot the chickpeas with a paper towel to dry them. On a large baking sheet, toss the chickpeas with the oil and sprinkle with the cumin and salt. Stir to coat.

2. Bake for 20 to 30 minutes, shaking the baking sheet occasionally, or until golden brown and crunchy.

MAKES 4 SERVINGS

Per serving: 124 calories, 4 g protein, 28 g carbohydrates, 4 g total fat, 1 g saturated fat, 0 mg cholesterol, 4 g dietary fiber, 220 mg sodium

Papaya and Plum Salsa

A perfect alternative to spicy tomato salsas, this fruity combination is laced with the flavors of the Caribbean. Serve with multigrain chips or on top of grilled chicken or fish.

Prep time: 18 minutes   Chill time: 30 minutes

2 papaya, peeled, seeded, and diced, about 2 cups

4 small red plums, pitted and diced, 1¼ cups

¼ cup fresh lime juice

2 tablespoons brown sugar

2 tablespoons chopped red onion

⅛ teaspoon ground allspice

⅛ teaspoon ground red pepper

In a serving bowl, mix the papaya, plums, lime juice, sugar, onion, allspice, and pepper. Cover and chill for 30 minutes, or until ready to serve.

MAKES 12 SERVINGS

Per serving: 30 calories, 0 g protein, 8 g carbohydrates, 0 g total fat, 0 g saturated fat, 0 mg cholesterol, 1 g dietary fiber, 2 mg sodium

Red, Black, and Yellow Salsa

This bright, colorful salsa draws its fiber power from black beans. A hint of fresh ginger adds a bit of heat. Serve with Spiced Sweet Potato Chips (page 91) or baked pita triangles dusted with ground red pepper.

Prep time: 10 minutes   Standing time: 30 minutes

1 large ripe mango

1 can (15–16 ounces) black beans, rinsed and drained

1 large red bell pepper, chopped

¼ cup coarsely chopped fresh cilantro

¼ cup chopped sweet red or white onion

3 tablespoons fresh lemon juice

1 tablespoon olive oil

1 tablespoon honey

½ teaspoon finely grated peeled fresh ginger

Pinch of salt

1. With a vegetable peeler, remove the peel from the mango. Cut the fruit off the flat pit and chop coarsely. Put in a medium bowl.

2. Add the beans, pepper, cilantro, onion, lemon juice, oil, honey, ginger, and salt. Stir gently to mix. Cover and let stand for 30 minutes before serving.

MAKES 12 SERVINGS

Per serving: 53 calories, 2 g protein, 10 g carbohydrates, 1 g total fat, 0 g saturated fat, 0 mg cholesterol, 2 g dietary fiber, 105 mg sodium

Broccoli Spears with Light Cheese Fondue

You can serve this fondue with broccoli, of course, but it is also delicious with apple slices or multigrain crackers. Blanching the broccoli renders it more tender and flavorful than raw.

Prep time: 10 minutes   Cook time: 10 minutes

1 pound broccoli

¾ cup milk

2 teaspoons flour

½ clove garlic, crushed

1 tablespoon white wine

2 ounces goat cheese

2 ounces low-fat sharp Cheddar cheese, shredded, about ½ cup

1. Cut the broccoli into long spears. Fill a large bowl with ice cubes and water to cover. Bring a large saucepan of salted water to a boil. Add the broccoli spears and cook just until crisp-tender, about 4 minutes. Drain and immediately transfer the broccoli to the cold water to stop the cooking. When cool, drain well and blot dry.

2. In a small saucepan, combine the milk, flour, and garlic and whisk to blend. Heat over medium heat, stirring constantly, until boiling. Boil until creamy and thickened, 3 to 4 minutes. Add the wine and cook 1 minute. Add the goat cheese and Cheddar and stir until melted.

3. Transfer to a small bowl or fondue pot over a low flame and serve immediately with the broccoli spears.

MAKES 4 SERVINGS

Per serving: 158 calories, 11 g protein,
11 g carbohydrates, 8 g total fat, 5 g saturated fat,
21 mg cholesterol, 3 g dietary fiber, 230 mg sodium

Crisp Broccoli Spears
with Asian Peanut Dipping Sauce

This savory peanut sauce is a perfect dip for broccoli spears or carrot sticks and can also be used as a salad dressing. The Asian chile sauce used in this recipe is called sriracha, but you can use sambal olek or any other traditional chile or chile-and-garlic sauce.

Prep time: 10 minutes   Cook time: 3 minutes

---

1 pound broccoli

¼ cup smooth or chunky peanut butter

2 tablespoons rice vinegar

1 tablespoon reduced-sodium soy sauce

1½ teaspoons brown sugar

1 clove garlic, minced

½–1 teaspoon Asian chile sauce

2 tablespoons hot water

1. Cut the broccoli into long spears. Fill a large bowl with ice cubes and water to cover. Bring a large saucepan of salted water to a boil. Add the broccoli spears and cook just until bright green and slightly tender, about 3 minutes. Drain and immediately transfer the broccoli to the cold water to stop the cooking. When cool, drain well and blot dry.

2. In a medium bowl, combine the peanut butter, vinegar, soy sauce, sugar, garlic, and chile sauce. Whisk together, adding hot water as necessary to make a sauce. Serve with the broccoli spears.

MAKES 4 SERVINGS

Per serving: 141 calories, 7 g protein, 13 g carbohydrates, 9 g total fat, 2 g saturated fat, 0 mg cholesterol, 4 g dietary fiber, 343 mg sodium

Smoked Paprika Hummus
with Broccoli and Red Pepper Dippers

Smoked paprika imparts a solid, smoky flavor without a lot of heat. As with all herbs and spices, paprika should be stored in a cool, dark place for no more than 6 months.

Prep time: 15 minutes   Chill time: 30 minutes   Cook time: 8 minutes

2 cans (15–16 ounces each) chickpeas, drained; reserve 2 tablespoons liquid

6 tablespoons fresh lemon juice

2 cloves garlic, peeled

2 tablespoons + 1 teaspoon olive oil

¾ teaspoon smoked paprika

¼ teaspoon ground black pepper

⅛ teaspoon salt

⅛ teaspoon ground red pepper

4 cups broccoli florets, steamed and cooled

2 large red bell peppers, cut into wedges

1. In a food processor, combine the chickpeas, reserved chickpea liquid, lemon juice, garlic, 2 tablespoons of the oil, ½ teaspoon of the paprika, black pepper, salt, and red pepper. Process until very smooth, scraping the sides once or twice. Scrape into a serving bowl; cover and chill for at least 30 minutes, or until ready to serve.

2. To serve, place the bowl on a platter and surround it with the broccoli and bell peppers. Garnish the dip with the remaining 1 teaspoon oil and ¼ teaspoon paprika.

MAKES 12 SERVINGS

Per serving: 99 calories, 4 g protein, 16 g carbohydrates, 3 g total fat, 0.5 g saturated fat, 0 mg cholesterol, 4 g dietary fiber, 187 mg sodium

Instant Black Bean Dip

This black bean dip is super fast and easy to put together, so it's perfect for impromptu company. Of course, it is tasty with multigrain tortilla chips, but try it with carrot sticks, as well.

Prep time: 5 minutes

---

1 can (15.5 ounces) black beans, rinsed and drained

½ cup thick and chunky salsa

1 tablespoon lime juice

½ teaspoon ground cumin

Mash ½ cup of the black beans with a potato masher in a medium bowl. Add the remaining beans, salsa, lime juice, and cumin. Mix well.

MAKES 4 SERVINGS

Per serving: 72 calories, 4 g protein, 16 g carbohydrates, 0.5 g total fat, 0 g saturated fat, 0 mg cholesterol, 4 g dietary fiber, 300 mg sodium

Roasted Eggplant Dip with Miso

Serve as a dip with baked multigrain chips or little triangles of warmed whole wheat pitas.

Prep time: 15 minutes   Bake time: 35–45 minutes   Chill time: 30 minutes

1 large eggplant, 1¼ pounds

3 tablespoons mellow white miso

3 tablespoons lemon juice

1 tablespoon olive oil

2 teaspoons honey

1 clove garlic, minced

1½ teaspoons finely grated, peeled fresh ginger

¼ cup finely chopped, well-drained, jarred roasted red peppers

¼ cup finely chopped sweet white onion

2 tablespoons chopped fresh flat-leaf parsley

1. Preheat the oven to 425°F. Poke the eggplant several times with a skewer and place in a baking pan.

2. Bake for 35 to 45 minutes, or until the eggplant has collapsed and is very tender. Let it stand until cool enough to handle, then peel off the skin and trim the top. Chop the eggplant coarsely, then transfer to a medium bowl and mash with a potato masher until nearly smooth.

3. In a small bowl, with a fork, stir together the miso, lemon juice, oil, honey, garlic, and ginger. Add the miso mixture, peppers, onion, and parsley to the eggplant and stir to mix.

4. If possible, cover and refrigerate for 30 minutes to blend the flavors before serving.

MAKES 8 SERVINGS

Per serving: 56 calories, 1 g protein, 9 g carbohydrates, 2 g total fat, 0.5 g saturated fat, 0 mg cholesterol, 3 g dietary fiber, 198 mg sodium

Broccoli-Artichoke Dip
with Toasted Whole Wheat Pita Chips

When dining out, forget about ordering a fat-laden appetizer the next time you're tempted. Just remember you can go home and whip up your own version with seven simple ingredients and reap the reward of 3 grams of fiber in less than 100 calories.

Prep time: 12 minutes   Bake time: 40 minutes

CHIPS
3 mini whole wheat pitas (6" diameter)

DIP
1 can (14 ounces) artichoke hearts in water, drained

¼ cup reduced-calorie mayonnaise

1 small clove garlic, peeled

1 package (10 ounces) frozen chopped broccoli, thawed and drained, excess moisture gently pressed out

½ cup part-skim ricotta cheese

¼ cup shredded Parmesan cheese

1. *To make the chips:* Preheat the oven to 350°F. With kitchen shears, cut each pita in half, cutting around the edge, making 2 rounds. Stack the rounds and cut into 8 wedges. Arrange the wedges rough side up in single layers on 2 baking sheets. Bake until the wedges are crisp and golden brown, about 10 minutes, reversing the position of the sheets halfway through baking. Let cool on the sheets on wire racks. Leave the oven on.

2. *To make the dip:* Meanwhile, in a food processor, combine the artichokes, mayonnaise, and garlic. Process until smooth. Add the broccoli and ricotta and pulse to form a chunky dip; do not puree. Scrape the mixture into a 9" glass pie plate. Sprinkle with the Parmesan.

3. Bake for 25 to 30 minutes, until the dip is heated through and begins to brown at the edges. Let cool for a few minutes before serving with the chips.

MAKES 12 SERVINGS

Per serving: 93 calories, 5 g protein, 12 g carbohydrates, 3 g total fat, 1 g saturated fat, 6 mg cholesterol, 3 g dietary fiber, 322 mg sodium

Broccoli Dip with Multigrain Chips

Inspired by the classic French onion dip, this healthier version of the popular party food is vivid to both eye and palate. Flecked with bright green pieces of fiber-rich broccoli and the complex flavor of caramelized onion, there's no need to wait for a party to enjoy this delicious snack.

Prep time: 10 minutes   **Cook time: 18 minutes**   **Cool time: 10 minutes**

4 cups fresh broccoli florets

2 teaspoons extra virgin olive oil

2 onions, chopped, 2 cups

2 cloves garlic, minced

2 teaspoons sugar

¾ cup light sour cream

½ cup low-fat mayonnaise

1 teaspoon grated fresh orange peel

¾ teaspoon salt

⅛ teaspoon ground black pepper

6 multigrain tortillas (7"–8" diameter), cut into 8 wedges each

1. Preheat the oven to 400°F. Coat 2 baking sheets with cooking spray.

2. Bring a large saucepan of lightly salted water to a boil over high heat. Add the broccoli, return to a boil, and cook until bright green, about 3 minutes. Drain, rinse under cold water, and drain again. Pat the broccoli with paper towels to remove excess water. Finely chop.

3. Meanwhile, heat the oil in a medium nonstick skillet over medium-high heat. Add the onions, garlic, and sugar. Cook, stirring often, until the onions are lightly golden, 7 to 9 minutes. Remove from the heat and let cool for 10 minutes. Transfer to a bowl and stir in the broccoli, sour cream, mayonnaise, orange peel, salt, and pepper.

4. Meanwhile, arrange the tortilla wedges in a single layer on the prepared baking sheets and coat lightly with cooking spray. Bake until lightly browned and crisp, about 7 to 8 minutes. Cool before serving with the dip.

MAKES 12 SERVINGS

Per serving: 118 calories, 3 g protein, 16 g carbohydrates, 5 g total fat, 1 g saturated fat, 5 mg cholesterol, 3 g dietary fiber, 365 mg sodium

Caramelized Onion and Lentil Spread

This spread is similar to a vegetarian version of pâté. It is great on crackers or pita chips, but you could also use it in a sandwich or even as a side dish with chicken or meat.

Prep time: 10 minutes**Cook time: 1 hour 20 minutes**

3 cups diced onions

1 tablespoon olive oil

3 tablespoons + 1½ cups water

½ cup lentils

2 tablespoons sherry

½ teaspoon salt

½ teaspoon ground black pepper

1 teaspoon chopped fresh sage

2 tablespoons chopped fresh parsley

1. In a medium heavy-bottomed saucepan, combine the onions, oil, and 3 tablespoons of the water. Cook over medium heat, stirring occasionally, until the onions are just golden, about 15 minutes.

2. Add the lentils and remaining 1½ cups water, cover, and cook over very low heat for 1 hour, stirring occasionally.

3. Stir in the sherry, salt, and pepper and cook, uncovered, over medium heat until the compote is thick, about 5 minutes. Remove from the heat, add the sage and parsley, and let cool.

MAKES 12 SERVINGS

Per serving: 56 calories, 3 g protein, 9 g carbohydrates, 1 g total fat, 0.5 g saturated fat, 0 mg cholesterol, 3 g dietary fiber, 101 mg sodium

Texas Caviar

This Texas favorite comes together extra fast when using frozen peas. You can control the heat in this dish by paying careful attention to how many seeds are added (wear plastic gloves when handling jalapeños).

Prep time: 10 minutes   Cook time: 20 minutes, for frozen peas   Chill time: 30 minutes

2 cups cooked black-eyed peas (from frozen and cooked according to package directions, or rinsed and drained canned)

½ cup corn kernels, cut from fresh ears, or drained canned

¼ cup light Italian dressing

2 scallions, thinly sliced

1 large jalapeño chile pepper, diced (with some seeds)

2 or 3 large heads Belgian endive, trimmed and leaves separated for dippers, or small inner romaine leaves or baked tortilla chips

1. In a medium serving bowl, mix the peas, corn, dressing, scallions, and pepper. Cover and chill for 30 minutes to blend the flavors.

2. To serve, place the bowl in the center of a large platter. Surround with the endive or romaine leaves or with the chips.

MAKES 12 SERVINGS

Per serving (with endive): 56 calories, 3 g protein, 9 g carbohydrates, 1 g total fat, 0 g saturated fat, 0 mg cholesterol, 3 g dietary fiber, 40 mg sodium

Brown Rice California Rolls

California rolls take on a new twist when prepared with brown rice. Wait until the rice is completely cooled before assembling or it won't stick properly. If pressed for time, spread the cooked rice on a baking sheet to speed cooling.

Prep time: 20 minutes   **Cook time: 20 minutes**   **Stand and cool time: 25 minutes**

1 cup short-grain brown rice

2 cups water

3 tablespoons seasoned rice vinegar

1 tablespoon sugar

6 sheets nori

1 Hass avocado, peeled, pitted, and cut into 18 slices

8 ounces imitation crab stick (surimi), cut into 6 equal portions

Wasabi paste

Reduced-sodium soy sauce

1. In a medium saucepan, combine the rice and water and bring to a boil over medium-high heat. Reduce the heat to medium-low, cover, and simmer until the water is absorbed, 20 minutes. Remove from the heat and let stand for 10 minutes. In a small bowl, combine the vinegar and sugar and stir into the rice. Let stand for 15 minutes.

2. Place a bamboo sushi mat on a work surface. Place a sheet of nori on the mat with a long side closest to you. With slightly damp hands, spread ½ cup of the rice on the nori, leaving a 1" border along the top edge. Arrange 3 avocado slices end to end in a horizontal line about 1½" from the edge closest to you. Top with ⅙ of the crab. Grasp the edges of the nori and the mat closest to you. Fold the bottom over the filling and roll up, jelly roll–style, pressing down slightly with each quarter turn. Seal the roll with a few drops of water or grains of rice on the edge of the nori. Repeat with the remaining ingredients to make 6 rolls. Transfer the rolls to a cutting board. With a serrated knife dipped in hot water, cut each roll crosswise into 6 pieces. Serve with wasabi and soy on the side.

MAKES 6 SERVINGS (1 ROLL PER SERVING)

Per serving: 197 calories, 5 g protein, 33 g carbohydrates, 5 g total fat, 1 g saturated fat, 1 mg cholesterol, 4 g dietary fiber, 241 mg sodium

Black Bean Hummus, Cilantro, Carrot, and Red Pepper Roll-Ups

Black beans are loaded with extra antioxidants, which make this hummus extra special. If you like, swap out different vegetables for a change of pace.

Prep time: 20 minutes

1 can (15 ounces) chickpeas, rinsed and drained

1 cup canned black beans, rinsed and drained

1 clove garlic

2 tablespoons water

1 tablespoon extra virgin olive oil

2 teaspoons tahini

2 teaspoons lime juice

1 teaspoon grated fresh lime peel

¼ teaspoon hot-pepper sauce

¼ teaspoon salt

3 multigrain wraps

2 carrots, grated, about 1 cup

1 cup thinly sliced cucumber

½ cup jarred sliced roasted red pepper

3 tablespoons chopped fresh cilantro

1. In the bowl of a food processor, combine the chickpeas, black beans, garlic, water, oil, tahini, lime juice, lime peel, hot-pepper sauce, and salt; puree.

2. Arrange the wraps on a work surface and spread each with one-third of the hummus mixture, ⅓ cup of the carrots, ⅓ cup of the cucumber, one-third of the roasted peppers, and 1 tablespoon of the cilantro. Roll up jelly roll–style and cut each into 8 cross sections. Arrange on a plate and serve.

MAKES 6 SERVINGS

Per serving: 178 calories, 8 g protein, 30 g carbohydrates, 6 g total fat, 1 g saturated fat, 0 mg cholesterol, 9 g dietary fiber, 507 mg sodium

Bite-Size Bean and Cheese Quesadillas

It's hard to believe, but filling snacks like this one, enjoyed between lunch and dinner, can actually help you eat less food overall. The fiber in the whole grain and beans keeps your blood sugar and insulin levels steady.

Prep time: 10 minutes   Cook time: 8 minutes per quesadilla

3 multigrain tortillas (7"–8" diameter)

1 cup fat-free refried beans

½ teaspoon ground cumin

½ teaspoon chili powder

1 cup reduced-fat shredded Mexican cheese blend

½ cup bottled mild salsa

1. Arrange the tortillas on a work surface. In a small bowl, combine the beans, cumin, and chili powder. Spread the bean mixture over the lower half of each tortilla and top each with ⅓ cup of the cheese. Fold the plain half over the filling to form a semicircle.

2. Heat a large nonstick skillet over medium heat until hot. Add 2 of the tortillas and cook until lightly browned and heated through, about 3 to 4 minutes per side. Transfer to a cutting board and repeat with the remaining tortilla. Cut each into 4 wedges and serve with the salsa.

MAKES 6 SERVINGS

Per serving: 157 calories, 9 g protein, 19 g carbohydrates, 5 g total fat, 2 g saturated fat, 13 mg cholesterol, 5 g dietary fiber, 522 mg sodium

Chicken, Mango, and Cheese Quesadillas

Slices of golden sweet mango make this snack distinctive. In season, replace the mango with ripe peach, nectarine, or apricot if you prefer.

Prep time: 15 minutes   Cook time: 8 minutes per quesadilla

---

2 multigrain wraps (10" diameter), such as Mission brand

1 cup shredded cooked chicken breast

1 medium mango, sliced, 1 cup

1 tablespoon chopped fresh cilantro

¼ avocado, about 1 ounce, cut into 6 slices

½ cup shredded reduced-fat Cheddar cheese

1. Arrange the wraps on a work surface. Top the lower half of each wrap with ½ cup chicken, ½ cup mango, ½ tablespoon cilantro, 3 slices avocado, and ¼ cup cheese. Fold the top half of each wrap over the filling to form a semicircle.

2. Heat a large nonstick skillet over medium heat. Add the quesadillas and cook until lightly browned and the filling is hot, about 4 minutes per side. Transfer to a cutting board, let stand 1 minute, then cut each into 4 wedges.

MAKES 4 SERVINGS

Per serving: 191 calories, 17 g protein,
21 g carbohydrates, 7 g total fat, 2 g saturated fat,
40 mg cholesterol, 5 g dietary fiber, 307 mg sodium

Spiced Sweet Potato Chips

Dusted with a blend of sweet and hot seasonings, these crunchy chips never stay around for long. Stick to making them in small batches and enjoy right away.

Prep time: 10 minutes   Bake time: 14 minutes

1 sweet potato, peeled, 12 ounces

½ teaspoon ground cumin

¼ teaspoon sugar

¼ teaspoon chili powder

¼ teaspoon salt

1. Preheat the oven to 375°F.

2. With a V-slicer or mandoline, cut the potato into very thin slices. Spray 2 baking sheets with cooking spray. Arrange the potato slices on the baking sheets in a single layer. Coat the slices lightly with cooking spray. Bake for 7 minutes, or until barely starting to brown. Turn the potato slices over and return to the oven. Bake until lightly browned, about 7 to 10 minutes. Transfer to a bowl and repeat with remaining potato slices, if necessary.

3. Meanwhile, in a small bowl, combine the cumin, sugar, chili powder, and salt. Pour over the chips and toss well before serving.

MAKES 2 SERVINGS

Per serving: 157 calories, 4 g protein, 36 g carbohydrates, 0.5 g total fat, 0 g saturated fat, 0 mg cholesterol, 6 g dietary fiber, 354 mg sodium

Chipotle Bean Nachos

Chipotles are jalapeño chile peppers that are dried and smoked, giving them an intense flavor. One convenient way to buy them is canned in adobo sauce, a paste of ground chiles, herbs, and vinegar. Store leftover chipotles in adobo in a tightly sealed container in the refrigerator for up to 3 months.

Prep time: 15 minutes   Cook time: 20 minutes

1 teaspoon vegetable oil

1 onion, chopped

1 clove garlic, minced

½ pound extra-lean ground beef

1 can (10 ounces) diced tomatoes

1 can (15.5 ounces) black beans, rinsed and drained

2 chipotle peppers, chopped, plus 1 tablespoon adobo sauce

1 teaspoon ground cumin

1 teaspoon chili powder

¼ teaspoon salt

24 multigrain tortilla chips

¼ cup shredded reduced-fat Cheddar cheese

Sliced pickled jalapeños (optional)

Nonfat sour cream (optional)

1. Warm the oil in a large nonstick skillet over medium heat. Add the onion and garlic and cook, stirring frequently, until tender. Add the beef and cook until no longer pink. Add the tomatoes, beans, chipotle peppers and adobo sauce, cumin, chili powder, and salt. Simmer until thickened, about 10 minutes.

2. Preheat the oven to 450°F. Arrange the tortilla chips on a baking sheet. Spoon 2 tablespoons of the bean mixture onto each chip and top with the cheese. Bake for 5 minutes, or until the cheese is melted. Serve topped with pickled jalapeños and sour cream, if desired.

MAKES 6 SERVINGS

Per serving: 158 calories, 13 g protein, 18 g carbohydrates, 4 g total fat, 1 g saturated fat, 23 mg cholesterol, 4 g dietary fiber, 557 mg sodium

Snack-Size Sweet Corn Muffins with Pineapple

These tender muffins yield a natural sweetness from the stunning combination of corn and crushed pineapple. Delicious on their own, they also make a nice accompaniment to a garden salad and a bowl of Butternut Squash, Pear, and Sweet Potato Soup (page 133).

Prep time: 15 minutes   Bake time: 18 minutes

1 cup whole wheat flour

¾ cup yellow cornmeal

½ cup ground flaxseed

⅓ cup sugar

1 teaspoon baking powder

½ teaspoon baking soda

½ teaspoon salt

¾ cup buttermilk

⅔ cup fresh corn kernels, cut from 1 large ear of corn

1 can (8 ounces) crushed pineapple in juice

2 eggs, lightly beaten

1 egg white, lightly beaten

2 tablespoons unsalted butter, melted

1. Preheat the oven to 400°F. Coat a 12-cup muffin tin with cooking spray.

2. In a large bowl, combine the flour, cornmeal, flaxseed, sugar, baking powder, baking soda, and salt; mix well. In a separate bowl, combine the buttermilk, corn, pineapple with juice, eggs, egg white, and butter. Stir the buttermilk mixture into the cornmeal mixture until moistened.

3. Spoon the batter into the muffin cups. Bake for 18 to 20 minutes, or until the muffins are lightly browned around the edges and have pulled away from the sides of the pan. Remove the muffins and let cool on a wire rack.

MAKES 12 SERVINGS

Per serving: 161 calories, 5 g protein, 25 g carbohydrates, 5 g total fat, 2 g saturated fat, 41 mg cholesterol, 3 g dietary fiber, 219 mg sodium

Grown-Up French Bread Pizza

Ditch the bottled red sauce with its high sodium and high fructose corn syrup. Create a more sophisticated pizza topped with a colorful mix of red and yellow garden tomatoes, Italian seasonings, and tangy cheese.

Prep time: 10 minutes   **Bake time: 10 minutes**

2 medium red or yellow tomatoes, chopped, about 2 cups

1 clove garlic, minced

2 teaspoons balsamic vinegar

½ teaspoon dried oregano

2 ounces shredded reduced-fat mozzarella cheese

2 ounces reduced-fat feta cheese, crumbled

1 whole wheat or multigrain baguette (8 ounces), halved lengthwise

1. Preheat the oven to 400°F.

2. In a bowl, combine the tomatoes, garlic, vinegar, and oregano. In a separate bowl, combine the mozzarella and feta.

3. Place the bread, cut side up, on a baking sheet. Top each with one-half of the tomato mixture and one-half of the cheese mixture (don't worry if a little falls off). Bake until the cheese melts and the bread is crisp, 10 to 12 minutes. Transfer to a cutting board and cut each half into 3 pieces.

MAKES 6 SERVINGS

Per serving: 152 calories, 10 g protein, 21 g carbohydrates, 4 g total fat, 2 g saturated fat, 8 mg cholesterol, 3 g dietary fiber, 344 mg sodium

Curried Snack Mix with Golden Raisins

Dried cereal, fruit, and nuts enter an intriguing new flavor dimension when sprinkled with curry, coriander, and ground red pepper.

Prep time: 15 minutes   Bake time: 50 minutes   Cool time: 10 minutes

1 multigrain pita, halved crosswise and thinly sliced

2 cups Wheat Chex cereal

1 cup mini pretzels, about 2 ounces

¼ cup whole roasted almonds

1 tablespoon unsalted butter

½ tablespoon curry powder

½ tablespoon sugar

¾ teaspoon Worcestershire sauce

½ teaspoon garlic powder

¼ teaspoon paprika

¼ teaspoon ground coriander

¼ teaspoon salt

⅛ teaspoon ground red pepper

½ cup golden raisins

1. Preheat the oven to 400°F. Coat a baking sheet with cooking spray.

2. Spread the pita strips on the baking sheet and bake until crisp, about 7 to 8 minutes. Remove from the oven, transfer to a bowl, and let cool for 5 minutes. Stir in the cereal, pretzels, and almonds. Reduce the oven temperature to 200°F.

3. In a small saucepan over medium heat, combine the butter, curry powder, sugar, Worcestershire sauce, garlic powder, paprika, coriander, salt, and pepper. Cook, stirring often, until the butter melts and the spices toast slightly, about 3 to 4 minutes. Stir into the cereal mixture and toss well to coat. Pour the mixture onto a baking sheet and bake until crisp, 40 to 45 minutes. Remove from the oven, stir in the raisins, and cool completely before serving.

MAKES 16 SERVINGS

Per serving: 139 calories, 3 g protein, 23 g carbohydrates, 4 g total fat, 1 g saturated fat, 4 mg cholesterol, 3 g dietary fiber, 253 mg sodium

Trail Mix

Fiber is an effective energy booster, but it's sure to supercharge your day when it tastes great, too. This sweet and crunchy snack will stop a midday slump in its tracks.

Prep time: 10 minutes

---

2 cups Cheerios cereal

1 cup dried pineapple, chopped

1 cup dried blueberries

1 cup dried apricots, sliced

1 bag (1 ounce) freeze-dried strawberries

⅓ cup unsalted dry-roasted peanuts

¼ cup semisweet chocolate chips

¼ cup dry-roasted sunflower seeds

In a bowl, combine the cereal, pineapple, blueberries, apricots, strawberries, peanuts, chocolate chips, and sunflower seeds. Store in an airtight container for up to 1 week.

MAKES 12 SERVINGS

Per serving: 198 calories, 3 g protein, 37 g carbohydrates, 5.2 g total fat, 1.3 g saturated fat, 0 mg cholesterol, 4 g dietary fiber, 48 mg sodium

Stuffed Apricots

Don't use Turkish dried apricots for this dish because they're not halves;
they're the whole fruit and very hard to stuff.

Prep and assemble time: 15 minutes　　**Standing time: 10 minutes**　　**Cook time: 3 minutes**

32 California dried apricot halves (choose large, uncurled halves)

½ cup boiling water

3 tablespoons slivered almonds

¼ cup light cream cheese from a tub (not whipped)

1 tablespoon wheat germ

1 tablespoon honey

Pinch of ground cinnamon

1. Put the apricots in a small bowl and pour the boiling water over them. Let stand for 10 minutes to soften. Drain the apricots, place on a layer of paper towels, and pat dry.

2. Meanwhile, in a small skillet, toss the almonds over medium heat until lightly toasted, about 3 minutes. Tip onto a plate and let cool.

3. In another small bowl, combine the cream cheese, wheat germ, honey, and cinnamon. Spoon a heaping ¼ teaspoon of the cream cheese mixture inside each apricot half, making sure the mixture stays in the apricot. Sprinkle 2 or 3 pieces of almonds over each. Cover loosely and refrigerate until ready to serve.

MAKES 8 SERVINGS (4 APRICOT HALVES PER SERVING)

Per serving: 123 calories, 2 g protein, 23 g carbohydrates, 2.6 g total fat, 1 g saturated fat, 4 mg cholesterol, 4 g dietary fiber, 38 mg sodium

Oatmeal-Granola Marshmallow Treats

Eating healthier does not have to equate to deprivation, as these sticky sweet morsels attest.

Prep time: 10 minutes   **Cook time: 6 minutes**   **Cool time: 60 minutes**

2 tablespoons unsalted butter

30 marshmallows

3 cups Cheerios cereal

3 cups Mixed Fruit Granola (see page 37)

1. Coat an 8" x 8" square baking dish with cooking spray.

2. Melt the butter in a large saucepan over medium heat. Add the marshmallows and cook, stirring, until melted, about 6 to 7 minutes. Remove from the heat and stir in the cereal and granola, stirring until well coated. Pour the mixture into the prepared pan, using a rubber spatula if needed. Place a piece of waxed paper over the cereal mixture and press down firmly with the palm of your hand to flatten. Let cool in the pan for 30 minutes. Remove from the pan and set on a cutting board and cool completely, 30 minutes. Cut into 16 squares. Store in an airtight container up to 5 days.

MAKES 16 SERVINGS

Per serving: 163 calories, 3 g protein, 31 g carbohydrates, 4 g total fat, 1 g saturated fat, 4 mg cholesterol, 2 g dietary fiber, 73 mg sodium

CHAPTER 6

LUNCH

To reach your daily fiber quota, it's good to aim for 5 to 10 grams of fiber at each meal and snack. After reading about high-fiber breakfasts and snacks, you've probably come to realize that getting to 5 grams is easier than expected. And getting at least 5 grams at lunch is even easier than at breakfast or snack time. If you love sandwiches, for example, you can get to 5 just by swapping your refined white bread for a whole wheat variety. Fill that sandwich with some veggies, have a piece of fruit on the side, and you're already closer to 10!

Not only is it easy, the payoffs of a high-fiber midday meal are huge. Foods that are rich in fiber tend to break down and digest slowly, meaning they tend to be "low glycemic," or low blood glucose–raising. Studies show that eating a low–glycemic index (GI) lunch is more satisfying than consuming a high-glycemic lunch. In one study done at Children's Hospital in Boston, obese teens who ate high-GI lunches snacked on 81 percent more calories over the course of the afternoon than teens who ate a low-GI lunch. The fast-digesting meal also spiked levels of the hunger hormone insulin and the stress hormone epinephrine.

By normalizing insulin levels, a high-fiber lunch ensures that you're less likely to lust after the doughnuts and chocolate chunk cookies during the afternoon. You'll also have more energy and better focus and be more likely to stay awake at your desk. If you exercise after work and before dinner, you'll have more oomph in every step. Finally, a high-fiber lunch paired with a fiber-rich midafternoon snack ensures that you are only mildly hungry come six or seven o'clock. So you'll eat dinner at a leisurely pace, enjoying each bite and stopping before you've overeaten.

PACK IN THE FIBER

If you work outside the home, the best way to guarantee a fiber-rich lunch plate is to bring your own. Various studies show that we tend to eat more and make poorer choices when confronted with cafeteria-style or buffet options. If you are rushed in the morning, make your lunch the night before so you can grab it on your way out the door. Buy a lunch box or cooler, and use these smart lunch-packing tips.

- Pack small whole grain crackers, trail mix, or other loose snack foods in small plastic containers with lids or in paper cups covered with plastic bags or pieces of foil. This will prevent them from turning into dust by lunchtime.

- Wrap a paper towel around whole pieces of fruit, such as pears or nectarines, to keep them from bruising. Once you unwrap your fruit, you can use the paper towel as a napkin.

- Rather than using plastic bags, pack sandwiches in hard plastic containers to prevent mashing.

- Separate wet foods from dry foods. For instance, place lettuce and sliced tomato in a container separate from your bread, and then assemble your sandwich when you're ready to eat so the bread doesn't get soggy.

Below you'll find some ways to pump up the fiber content of a few quintessential "brown-bag" lunch options.

Sandwiches. Start with a whole grain wrap, pita, bagel, roll, or bread. Substitute veggies (sliced cucumbers, lettuce, sprouts, sliced bell pepper, sliced avocado, sliced jicama, tomato) for some of the meat you usually put in your sandwich. Spread the bread with a bean dip or guacamole rather than mustard or mayo.

To determine whether or not you have found truly "whole grain" bread, check the ingredient list on the package. If the first ingredient is "whole wheat flour" or "100% whole wheat flour," you have found a whole grain product. Products simply labeled "wheat flour" or "stone-ground wheat flour" are not necessarily whole grain. The key word is *whole*. Be sure to consult the list of recommended brands of bread in the Appendix on page 330 for more direction.

Soups. In a study of 150 overweight people, researchers found that those who ate soup every day for a year lost 50 percent more weight than people who didn't. The fiber

FIBER BENEFIT #3

GET SICK LESS OFTEN

One of the unfortunate side effects of dieting is that it generally makes you sick—literally. Various studies have shown that different types of weight-loss diets reduce the effectiveness of natural killer cells, important immune system players that protect us against viruses and cancer. In one study, when eight young and healthy women cut their calorie intake in half for 15 weeks, their natural killer cells got sluggish, working only 20 percent as effectively as they had before the women began dieting.

Fiber reverses this dieting dilemma. In one study, a high-fiber diet made white blood cells stronger and more effective disease fighters. Fiber bolsters immunity in part by nourishing immunity-boosting intestinal bacteria. These bacteria secrete substances that improve health and immunity. One of these substances, butyric acid, is absorbed into the bloodstream, where it stimulates the production of antibodies and many different types of immune cells. Most high-fiber foods are also high in immunity-boosting nutrients such as various types of antioxidants. In addition to neutralizing free radicals, certain types of antioxidants have been shown to fight off harmful bacteria, yeast, and viruses.

and water in the soup weighs down the stomach, which triggers stretch receptors to flip off your hunger switch. Use either a homemade or commercially prepared soup, toting the can and can opener with you to work. Then heat it in a microwave-safe container. Look for low-sodium, clear broth varieties that are chock-full of veggies and beans. Vegetable soup and minestrone are great options. Pump up the fiber content even more by adding canned beans (rinsed and drained) or frozen vegetables to commercially prepared soup.

Salads. For convenience, use a bagged, prewashed lettuce mix, along with your choice of precut veggies. Then pump up the fiber grams and satisfaction level by adding beans. One cooked cup of beans provides as much as 17 grams of fiber. Avocado is another great fiber star for salads. Peel and slice just before eating to prevent browning. Finally, pumpkin or sunflower seeds add a nice fiber-rich crunch, as well as potassium and vitamin E, to salads.

Leftovers. Last night's dinner can become today's lunch. Toss leftover steamed vegetables and a little dressing into a storage container. Mix leftover cooked grains (brown rice, quinoa, bulgur) with canned beans or frozen veggies and cook in the office microwave.

THE HIGH-FIBER POWER LUNCH

Even though packing your own lunch is the best strategy for getting the fiber you need, there are still plenty of ways to maximize your fiber when restaurants are the only option. In fact, going high fiber when eating out may be even more important than when eating a packed lunch—fiber can be an important ally in preventing the seemingly inevitable overeating that tends to occur when the restaurant serves you portions that could feed a family of 10. To get a healthy amount of fiber, whether at a sit-down place or from a take-out counter, use these ordering tricks:

- Ask for a side of fruit, steamed vegetables, or salad in place of french fries, potato chips, or any other refined food that may accompany your main course.

- If you are ordering a sandwich at a deli, request a whole grain wrap, pita, or bread. Also ask for extra lettuce, peppers, and other veggies if the sandwich isn't already packed with them.

- If you're doing Chinese, request brown rice and opt for dishes that contain vegetables and/or nuts, such as chicken with cashews and snow peas.

- If you're going Tex-Mex, think about getting the bean chili, a quesadilla covered with beans and/or veggies, or a bean and chicken burrito.

- If you're at a diner, order the vegetable soup, a big salad, or a veggie-packed omelet.

- If you're doing pizza, top yours with lots of veggies, stick to one slice, and have a salad on the side.

- If you're at a burger place, choose a burger with high-fiber toppings such as avocado, guacamole, onion, tomato, lettuce, and other veggies. Give yourself bonus points for ordering a soy burger.

Getting more fiber at lunch, whether you eat out or at home, can be as simple as making the following switches and substitutions.

IF YOU NORMALLY EAT ...	SWITCH TO THIS HIGH-FIBER ALTERNATIVE ...
Beef burrito	Beef and bean burrito
Applesauce on the side	Apple on the side
Chips on the side	Whole grain crackers, dry whole grain cereal, or trail mix on the side
Sandwich made with white bread	Sandwich made with whole grain bread
Pizza slice with fries	Pizza slice topped with veggies and a side salad or minestrone soup
Tuna salad sandwich	Tuna salad made with shredded carrots, diced apples, and raisins and served over a bed of greens or between two slices of whole grain bread
Egg salad sandwich	Egg and Black-Bean Salad Wraps (page 113) or egg salad made with celery, cucumber, bell pepper, and other veggies and served over a bed of greens or between two slices of whole grain bread
Burger	Portobello Burgers with Roasted Peppers, Swiss, and Caramelized Onions (page 124) or soy burger on a whole grain bun, topped with lots of veggies and guacamole or hummus as a spread instead of ketchup
Plain baked potato	Baked potato stuffed with broccoli, beans, and other veggies

Lunch Recipes

(continued)

Tomato-Avocado Open-Faced Sandwiches

If ever a sandwich could be called luxurious, this one is it. Buttery avocado, nutty hummus, and juicy tomatoes just melt on the tongue.

Prep time: 10 minutes

---

8 slices whole grain bread, toasted

8 tablespoons prepared hummus

1 large ripe avocado, halved, peeled, pitted, and cut into thin slices

2 medium tomatoes (each about 6 ounces), sliced

Coarse salt and ground black pepper, to taste

Spread each slice of toast with 1 tablespoon of the hummus. Layer each with avocado and tomato slices and season to taste with salt and pepper. Cut each slice in half on an angle.

MAKES 4 SERVINGS (4 TRIANGLES PER SERVING)

Per serving: 271 calories, 8 g protein, 37 g carbohydrates, 11 g total fat, 2 g saturated fat, 0 mg cholesterol, 8 g dietary fiber, 366 mg sodium

California Club Sandwich

A native of subtropical America, the avocado has been cultivated for more than 7,000 years. More than 500 varieties are in existence, but the Hass and Fuerte are the most popular types in the United States.

Prep time: 10 minutes

---

4 slices country-style multigrain bread, such as La Brea brand

1½ teaspoons Dijon mustard

½ cup thinly sliced cucumber

½ medium avocado, sliced, about 3 ounces

½ jarred roasted red pepper, drained and halved

1 ounce soft goat cheese, crumbled

¼ cup alfalfa sprouts

Place 2 slices of the bread on a work surface. Spread one side of each with the mustard. Top each with ¼ cup cucumber, one-half of the avocado, one-half of the roasted pepper, ½ ounce goat cheese, 2 tablespoons of the sprouts, and 1 of the remaining bread slices. Cut each in half.

MAKES 2 SERVINGS

Per serving: 216 calories, 8 g protein, 29 g carbohydrates, 11 g total fat, 3 g saturated fat, 11 mg cholesterol, 9 g dietary fiber, 387 mg sodium

Broccoli Rabe and Roasted Red Pepper Wraps

Although there's no definition of the edible "wrap" in Webster's Dictionary, it's a sandwich concept that seems here to stay. Boiling the broccoli rabe helps tame the vegetable's natural bitterness, rendering it a perfect complement to the sweetness of roasted red pepper.

Prep time: 10 minutes   Cook time: 8 minutes

1 pound broccoli rabe, woody stems trimmed (trimmed weight about 8 ounces)

1 tablespoon extra virgin olive oil

3 cloves garlic, thinly sliced

⅛ teaspoon red-pepper flakes, optional

¼ teaspoon salt

1 tablespoon balsamic vinegar

2 multigrain wraps (10" diameter), such as Mission brand

1 jarred roasted red pepper, drained, patted dry, and cut into strips

½ cup shredded reduced-fat mozzarella cheese

1. Bring a large pot of lightly salted water to a boil. Add the broccoli rabe, return to a boil, and cook for 3 minutes. Drain, rinse with cold water, and drain again.

2. Heat the oil in a large nonstick skillet over medium-high heat. Add the garlic and red-pepper flakes, if using, and cook until the garlic begins to brown slightly, about 1 minute. Stir in the broccoli rabe and salt; cook until hot, 1 to 2 minutes. Add the vinegar and cook 1 minute longer; remove from the heat.

3. Place the wraps on a work surface and make a line across the center of each, leaving a 1½" border on each end, with the broccoli rabe, pepper strips, and cheese. Fold the right and left sides of the wrap so that they just cover the very edges of the filling, and then fold the bottom over and roll up jelly roll–style. Cut each in half on an angle.

MAKES 4 SERVINGS

Per serving: 151 calories, 9 g protein, 18 g carbohydrates, 7 g total fat, 2 g saturated fat, 8 mg cholesterol, 4 g dietary fiber, 506 mg sodium

Egg and Black-Bean Salad Wraps

If you're in a cold-cut rut, turn to convenient canned beans to pack flavor, nutrients, and fiber into your midday meal. This sprightly wrap will keep you energized all afternoon.

Prep time: 20 minutes   Cook time: 18 minutes   Cool time: 10 minutes

6 large eggs

1 can (15–16 ounces) no-salt-added black beans, rinsed and drained

¼ cup chopped cucumber

¼ cup chopped radishes

¼ cup chopped fresh cilantro

¼ cup reduced-calorie mayonnaise

2 tablespoons fresh lime juice

¼ teaspoon ground black pepper

4 whole wheat tortillas or multigrain wraps (9" diameter)

2 cups baby spinach, loosely packed

1. Put the eggs in a large saucepan and add water to cover. Bring to a boil over high heat; remove from the heat, cover, and let stand for 15 minutes. Drain off the hot water; fill the saucepan with cold water and let stand until the eggs have cooled, about 10 minutes.

2. Shell the eggs, discarding 3 of the yolks. Chop the eggs and put in a medium bowl. Stir in the beans, cucumber, radishes, cilantro, mayonnaise, lime juice, and pepper.

3. Warm the tortillas or wraps in the microwave according to package directions. Spoon one-quarter of the egg salad onto the bottom of a wrap. Place ½ cup of the spinach leaves on top. Roll the wrap tightly around the filling, folding in the sides. Cut the wrap in half on an angle. Repeat with the remaining wraps, egg mixture, and spinach.

MAKES 4 SERVINGS

Per serving: 327 calories, 16 g protein,
35 g carbohydrates, 13 g total fat, 3 g saturated fat,
321 mg cholesterol, 7 g dietary fiber, 467 mg sodium

Thai Beef Salad Wraps

The complex interplay of sweet and sour, hot and herbal makes this sandwich a memorable way to take a midday break.

Prep time: 15 minutes   **Cook time: 8 minutes**

---

12 ounces flank steak, trimmed

1½ teaspoons Asian chile sauce

3 tablespoons lime juice

1 teaspoon fish sauce

2 teaspoons light brown sugar

1 cucumber, halved, seeded, and thinly sliced, 1½ cups

1 cup shredded carrots

2 cups Boston or Bibb lettuce, torn in bite-size pieces

¼ cup fresh mint leaves (packed), large leaves torn in half

4 multigrain wraps (9" diameter)

¼ cup chopped unsalted peanuts

1. Heat the broiler with the oven rack about 4 inches from the heat. Pat the steak dry and sprinkle each side with ½ teaspoon of the chile sauce. Place the steak on a baking sheet and broil for 4 minutes per side. Set aside.

2. In a large bowl, whisk together the lime juice, fish sauce, sugar, and remaining ½ teaspoon chile sauce. Add the cucumber, carrots, lettuce, and mint and toss well.

3. Slice the steak across the grain as thinly as possible, cutting the longer pieces in half as necessary, for 6 to 8 slices per wrap. Divide between the 4 wraps, placing slices in the upper two-thirds of each wrap. Top with the salad mixture (about 1¼ cups each) and sprinkle with the peanuts. Fold up the bottom one-third and then roll in the sides, similar to a burrito with an open top.

MAKES 4 SERVINGS

Per serving: 338 calories, 27 g protein, 36 g carbohydrates, 13 g total fat, 3 g saturated fat, 30 mg cholesterol, 11 g dietary fiber, 530 mg sodium

Black Bean, Mango, Corn, and Brown Rice Wraps

A little bit of advance planning can make quick work of interesting lunches like this one. Instead of cooking the rice from scratch, make some extra rice the next time you prepare it for a side dish. Cool and pack into a quart-size resealable plastic freezer bag and place in the freezer.

Prep time: 15 minutes   Cook time: 15 minutes

½ cup quick-cooking brown rice (cooks in 10 minutes), such as Uncle Ben's

1 teaspoon olive oil

½ cup chopped red onion

1 clove garlic, minced

1 can (15 ounces) reduced-sodium black beans, rinsed and drained

1 cup frozen corn kernels

1 teaspoon ground cumin

½ teaspoon chili powder

½ cup mild chunky salsa

1 cup chopped mango

2 tablespoons chopped fresh cilantro

4 low-sodium multigrain wraps (10" diameter)

4 tablespoons fat-free sour cream

1. Cook the rice according to package directions, omitting any fat.

2. Heat the oil in a large nonstick skillet over medium-high heat. Add the onion and garlic and cook until starting to soften, 2 to 3 minutes. Stir in the beans, corn, cumin, and chili powder; cook until hot, 2 to 3 minutes. Stir in the salsa and cook for 30 seconds. Add the rice and cook until well combined, 1 minute. Remove from the heat and stir in the mango and cilantro.

3. Arrange the wraps on a work surface and spread 1 cup of the rice mixture across the center of each, leaving a 1½" border on each end. Fold the right and left sides of the wrap so that they just cover the very edges of the filling, and then fold the bottom over and roll up jelly roll–style. Cut each in half on an angle. Top each with 1 tablespoon of the sour cream.

MAKES 4 SERVINGS

Per serving: 276 calories, 13 g protein, 60 g carbohydrates, 5 g total fat, 0.5 g saturated fat, 1 mg cholesterol, 14 g dietary fiber, 580 mg sodium

Tex-Mex Turkey, Mango, and Pineapple Wraps

This sandwich— comprised of grainy flat bread, tangy Cheddar, sweet fruits, and pickled peppers—is a long way from the days of pallid turkey on white bread with mayonnaise.

Prep time: 10 minutes   Cook time: 4 minutes

1 multigrain wrap (10" diameter), such as Mission brand

4 teaspoons low-fat mayonnaise

¼ cup shredded reduced-fat Cheddar cheese

4 ounces deli-sliced salt-free turkey breast

½ cup chopped romaine lettuce

⅓ cup chopped fresh pineapple

¼ cup chopped fresh mango

1 tablespoon pickled jalapeño chile pepper slices, optional

1. Place the wrap on a work surface and spread the side facing you with the mayonnaise. Spread the cheese across the center of the wrap (so that the line is parallel to the edge of the counter closest to you), leaving a 1½" border at each end. Top with the turkey, lettuce, pineapple, mango, and jalapeño slices, if using. Fold the right and left sides of the wrap so that they just cover the very edges of the filling, and then fold the bottom over and roll up jelly roll–style.

2. Heat a small nonstick skillet over medium heat. When hot, add the wrap and cook until lightly browned on the outside, about 1 to 2 minutes per side. Transfer to a cutting board and cut the wrap in half on an angle.

MAKES 2 SERVINGS

Per serving: 190 calories, 21 g protein, 20 g carbohydrates, 6 g total fat, 2 g saturated fat, 40 mg cholesterol, 5 g dietary fiber, 424 mg sodium

Almond, Tarragon, and Chicken Salad Sandwiches

Tarragon is popular in the cook's perennial herb garden, and it's also now readily available in supermarkets. Look for bunches of the herb with sprightly dark green leaves that smell mildly of anise. If you have leftover leaves from this recipe, chop them finely and mix with extra virgin olive oil or softened butter. Store in an airtight container or wrap in plastic and refrigerate for several weeks to use as an instant sauce for seared chicken breasts.

Prep time: 10 minutes   Cook time: 15 minutes   Cool time: 10 minutes

---

3 boneless, skinless chicken breast halves (4 ounces each)

3 tablespoons sliced almonds

⅓ cup chopped red bell pepper

1 scallion, chopped, about ¼ cup

⅓ cup low-fat mayonnaise

2 tablespoons honey

1 tablespoon chopped fresh tarragon

⅛ teaspoon salt

⅛ teaspoon black pepper

8 slices multigrain bread

1. Fill a 10" skillet three-quarters of the way with water and bring to a boil over high heat. Add the chicken, return to a simmer, reduce the heat to medium, and cook for 12 to 15 minutes, turning occasionally, until a thermometer inserted into the thickest portion registers 160°F and the juices run clear. Remove from the heat and let the chicken cool in the water for 10 minutes. Cut the chicken into ¼" cubes and transfer to a medium bowl.

2. Meanwhile, heat a small skillet over medium heat. Add the almonds and cook, shaking the pan often, until lightly browned, about 5 to 6 minutes. Add to the bowl with the chicken and stir in the bell pepper, scallion, mayonnaise, honey, tarragon, salt, and black pepper; mix well.

3. Toast the bread and then top 4 of the slices with ½ cup of the chicken mixture. Top with the remaining bread slices and cut each in half on an angle.

MAKES 4 SERVINGS

Per serving: 350 calories, 29 g protein, 41 g carbohydrates, 8 g total fat, 1 g saturated fat, 49 mg cholesterol, 9 g dietary fiber, 573 mg sodium

Turkey, Pear, and Arugula Panini

For all their sophistication, panini are actually just the Italian version of a grilled cheese sandwich. This one's dressed up with pear, arugula, and Dijon mustard.

Prep time: 10 minutes   Cook time: 6 minutes

2 teaspoons low-fat mayonnaise

1 teaspoon Dijon mustard

4 slices country-style multigrain bread, such as La Brea brand

8 thin pear slices, about ½ medium pear

4 ounces deli-sliced no-salt turkey breast

¼ cup fresh arugula

2 slices reduced-fat Swiss cheese, about 1 ounce

1. In a small bowl, combine the mayonnaise and mustard. Spread the mixture over 1 side of 2 slices of bread. Top each with 4 pear slices, 2 ounces of turkey, 2 tablespoons of arugula, 1 slice of cheese, and 1 of the remaining bread slices.

2. Heat a medium nonstick skillet over medium heat. Add the sandwiches and place a second skillet on top, pressing down slightly. Cook until slightly flattened and toasted, about 2 to 3 minutes per side.

MAKES 2 SERVINGS

Per serving: 343 calories, 32 g protein, 40 g carbohydrates, 9 g total fat, 3 g saturated fat, 44 mg cholesterol, 10 g dietary fiber, 473 mg sodium

BLTA

You can search the world over, but you won't find a better sandwich than this one. Just be sure to use local summer tomatoes and a carefully ripened avocado. If it's a bit firm when you purchase it, store it in a brown paper bag with some bananas for a day or two.

Prep time: 4 minutes   Cook time: 6 minutes

4 slices center-cut (30% less fat) bacon, such as Oscar Mayer

4 slices multigrain bread

2 teaspoons fat-free mayonnaise

4 leaves Boston lettuce

4 tomato slices

¼ small avocado, about 1 ounce, cut into 4 slices

1. Heat a medium nonstick skillet over medium-high heat. Add the bacon and cook for 5 to 6 minutes, turning once, or until crisp. Remove from the pan and drain on paper towels.

2. Meanwhile, toast the bread slices and spread one side of 2 of the slices with the mayonnaise. Top the mayonnaise with 2 lettuce leaves, 2 tomato slices, 2 bacon slices, 2 avocado slices, and the remaining bread slices. Cut each in half on a diagonal.

MAKES 2 SERVINGS

Per serving: 302 calories, 13 g protein, 33 g carbohydrates, 14 g total fat, 3 g saturated fat, 14 mg cholesterol, 10 g dietary fiber, 555 mg sodium

Turkey and Barbecue-Slaw Buns

For best flavor contrast with the crunchy slaw that tops these sandwiches, use a barbecue sauce with a strong tomato presence instead of something smoky. Enjoy the remaining slaw on the side.

Prep time: 10 minutes

1½ cups slaw mix

1 medium Granny Smith apple, cut into very thin matchstick strips

¼ cup reduced-calorie mayonnaise

3 tablespoons barbecue sauce

3 tablespoons dark raisins

¼ teaspoon coarse-ground black pepper

4 whole wheat hamburger buns

1½ tablespoons grainy mustard

½ pound shaved no-salt deli turkey

1. In a medium bowl, stir together the slaw mix, apple, mayonnaise, barbecue sauce, raisins, and pepper.

2. Spread the buns with the mustard and top each with one-quarter of the turkey. Spoon a heaping spoonful of slaw over each and sandwich with a bun top, pressing down to close the sandwich.

MAKES 4 SERVINGS

Per serving: 278 calories, 19 g protein, 43 g carbohydrates, 5 g total fat, 1 g saturated fat, 34 mg cholesterol, 5 g dietary fiber, 594 mg sodium

Chicken Gyros in Pitas
with Yogurt and Cucumber Sauce

Whether you pronounce the name of this sandwich as *JI-row* or *YEE-ro*, you'll declare that the taste is indisputably good.

Prep time: 15 minutes   Cook time: 15 minutes

---

3 boneless, skinless chicken breast halves (4 ounces each)

1 teaspoon extra virgin olive oil

½ teaspoon dried oregano

⅛ teaspoon ground black pepper

4 multigrain pitas

1 cup chopped romaine lettuce

½ cup chopped tomato

⅓ cup thinly sliced red onion

¼ cup crumbled reduced-fat feta cheese

½ cup plain nonfat yogurt

½ cucumber, peeled, seeded, and grated, excess liquid squeezed out

½ clove garlic, minced

1. Coat a grill pan with cooking spray and heat over medium-high heat. In a bowl, combine the chicken, oil, oregano, and pepper. Place on the pan and grill for 5 to 6 minutes per side, or until a thermometer inserted into the thickest portion registers 160°F and the juices run clear. Transfer to a cutting board and cut into thin slices.

2. Meanwhile, toast the pitas. With the tip of a knife, cut an opening in one side of each pita. Fill each pita with ¼ cup romaine, 2 tablespoons tomato, 2 tablespoons onion, 1 tablespoon feta, and one-fourth of the chicken.

3. In a small bowl, combine the yogurt, cucumber, and garlic and spoon over the chicken.

MAKES 4 SERVINGS

Per serving: 321 calories, 30 g protein,
41 g carbohydrates, 5 g total fat, 2 g saturated fat,
54 mg cholesterol, 6 g dietary fiber, 579 mg sodium

Red Bean and Corn Sloppy Janes

Spicy hot beans and Italian sausage make this quick-to-fix dish a great crowd pleaser.

Prep time: 3 minutes   **Cook time: 16 minutes**

1 can (15–16 ounces) hot chili beans, drained

1 can (14½ ounces) salt-free diced tomatoes

½ cup drained, canned corn kernels

1 hot Italian-style fully cooked chicken sausage, halved lengthwise and thinly sliced

4 whole wheat hamburger buns

1. In a large nonstick skillet, stir together the beans, tomatoes, corn, and chicken sausage. Bring to a boil over medium-high heat. Reduce the heat to low, cover, and simmer for 10 minutes to blend the flavors. Remove the cover and simmer for 2 to 3 minutes longer to thicken the juices.

2. Toast the buns. Place a bun bottom on each of 4 plates. Spoon the bean mixture evenly over bun bottoms and top each with a bun top.

MAKES 4 SERVINGS

Per serving: 269 calories, 16 g protein, 39 g carbohydrates, 5 g total fat, 1 g saturated fat, 19 mg cholesterol, 9 g dietary fiber, 599 mg sodium

Portobello Burgers with Roasted Peppers, Swiss, and Caramelized Onions

Transitioning to healthier eating is easier if you prepare familiar dishes with better ingredients. This grilled "burger" with all the trimmings will satisfy even devoted beef fans. Serve some oven sweet potato fries on the side.

Prep time: 10 minutes   Cook time: 19 minutes

---

1 tablespoon extra virgin olive oil

1 onion, thinly sliced, 1 cup

1 teaspoon sugar

1 tablespoon balsamic vinegar

4 portobello mushroom caps, about 3½–4 ounces each

¼ teaspoon salt

¼ teaspoon ground black pepper

4 slices reduced-fat Swiss cheese, about 2 ounces

4 (100-calorie) light multigrain English muffins, such as Thomas', split

2 jarred roasted red peppers, drained and cut into strips

1. Preheat the grill.

2. Heat 1 teaspoon of the oil in a small nonstick skillet over medium-high heat. Add the onion and sugar and cook, stirring occasionally, until lightly browned, about 5 to 6 minutes. Remove from the heat.

3. Combine the remaining 2 teaspoons oil and the vinegar in a small bowl. Brush the mixture over the mushroom caps and sprinkle with the salt and pepper. Grill, covered, turning occasionally, until tender, 9 to 11 minutes. Top each with 1 slice of the cheese and grill until the cheese melts, about 1 to 2 minutes longer. Transfer to a plate and keep warm.

4. Toast the English muffins. Place the bottom half of each muffin on a plate and top with 1 portobello cap, one-fourth of the roasted peppers, and one-fourth of the onion. Top with the remaining muffin halves.

MAKES 4 SERVINGS

Per serving: 225 calories, 13 g protein, 36 g carbohydrates, 7 g total fat, 2 g saturated fat, 9 mg cholesterol, 10 g dietary fiber, 494 mg sodium

Open-Faced Grilled Vegetable Sandwiches

Fruity olive oil and tart lemon juice moisten this salad inside a bun. Aromatic fresh basil leaves provide the crowning touch.

Prep time: 10 minutes   Cook time: 15 minutes

---

1 small eggplant, 8 ounces, cut into 8 slices

1 zucchini, 8 ounces, cut lengthwise into 4 slices

1 red onion, cut into 4 slices

1 red bell pepper, cut into 4 panels

5 teaspoons extra virgin olive oil

¼ teaspoon salt

¼ teaspoon ground black pepper

1 cup cooked cannellini beans

1 tablespoon lemon juice

2 multigrain submarine rolls or multigrain baguette sections (3 ounces each), halved lengthwise

8 fresh basil leaves

1. Preheat the grill.

2. Lightly brush the eggplant, zucchini, onion, and bell pepper with 4 teaspoons of the oil; sprinkle with the salt and pepper. Grill the eggplant and zucchini slices until tender and well marked, 4 to 5 minutes per side. Grill the onion and bell pepper until tender and well marked, 6 to 7 minutes per side. Separate the onion slices into rings and slice the peppers into strips.

3. Meanwhile, in a small bowl, place the beans, lemon juice, and the remaining 1 teaspoon olive oil and lightly mash with the tines of a fork until combined.

4. Grill the rolls until lightly toasted, 45 seconds per side. Spread the cut halves with the bean mixture and top each with 2 eggplant slices, 1 zucchini slice, one-fourth of the onion rings and pepper strips, and 2 basil leaves.

MAKES 4 SERVINGS

Per serving: 249 calories, 9 g protein, 41 g carbohydrates, 8 g total fat, 1 g saturated fat, 0 mg cholesterol, 10 g dietary fiber, 578 mg sodium

Veggie Pitas with Hummus Dressing

You get plenty of protein in these vegetarian sandwiches, thanks to the chickpeas.

Prep time: 15 minutes

HUMMUS DRESSING

1 can (15.5 ounces) chickpeas, rinsed and drained

1½ tablespoons Asian toasted sesame oil

3 tablespoons lemon juice

1 small clove garlic, peeled

½–1 teaspoon hot-pepper sauce

½ teaspoon salt

5 tablespoons water

SALAD

2 medium cucumbers, peeled, halved lengthwise, seeded, and cut into ¼"-thick slices (2 packed cups)

6 small radishes, halved and sliced

½ cup shredded carrots

4 large whole wheat pitas, halved

4 cups thinly sliced romaine lettuce

1. *To make the dressing:* In a food processor or blender, combine the chickpeas, oil, lemon juice, garlic, hot-pepper sauce, salt, and water until smooth.

2. *To make the salad:* In a large bowl, combine the cucumbers, radishes, and carrots. Toss with 1 cup of the hummus dressing.

3. Fill each pita half with ½ cup lettuce and about ½ cup vegetable mixture. Drizzle a little more hummus dressing over the top of each pita. Serve immediately.

MAKES 4 SERVINGS

Per serving: 282 calories, 11 g protein,
44 g carbohydrates, 8 g total fat, 1 g saturated fat,
0 mg cholesterol, 9 g dietary fiber, 577 mg sodium

Spring Pea Soup

Peas are a vegetable that benefits from freezing because their essential sugars are captured right after harvest, before they turn to starch. Look for baby or petite peas for best flavor.

Prep time: 10 minutes   Cook time: 30 minutes   Cool time: 5 minutes

1 tablespoon olive oil

2 large shallots, chopped, about 1 cup

1 carrot, chopped

4 cups lower-sodium, fat-free chicken broth

2 packages (10 ounces each) frozen peas

1 tablespoon chopped fresh tarragon

¼ teaspoon salt

¼ teaspoon ground black pepper

1. Heat the oil in a large saucepan over medium heat. Add the shallots and carrot; cook, stirring occasionally, until the vegetables are soft, about 8 to 9 minutes. Stir in the broth and peas; increase the heat to high and bring to a boil. Reduce the heat to medium-low and simmer, covered, until the peas are very tender, about 20 minutes.

2. Remove the saucepan from the heat, stir in the tarragon, and cool for 5 minutes. Transfer the soup in batches to a blender and puree. Stir in the salt and pepper.

MAKES 4 SERVINGS

Per serving: 175 calories, 12 g protein,
23 g carbohydrates, 5 g total fat, 1 g saturated fat,
5 mg cholesterol, 7 g dietary fiber, 455 mg sodium

Sausage and Bean Stew

This easy stew is like a cassoulet turned inside out! Instead of smoked pork, it has a smoky low-fat turkey kielbasa. Instead of high-fat duck confit, it uses lean pork tenderloin. Same hearty flavor, but high fiber and low fat.

Prep time: 15 minutes   Cook time: 25 minutes

2 teaspoons olive or vegetable oil

1 pork tenderloin (12 ounces), cut into 1" chunks

1 cup chopped onion

2 cups diced carrots

3 cloves garlic, sliced

½ cup dry red wine

4 tablespoons tomato paste

1 can (14 ounces) reduced-sodium chicken broth

¼ pound low-fat turkey kielbasa, chopped

2 cans (15.5 ounces each) white kidney (cannellini) beans, rinsed and drained

3 teaspoons chopped thyme leaves

⅛ teaspoon ground black pepper

1. Heat the oil in a large nonstick skillet over medium-high heat. Add the pork and cook until just golden on all sides, about 5 minutes. Remove the pork from the pan and set aside.

2. Reduce the heat to medium and add the onion, carrots, and garlic and cook until the onion is tender, about 5 minutes. Add the wine and cook for 1 minute. Add the tomato paste and cook, stirring until the mixture is dry, about 2 minutes. Add the broth, kielbasa, beans, 2 teaspoons of the thyme, and pepper. Simmer until thickened, 10 minutes, stirring occasionally.

3. Add the pork and any juices that have accumulated to the bean mixture and cook until heated through, 1 to 2 minutes. Spoon into serving bowls and sprinkle with the remaining 1 teaspoon thyme.

MAKES 6 SERVINGS

Per serving: 212 calories, 19 g protein, 18 g carbohydrates, 5 g total fat, 1 g saturated fat, 49 mg cholesterol, 5 g dietary fiber, 574 mg sodium

Corn and Green Chile Soup with Tomato-Avocado Salad

If you simply can't decide whether to dine on soup or salad, this is the meal for you. A salsalike condiment floats atop a vegetable chowder.

Prep time: 5 minutes   Cook time: 15 minutes

SOUP

1 tablespoon olive oil

1 medium onion, chopped

3 cans (11 ounces each) corn, drained

2½ cups water

2 cups reduced-sodium, fat-free chicken broth

1 can (4.25 ounces) chopped mild green chiles, undrained

½ teaspoon dried oregano

¾ teaspoon ground black pepper

SALAD

1 ripe medium avocado, pitted, peeled, and cut into small chunks

2 medium tomatoes, diced

3 scallions, thinly sliced

1. Heat the oil in a heavy Dutch oven over medium heat. Add the onion and cook, stirring often, until tender, about 5 minutes. Stir in the corn, water, broth, chiles, oregano, and pepper. Bring to a boil over high heat. Reduce the heat to low, cover, and simmer for 10 minutes to blend the flavors.

2. Remove the soup from the heat and use an immersion blender to process it to a coarse puree. Or, puree half the soup, in batches, in a food processor until nearly smooth. Stir the pureed mixture back into the soup. Reheat if necessary.

3. *To make the salad:* In a small bowl, combine the avocado, tomatoes, and scallions. Ladle the soup into deep bowls and top each with some of the salad.

MAKES 6 SERVINGS

Per serving: 123 calories, 4 g protein, 24 g carbohydrates, 3 g total fat, 0.5 g saturated fat, 0 mg cholesterol, 3 g dietary fiber, 557 mg sodium

Butternut Squash, Pear, and Sweet Potato Soup

A leek may look like an overgrown scallion, but its gentle, sweet nature belies its size. It's a natural for the soup pot, where its mild onion flavor mingles with all the other ingredients.

Prep time: 20 minutes   Cook time: 55 minutes   Cool time: 10 minutes

3 slices center-cut (30% less fat) bacon, such as Oscar Mayer, chopped

3 leeks, white and light green parts only, chopped, 2 cups

2 pounds butternut squash, peeled, seeded, and chopped

1 pound sweet potatoes, peeled and chopped

2 pears, peeled, cored, and chopped

2 carrots, chopped, ½ cup

1 teaspoon chopped fresh thyme

⅛ teaspoon ground nutmeg

4 cups lower-sodium, fat-free chicken broth

½ cup light cream

¼ teaspoon salt

⅛ teaspoon ground black pepper

1. Heat a large saucepan over medium-high heat. Add the bacon and cook until crisp, 5 to 6 minutes. Stir in the leeks and cook until they start to soften, 2 to 3 minutes. Add the squash, sweet potatoes, half of the pears, the carrots, and thyme; cook, stirring occasionally, until the vegetables are slightly softened, about 9 to 10 minutes. Stir in the nutmeg and cook for 30 seconds. Pour in the broth; bring to a boil, reduce the heat to medium-low, cover, and simmer until the vegetables are tender, about 30 minutes. Remove the saucepan from the stove and cool for 10 minutes.

2. Transfer the soup, in batches, to a blender and puree. Return the soup to the saucepan over medium heat. Stir in the cream, salt, and pepper and heat until hot, 1 to 2 minutes. Divide the soup among 8 bowls and garnish each with some of the remaining pear.

MAKES 8 SERVINGS

Per serving: 183 calories, 6 g protein, 33 g carbohydrates, 4 g total fat, 2 g saturated fat, 15 mg cholesterol, 6 g dietary fiber, 243 mg sodium

Thai Sweet Potato and Peanut Soup

This exotic blend of flavors is alluring. Any leftover canned coconut milk can be frozen for up to 3 months in resealable plastic storage bags.

Prep time: 10 minutes   Cook time: 40 minutes

1 teaspoon dark sesame oil

1 tablespoon grated fresh ginger

2 cloves garlic, minced

1 onion, chopped, 1 cup

2 pounds sweet potatoes, peeled and cut into chunks

1 teaspoon curry powder

4 cups lower-sodium, fat-free chicken broth

3 tablespoons packed brown sugar

⅓ cup peanut butter

½ cup light coconut milk

1 tablespoon fish sauce

2 tablespoons chopped fresh cilantro

4 teaspoons lime juice

1. Heat the oil in a large saucepan over medium heat. Add the ginger, garlic, and onion and cook, stirring occasionally, until starting to soften, about 3 to 4 minutes. Add the sweet potatoes and curry powder; cook for 1 minute, or until fragrant. Stir in the broth and sugar; increase the heat to high, cover, and bring to a boil. Reduce the heat to medium low and simmer until the potatoes are almost tender, 15 minutes. Stir in the peanut butter and cook until the sweet potatoes are tender, 8 minutes longer. Add the coconut milk and fish sauce and cook, uncovered, 3 minutes longer. Remove from the heat and cool for 10 minutes.

2. Transfer the soup, in batches, to a blender and puree. Return the soup to the saucepan and stir in the cilantro and lime juice. The soup should be thick. If you prefer a thinner consistency, stir in a little chicken broth or water to help thin it.

MAKES 6 SERVINGS

Per serving: 332 calories, 12 g protein, 53 g carbohydrates, 10 g total fat, 3 g saturated fat, 3 mg cholesterol, 6 g dietary fiber, 473 mg sodium

Lentil Soup with Butternut Squash and Swiss Chard

A new, wonderful convenience food is peeled, cubed butternut squash—sold fresh and frozen in bags. It saves time and the trouble of peeling the squash. Red-stemmed Swiss chard is an especially nice addition to this soup.

Prep time: 18 minutes   Cook time: 60 minutes

2 tablespoons olive oil

1 large onion, chopped

2 large carrots, sliced

3 medium ribs celery with leaves, sliced

4 cloves garlic, minced

1½ teaspoons dried thyme

½ teaspoon dried marjoram

1 teaspoon salt

1 teaspoon ground black pepper

1½ cups lentils, picked over and rinsed

8 cups water

1 package (10 ounces) frozen cubed butternut squash, or 2½ cups fresh peeled and cubed butternut squash

½ pound Swiss chard, large leaves halved lengthwise and sliced 1" thick; stems sliced ¼" thick (6 cups)

1 can (14½ ounces) salt-free diced tomatoes

1. Heat the oil in a large, heavy Dutch oven over medium heat. Add the onion, carrots, celery, and garlic and cook, stirring often, until nearly tender, about 8 minutes. Stir in the thyme, marjoram, salt, pepper, and lentils. Cook and stir for 30 seconds.

2. Add the water and bring to a boil over high heat. Reduce the heat to low, cover, and simmer until the lentils are very tender, 25 to 30 minutes.

3. Stir in the squash, Swiss chard, and tomatoes and return to a boil, breaking up the tomatoes with the side of a spoon. Cover and simmer until all of the vegetables are tender, about 10 minutes more.

MAKES 8 SERVINGS

Per serving: 171 calories, 8 g protein, 27 g carbohydrates, 4 g total fat, 1 g saturated fat, 0 mg cholesterol, 10 g dietary fiber, 412 mg sodium

Creamy Broccoli Soup with Parmesan Crisps

If you can, grate the cheese from a hunk for the best flavor. Parmigiano-Reggiano is the true Parmesan from Italy (and also the most expensive). Other good options are Grana Padano, a generic Italian hard grating cheese, or a Parmesan-style cheese from Wisconsin.

Prep time: 15 minutes   Cook time: 25 minutes

1 multigrain wrap (8" diameter)

⅓ cup grated Parmesan cheese

2 cups reduced-sodium chicken broth

1 cup 1% milk

2 teaspoons olive oil

1 cup chopped onion

2 cloves garlic, minced

2 tablespoons flour

6 cups chopped broccoli florets and peeled stems, steamed to crisp-tender

½ packed cup Italian (flat leaf) parsley leaves, chopped

1 tablespoon fresh thyme leaves, chopped

½ teaspoon ground black pepper

1. Heat the oven to 400°F. Place the wrap on a baking sheet and sprinkle with the cheese, spreading it out until near the edges. Bake for 8 to 10 minutes, until the cheese is melted and the wrap is crisp. Immediately cut into 8 wedges. Set aside.

2. In a small saucepan, heat the broth and milk until almost simmering. Meanwhile, heat the oil in a large saucepan over medium heat. Add the onion and garlic and cook for 3 to 5 minutes, until translucent. Add the flour and cook, stirring, for 1 minute. Add the hot broth and milk and simmer, constantly stirring with a whisk, until the mixture thickens, about 5 minutes. Add the broccoli and cook until tender, about 5 minutes. Remove from the heat and cool slightly.

3. Transfer the mixture to a blender or food processor. Add the parsley, thyme, and pepper. Puree until smooth, in batches as necessary.

4. Return the soup to the saucepan and reheat just to boiling. Serve with the Parmesan crisps.

MAKES 4 SERVINGS

Per serving: 190 calories, 13 g protein, 26 g carbohydrates, 6 g total fat, 2 g saturated fat, 10 mg cholesterol, 7 g dietary fiber, 468 mg sodium

Hearty Minestrone

How can you not feel healthy when you dip into a bowl of chunky minestrone? This mélange of beans, greens, and vegetables is just off the charts in nutrients.

Prep time: 20 minutes   Cook time: 40 minutes

2 tablespoons extra virgin olive oil

1 onion, chopped, 1 cup

4 cloves garlic, minced

1½ teaspoons dried basil

1 sweet potato, 8 ounces, peeled and cut into ½" pieces

1 zucchini, 8 ounces, cut into ½" pieces

1 yellow squash, 8 ounces, cut into ½" pieces

1 fennel bulb, 8 ounces, cut into ½" pieces

5 cups lower-sodium, fat-free chicken broth

1 can (14.5 ounces) diced tomatoes

1 bag (5 ounces) baby spinach

1 can (15 ounces) red kidney beans, rinsed and drained

¼ teaspoon ground black pepper

¼ cup grated Parmesan cheese

1. Heat the oil in a large saucepan over medium-high heat. Add the onion, garlic, and basil; cook, stirring occasionally, until starting to soften, 2 to 3 minutes. Add the sweet potato and cook for 1 minute. Stir in the zucchini, yellow squash, and fennel and cook until just starting to soften, 2 to 3 minutes. Add the broth and tomatoes; bring to a boil, reduce the heat to medium, and simmer, uncovered, until the vegetables are crisp-tender, about 25 minutes.

2. Stir in the spinach and cook until wilted, 5 minutes. Add the beans and pepper; cook until hot, 3 minutes. Remove from the heat and stir in the cheese.

MAKES 8 SERVINGS

Per serving: 154 calories, 7 g protein, 22 g carbohydrates, 5 g total fat, 1 g saturated fat, 2 mg cholesterol, 7 g dietary fiber, 500 mg sodium

Tuscan Ribolitta (Bread and Tomato Soup)

Ribolitta is the name of a Tuscan dish which means "reboiled." Cooks would reheat leftover minestrone and thicken it with dry bread to create a brand-new meal.

Prep time: 25 minutes   Cook time: 30 minutes

2 tablespoons extra virgin olive oil

1 onion, chopped, 1 cup

4 ribs celery, chopped, 1 cup

2 carrots, chopped, ¾ cup

2 cloves garlic, minced

2 cans (14.5 ounces each) lower-sodium, fat-free vegetable broth

½ pound escarole, about 4 cups, coarsely chopped

1 can (14.5 ounces) salt-free diced tomatoes

1 can (15 ounces) cannellini beans, rinsed and drained

6 slices stale multigrain bread, cut into cubes

½ cup fresh basil leaves

¼ cup grated Romano cheese

¼ teaspoon ground black pepper

1. Heat the oil in a large saucepan over medium-high heat. Add the onion, celery, carrots, and garlic; cook, stirring occasionally, until softened, 8 to 9 minutes. Stir in the broth, escarole, tomatoes, and beans. Bring to a boil and cook, stirring occasionally, until the escarole wilts, 3 to 4 minutes.

2. Add the bread and reduce the heat to medium; simmer, stirring occasionally, until the mixture becomes a thick porridgelike consistency, about 15 to 18 minutes. Remove from the heat and stir in the basil, cheese, and pepper.

MAKES 6 SERVINGS

Per serving: 236 calories, 10 g protein, 31 g carbohydrates, 8 g total fat, 2 g saturated fat, 5 mg cholesterol, 9 g dietary fiber, 590 mg sodium

Pasta Fagioli

Pasta and beans is pure Italian comfort food. A grating of Pecorino Romano cheese is a fine addition.

Prep time: 15 minutes   Cook time: 24 minutes

2 slices center-cut (30% less fat) bacon, such as Oscar Mayer, chopped

1 onion, chopped, 1 cup

4 cloves garlic, minced

3 ribs celery, chopped, ¾ cup

2 carrots, chopped, ½ cup

4 cups lower-sodium, fat-free chicken broth

1 can (14.5 ounces) salt-free diced tomatoes

6 ounces whole wheat blend rotini, such as Healthy Harvest (Ronzoni)

1 can (15 ounces) dark red kidney beans, rinsed and drained

¼ cup chopped fresh parsley

¼ cup chopped fresh basil

⅛ teaspoon ground black pepper

1. Heat a large saucepan over medium-high heat Add the bacon and cook until just starting to brown, 5 to 6 minutes. Add the onion, garlic, celery, and carrots and cook until just starting to soften, 2 to 3 minutes.

2. Pour in the broth, tomatoes, rotini, and beans. Cover and bring to a boil; uncover and cook until the rotini is tender, about 12 to 15 minutes. Remove from the heat and stir in the parsley, basil, and pepper.

MAKES 6 SERVINGS

Per serving: 210 calories, 10 g protein, 33 g carbohydrates, 4 g total fat, 1 g saturated fat, 3 mg cholesterol, 9 g dietary fiber, 490 mg sodium

North African Spiced Chickpea and Pasta Soup

In North America, cinnamon is used mostly in baked goods and sweet dishes, but in other cuisines it provides a sweet, spicy counterpoint to sharper seasonings in savory dishes. Here, it balances the bite of fresh ginger and the slight astringency of saffron.

Prep time: 15 minutes   Cook time: 30 minutes

2 tablespoons extra virgin olive oil

1 onion, chopped, 1 cup

2 ribs celery, chopped, ½ cup

2 teaspoons grated fresh ginger

1 teaspoon ground cumin

½ teaspoon ground cinnamon

⅛ teaspoon saffron threads, lightly crushed

4 cups lower-sodium, fat-free chicken broth

2 cans (15 ounces each) chickpeas, rinsed and drained

1 can (14.5 ounces) diced tomatoes

3 tablespoons tomato paste

3 ounces whole wheat elbow macaroni

⅓ cup chopped fresh cilantro

1 tablespoon lemon juice

1. Heat the oil in a large saucepan over medium-high heat. Add the onion, celery, and ginger; cook, stirring occasionally, until starting to soften, about 3 to 4 minutes. Add the cumin, cinnamon, and saffron and cook until fragrant, 45 seconds. Stir in the broth, chickpeas, tomatoes, and tomato paste. Bring to a boil, reduce the heat to medium, and simmer, uncovered, for 15 minutes.

2. Stir in the pasta and cook until tender, about 10 minutes. Remove from the heat and stir in the cilantro and lemon juice.

MAKES 6 SERVINGS

Per serving: 232 calories, 11 g protein, 33 g carbohydrates, 7 g total fat, 1 g saturated fat, 3 mg cholesterol, 7 g dietary fiber, 442 mg sodium

Super-Fast Herbed White Bean Soup

Don't be fooled by this easy recipe. With fresh rosemary, parsley, and extra virgin olive oil, you'll taste Tuscany in a bowl.

Prep time: 10 minutes   Cook time: 5 minutes

---

2 cans (15.5 ounces each) cannellini beans, rinsed and drained

1 can (14.5 ounces) low-sodium chicken broth

¼ cup chopped parsley

¾ teaspoon finely chopped rosemary

¼ teaspoon ground black pepper

¼ teaspoon salt

⅓ cup water

1 tablespoon lemon juice

4 teaspoons extra virgin olive oil

In a blender, combine 1 can of the beans, the broth, parsley, rosemary, pepper, and salt. Puree until smooth. Transfer to a small saucepan and add the second can of beans and the water. Bring to a boil. Remove from the heat, stir in lemon juice, and spoon into 4 bowls. Drizzle each with 1 teaspoon of the oil.

MAKES 4 SERVINGS

Per serving: 171 calories, 7 g protein, 22 g carbohydrates, 6 g total fat, 1 g saturated fat, 2 mg cholesterol, 6 g dietary fiber, 516 mg sodium

Mexican Chicken and Avocado Soup

Just reading the ingredients list of this savory soup is enticing: onion, garlic, oregano, chili powder, tomato, fresh lime, and cilantro—all the essentials of genuine Mexican cooking.

Prep time: 15 minutes   Cook time: 35 minutes

2 teaspoons olive oil

1 large white onion, chopped, about 1½ cups

4 ribs celery, chopped, about 1 cup

3 carrots, chopped, about 1 cup

3 cloves garlic, minced

1 pound boneless, skinless chicken breasts, cut crosswise into thin strips

½ teaspoon dried oregano

½ teaspoon chili powder

¼ teaspoon ground chipotle

4 cups lower-sodium, fat-free chicken broth

1½ cups chopped tomato

2 tablespoons chopped fresh cilantro

1 tablespoon lime juice

2 multigrain tortillas (7–8" diameter), such as Mission brand, cut into thin strips

½ medium avocado, diced (¾ cup), 4 ounces

1. Preheat the oven to 400°F. Coat a baking sheet with cooking spray and set aside.

2. Heat the oil in a large saucepan over medium-high heat. Add 1 cup of the onion, the celery, carrots, and garlic; cook, stirring occasionally, until the vegetables are almost soft, about 7 to 8 minutes. Stir in the chicken, oregano, chili powder, and chipotle; cook until the chicken is no longer pink, about 3 to 4 minutes. Add the broth and tomato; bring to a boil, reduce the heat to medium-low, cover, and simmer for 15 minutes. Remove from the heat and stir in the cilantro and lime juice.

3. Meanwhile, place the tortilla strips on the prepared baking sheet and spray with cooking spray. Bake until crisp, 6 to 7 minutes; remove from the oven and let cool.

4. To serve, divide the soup among 6 bowls and garnish each with the remaining onion, the tortilla strips, and the avocado.

MAKES 6 SERVINGS

Per serving: 206 calories, 21 g protein, 17 g carbohydrates, 6 g total fat, 1 g saturated fat, 44 mg cholesterol, 5 g dietary fiber, 468 mg sodium

Havana Black Bean Soup with Oranges and Sherry

Black beans and oranges have a real affinity. Add a touch of sherry and citrusy cilantro, and you have a meal worth sitting down to.

Prep time: 18 minutes   Cook time: 40 minutes

2 tablespoons olive oil

1 large onion, chopped

2 large carrots, thinly sliced

4 cloves garlic, minced

1½ teaspoons whole cumin seeds

½ teaspoon dried oregano

½ teaspoon salt

⅛ teaspoon ground red pepper

3 cans (15–16 ounces each) reduced-sodium black beans, rinsed and drained

4 cups water

¼ cup medium-dry sherry

ORANGE TOPPING

2 navel oranges, peeled, all white pith cut off, chopped

2 tablespoons chopped red onion

2 tablespoons chopped fresh cilantro

1. Heat the oil in a heavy Dutch oven over medium heat. Add the onion, carrots, and garlic and cook, stirring often, until tender, about 8 minutes. Add the cumin, oregano, salt, and pepper; cook and stir for 30 seconds.

2. Stir in the beans and water. Bring to a boil over high heat. Reduce the heat to low; cover and simmer until the flavors have blended, 10 minutes. Add the sherry and simmer, uncovered, for 5 minutes more. Use an immersion blender to puree the soup, or process it in a food processor, in batches. Return the soup to the pot; reheat if necessary, and cover to keep warm.

3. *To make the topping:* In a small bowl, mix the oranges, red onion, and cilantro. Ladle the soup into soup bowls and spoon some topping onto each.

MAKES 4 SERVINGS

Per serving: 267 calories, 11 g protein,
48 g carbohydrates, 7 g total fat, 1 g saturated fat,
0 mg cholesterol, 14 g dietary fiber, 495 mg sodium

Fruited Spinach Salad with Smoked Turkey and Toasted Walnuts

Cultured buttermilk makes a wonderful thick and tangy base for creamy dressings. It has much less fat than either cream or mayonnaise.

Prep time: 15 minutes   Cook time: 3 minutes

DRESSING

½ cup buttermilk

2 tablespoons reduced-calorie mayonnaise

1 tablespoon cider vinegar

1½ teaspoons grainy Dijon mustard

½ teaspoon coarse-ground black pepper

Pinch of salt

SALAD

1 package (6 ounces) prewashed baby spinach

1 large Granny Smith apple, quartered, cored, and thinly sliced crosswise

1 large ripe pear, quartered, cored, and thinly sliced crosswise

4 ounces sliced lean ham or smoked turkey, cut into 2" × ½" strips

¼ cup thinly sliced red onion

2 tablespoons pumpkin seeds

2 tablespoons golden raisins

2 tablespoons coarsely chopped walnuts, toasted

1. *To make the dressing:* In a salad bowl, whisk together the buttermilk, mayonnaise, vinegar, mustard, pepper, and salt.

2. *To make the salad:* Add the spinach, apple, pear, ham or turkey, onion, pumpkin seeds, raisins, and walnuts to the salad bowl. Toss until well coated with the dressing.

MAKES 4 SERVINGS

Per serving: 178 calories, 9 g protein, 26 g carbohydrates, 6 g total fat, 1 g saturated fat, 22 mg cholesterol, 5 g dietary fiber, 567 mg sodium

Italian Bread Salad (Panzanella)

This summer classic originated in Tuscany, where thrifty country cooks made use of every ingredient, including dry bread. In this version, day-old multigrain bread offers an important fiber boost as it soaks up all the summery flavors of fresh tomatoes, peppers, and onion.

Prep time: 10 minutes

4 slices day-old multigrain bread, 4 ounces, cut into ½" cubes

4 tomatoes, 1 pound, cut into 8 wedges each

1 cucumber, peeled, halved lengthwise, seeded, and thinly sliced, 2 cups

1 yellow bell pepper, thinly sliced, 1 cup

½ cup thinly sliced fresh basil

½ cup thinly sliced red onion

2 tablespoons red wine vinegar

2 tablespoons extra virgin olive oil

½ teaspoon salt

¼ teaspoon ground black pepper

In a large bowl, combine the bread, tomatoes, cucumber, bell pepper, basil, and onion. In a separate bowl, combine the vinegar, oil, salt, and black pepper and mix well. Add the vinegar mixture to the bread mixture and stir well. Let stand for 15 minutes before serving.

MAKES 4 SERVINGS

Per serving: 187 calories, 6 g protein, 24 g carbohydrates, 8 g total fat, 1 g saturated fat, 0 mg cholesterol, 7 g dietary fiber, 434 mg sodium

Avocado, Tomato, and Arugula Salad

Look for prewashed organic baby arugula in your grocer's organic section. Pumpkin seed kernels or slivered almonds can take the place of sunflower seeds if you like.

Prep time: 11 minutes

---

2 tablespoons extra virgin olive oil

1 tablespoon balsamic vinegar

1 small clove garlic, crushed through a press

¼ teaspoon salt

¼ teaspoon ground black pepper

4 cups baby arugula

3–4 ripe medium tomatoes (about 12 ounces total), cored and cut into wedges

1 large ripe avocado, halved, pitted, peeled, quartered, and sliced crosswise

¼ cup thinly sliced red onion

1 tablespoon toasted sunflower seeds

In a salad bowl, with a fork, mix the oil, vinegar, garlic, salt, and pepper. Add the arugula, tomatoes, avocado, and onion; toss gently to mix. Sprinkle with the sunflower seeds.

MAKES 4 SERVINGS

Per serving: 175 calories, 3 g protein, 10 g carbohydrates, 15 g total fat, 2 g saturated fat, 0 mg cholesterol, 5 g dietary fiber, 160 mg sodium

Fresh Corn and Tomato Bruschetta Salad

Some people may be surprised that corn doesn't have to be cooked. If it's freshly picked, just slice the sweet kernels off the cob. Then run the dull side of the cutting knife down the cob to release any remaining juices.

Prep time: 15 minutes

1 cup fresh corn kernels, cut from
2 ears corn

1 cup grape tomatoes, halved

1 cup yellow pear or cherry tomatoes, halved

1 cup seeded and chopped tomato

½ cup chopped Vidalia or other sweet onion

¼ cup chopped fresh mint

2 tablespoons chopped fresh basil

1½ tablespoons extra virgin olive oil

1 tablespoon balsamic vinegar

1 tablespoon drained nonpareil capers

½ teaspoon salt

⅛ teaspoon ground black pepper

4 slices (1 ounce each) peasant-style multigrain bread

1 clove garlic

1. In a large bowl, combine the corn, grape tomatoes, yellow tomatoes, chopped tomatoes, onion, mint, basil, oil, vinegar, capers, salt, and pepper; toss well.

2. Toast the bread slices. Rub 1 side of each slice briefly with the garlic clove. Place 1 slice of bread, rubbed side up, in the center of each of 4 plates. Top each with 1 cup of the corn mixture. Serve immediately.

MAKES 4 SERVINGS

Per serving: 187 calories, 6 g protein, 27 g carbohydrates, 7 g total fat, 1 g saturated fat, 0 mg cholesterol, 7 g dietary fiber, 488 mg sodium

Curried Lentil and Apricot Salad with Arugula

Plan on serving this dish often when apricots ripen in summer. Later in the season, replace the apricots with 2 ripe nectarines or peaches.

Prep time: 15 minutes   Cook time: 22 minutes

¾ cup brown lentils, picked over and rinsed

3 tablespoons lemon juice

2 tablespoons extra virgin olive oil

1 tablespoon honey

1 teaspoon curry powder

1 teaspoon grated lemon peel

½ teaspoon salt

¼ teaspoon ground black pepper

4 fresh apricots, pitted

½ cup chopped red bell pepper

3 scallions, chopped

3 tablespoons chopped fresh cilantro

1 bunch arugula, trimmed, washed, and spun dry, about 4 cups

1. Place the lentils in a medium saucepan with 3 cups water over medium-high heat. Bring to a boil, reduce the heat to medium, and simmer, partially covered, for 20 to 22 minutes, or until the lentils are tender but still hold their shape. Drain and transfer to a bowl.

2. Meanwhile, in a small bowl, combine the lemon juice, oil, honey, curry powder, lemon peel, salt, and black pepper. Slice 3 apricots and toss in a bowl with 2 teaspoons of the lemon juice mixture. Cut the remaining apricot into ¼" dice.

3. Add the diced apricot, bell pepper, scallions, cilantro, and 3 tablespoons of the lemon juice mixture to the lentils and toss well. Toss the arugula with 2 tablespoons of the dressing and arrange over a large serving platter. Top with the lentil mixture. Toss the sliced apricots with any remaining dressing and arrange around the lentil mixture.

MAKES 4 SERVINGS

Per serving: 197 calories, 8 g protein, 27 g carbohydrates, 8 g total fat, 1 g saturated fat, 0 mg cholesterol, 9 g dietary fiber, 300 mg sodium

Provençal Lentil Salad

This dish complements grilled Mediterranean vegetables. Brush sliced baby eggplant, colorful bell peppers, zucchini, and cipollini with olive oil and then brown them over direct heat. Move the vegetables away from the direct heat to cook through. Season with coarse salt and black pepper.

Prep time: 10 minutes   Cook time: 25 minutes

1 cup lentils

1 bay leaf

1 cup finely diced red bell pepper

½ cup chopped sweet white onion

½ cup chopped parsley

2 tablespoons extra virgin olive oil

1 tablespoon chopped fresh sage

1 tablespoon white wine vinegar

1 teaspoon salt

½ teaspoon ground black pepper

1. Wash the lentils and remove any debris. In a medium saucepan, cook the lentils with the bay leaf in plenty of boiling water until just tender, 20 to 25 minutes. Drain well and remove the bay leaf.

2. In a large bowl, toss the hot lentils with the bell pepper, onion, parsley, oil, sage, vinegar, salt, and black pepper. Cool to room temperature before serving.

MAKES 6 SERVINGS

Per serving: 174 calories, 10 g protein, 25 g carbohydrates, 5 g total fat, 1 g saturated fat, 0 mg cholesterol, 5 g dietary fiber, 392 mg sodium

Broccoli, Chickpea, and Cherry Tomato Salad

This recipe is especially welcome for times of the year when fresh lettuce isn't at its best.

Prep time: 10 minutes   **Cook time: 10 minutes**   **Chill time: 30 minutes**

3 cups small broccoli florets

1 tablespoon extra virgin olive oil

1 tablespoon cider vinegar

2 teaspoons grainy Dijon mustard

¼ teaspoon salt

¼ teaspoon ground black pepper

½ cup coarsely chopped and drained jarred, roasted red peppers

¼ cup sliced scallions

1½ cups halved cherry tomatoes or grape tomatoes

1 can (15–16 ounces) chickpeas, rinsed and drained

1. Place a steamer basket in a medium pot with 2" of water. Bring to a boil over high heat. Place the broccoli in the basket, cover, and steam for 5 to 6 minutes, or until crisp-tender. Drain and cool briefly under cold running water. Drain again.

2. In a salad bowl, with a fork, mix the oil, vinegar, mustard, salt, and black pepper. Stir in the roasted peppers and scallions. Add the broccoli, tomatoes, and chickpeas and stir to mix well. Cover and chill for at least 30 minutes before serving to blend the flavors.

MAKES 4 SERVINGS

Per serving: 128 calories, 6 g protein, 17 g carbohydrates, 5 g total fat, 1 g saturated fat, 0 mg cholesterol, 5 g dietary fiber, 353 mg sodium

Roasted Sweet and Russet Potato Salad

Potato fans will swoon over this concoction. It gives bland mayonnaise potato salad some stiff competition.

Prep time: 15 minutes   Cook time: 40 minutes

1 pound sweet potatoes, peeled and cut into 1" chunks

1 pound russet potatoes, peeled and cut into 1" chunks

2 tablespoons olive oil

1 red bell pepper, cut into strips

½ cup sliced Vidalia or other sweet onion

1 tablespoon white wine vinegar

2 teaspoons sugar

1 teaspoon Dijon mustard

½ teaspoon salt

1. Preheat the oven to 425°F. Coat a large baking sheet with cooking spray; set aside.

2. In a large bowl, combine the sweet potatoes and russet potatoes. Add 2 teaspoons of the oil and toss well to coat. Spread the mixture over the prepared baking sheet and roast, stirring occasionally, until the potatoes begin to brown slightly, about 25 minutes.

3. Meanwhile, toss the pepper and onion with 1 teaspoon of the oil. Stir into the potato mixture and roast for 12 to 15 minutes longer, or until the potatoes and vegetables are tender. Transfer to a large bowl.

4. In a small bowl, combine the remaining 1 tablespoon oil, the vinegar, sugar, mustard, and salt. Pour over the warm potato mixture and mix well.

MAKES 6 SERVINGS

Per serving: 170 calories, 3 g protein, 30 g carbohydrates, 5 g total fat, 1 g saturated fat, 0 mg cholesterol, 4 g dietary fiber, 230 mg sodium

Chopped Vegetable and Brown Rice Salad

Florence fennel, often mislabeled as anise in supermarkets, is a bulb vegetable that looks like chubby celery. Often, you can purchase it with the dark green fronds still attached to the top. You can cut them off and chop them as a garnish for this delightful salad.

Prep time: 15 minutes   **Cook time: 10 minutes**   **Standing time: 15 minutes**

1 cup quick-cooking brown rice (cooks in 10 minutes)

1 zucchini, cut into ½" cubes, about 2½ cups

1 red bell pepper, chopped

½ medium bulb fennel, chopped, about 1 cup

1 medium carrot, chopped

2 cups finely chopped romaine lettuce

1 cup rinsed and drained cannellini beans

⅓ cup finely chopped shallots

2 tablespoons red wine vinegar

2 tablespoons extra virgin olive oil

1 teaspoon Dijon mustard

½ teaspoon salt

¼ teaspoon ground black pepper

1. Cook the rice in a medium saucepan according to package directions, omitting any fat. When done, transfer to a bowl and allow to cool for 15 minutes.

2. Add the zucchini, bell pepper, fennel, carrot, lettuce, and beans to the rice and stir gently to combine. In a small bowl, combine the shallots, vinegar, oil, mustard, salt, and black pepper; mix well. Pour the shallot mixture over the rice and stir gently until combined.

MAKES 4 SERVINGS

Per serving: 248 calories, 7 g protein, 39 g carbohydrates, 8 g total fat, 1 g saturated fat, 0 mg cholesterol, 7 g dietary fiber, 496 mg sodium

Fruited Tabbouleh

This fresh take on the standard Middle Eastern wheat salad replaces some of the typical tomato with fresh juicy apricots, nectarines, and plums.

Prep time: 10 minutes   Standing time: 15 minutes

1½ cups water

1 cup bulgur

½ cup sliced fresh apricots

½ cup sliced fresh nectarines

½ cup sliced fresh plums

½ cup chopped tomato

½ cup thinly sliced fresh basil

¼ cup lemon juice

2 tablespoons extra virgin olive oil

½ teaspoon salt

¼ teaspoon ground black pepper

Bring the water to a boil in a small saucepan over high heat. Pour the bulgur into a medium bowl and add the boiling water; let stand until absorbed, about 15 minutes. Stir in the apricots, nectarines, plums, tomato, basil, lemon juice, oil, salt, and pepper; mix well. Serve immediately or store in an airtight container in the refrigerator for up to 2 days.

MAKES 4 SERVINGS

Per serving: 234 calories, 6 g protein, 39 g carbohydrates, 8 g total fat, 1 g saturated fat, 0 mg cholesterol, 10 g dietary fiber, 301 mg sodium

Roasted Pepper and Parsley Tabbouleh

Parsley really shines in this refreshing grain salad. For once, it steps out of the garnishing wings and takes a costarring role as a main ingredient. Be sure to choose flat-leaf parsley, which is more tender and flavorful than curly.

Prep time: 25 minutes   Standing time: 60 minutes

½ cup medium-grain bulgur wheat

2 cups boiling water

2–3 large tomatoes (12 ounces total), chopped, 1½ cups

1 cup packed chopped fresh flat-leaf parsley

1 cup drained canned chickpeas

¾ cup chopped hothouse cucumber

½ cup chopped, jarred, roasted red peppers, blotted dry

½ cup sliced fresh scallions

¼ cup chopped fresh mint

¼ cup fresh lemon juice

3 tablespoons olive oil

½ teaspoon salt

½ teaspoon ground black pepper

1. Place the bulgur in a medium bowl. Pour the boiling water over it and let stand for 30 minutes, or until softened. Drain through a fine-mesh colander. Dump the bulgur into the center of a thin cotton towel. Wrap the towel over the bulgur and twist the ends in opposite directions to get out all of the water. Transfer the bulgur to a large bowl. Fluff it with a fork or break up any clumps with your fingers.

2. Add the tomatoes, parsley, chickpeas, cucumber, roasted peppers, scallions, mint, lemon juice, oil, salt, and black pepper. Stir to mix well. Refrigerate for 30 minutes before serving, if possible.

MAKES 4 SERVINGS

Per serving: 246 calories, 7 g protein, 31 g carbohydrates, 12 g total fat, 2 g saturated fat, 0 mg cholesterol, 8 g dietary fiber, 460 mg sodium

Barley, Asparagus, and Cucumber Salad with Yogurt-Dill Dressing

Feel free to cook the barley and asparagus the day before. This is a great make-ahead picnic salad. After chilling, it might need another tablespoon of lemon juice to perk up the flavor.

Prep time: 8 minutes   Cook time: 50 minutes   Cooling time: 15 minutes

3 cups water

¾ teaspoon salt

½ pound asparagus, tough ends trimmed, cut diagonally into 2" pieces, 1½ cups

⅔ cup medium pearled barley

¾ cup plain nonfat yogurt

1 tablespoon olive oil

3 tablespoons snipped fresh dill

2 tablespoons fresh lemon juice

1 small clove garlic, crushed through a press

¼ teaspoon ground black pepper

1 cup thin half-moon slices hothouse cucumber

3 scallions, thinly sliced

1. Bring the water to a boil in a covered saucepan over high heat. Add ¼ teaspoon of the salt and the asparagus. Cook, stirring often, for 3 to 5 minutes, or until crisp-tender. With a skimmer or slotted spoon, lift the asparagus to a colander and rinse briefly under cold running water. Drain. Cover and refrigerate until ready to assemble the salad.

2. To the water, add the barley and return to a boil. Reduce the heat to low, cover, and simmer for about 35 minutes, or until the barley is tender. Drain in a colander. Place a piece of waxed paper on top of the barley and let it stand for about 15 minutes, or until lukewarm.

3. In a salad bowl, stir together the yogurt, oil, dill, lemon juice, garlic, the remaining ½ teaspoon salt, and the pepper. Add the cucumber, scallions, asparagus, and barley and toss gently to mix well. Cover and chill until ready to serve.

MAKES 4 SERVINGS

Per serving: 189 calories, 7 g protein, 35 g carbohydrates, 4 g total fat, 1 g saturated fat, 1 mg cholesterol, 7 g dietary fiber, 180 mg sodium

Grilled Nectarine and Watercress Salad

Cooking familiar foods in unfamiliar ways is intriguing for your tastebuds. Grilling nectarines heightens their sweet succulence, making this a perfect starter salad for a summer might.

Prep time: 10 minutes   Cook time: 10 minutes

SALAD

1 tablespoon + 1 teaspoon olive oil

1 tablespoon fresh lemon juice

1 teaspoon honey

⅛ teaspoon salt

⅛ teaspoon ground black pepper

2 tablespoons chopped red onion

4 cups loosely packed watercress, tough stems removed

2 tablespoons chopped walnuts

GRILLED NECTARINES

4 large firm-ripe nectarines, halved

2 teaspoons olive oil

Ground black pepper

1. Heat an outdoor grill to medium-low.

2. *To make the salad:* Meanwhile, in a salad bowl, with a fork, mix the oil, lemon juice, honey, salt, and pepper. Stir in the onion. Place the watercress in the bowl but don't toss it.

3. *To make the grilled nectarines:* Cut the fruit off the pits in large slabs. Drizzle with the oil and grind a little fresh pepper over the top. Place the nectarine pieces flesh-side down on the grill. Grill, turning once (the skin may stick), for 4 to 8 minutes, or until hot, lightly charred, and the color starts to become translucent. Transfer from the grill to a plate, and with a table knife, cut the nectarines into slices.

4. Add the nectarines and any juices to the salad; toss gently. Sprinkle with the walnuts and serve.

MAKES 4 SERVINGS

Per serving: 166 calories, 3 g protein, 20 g carbohydrates, 9 g total fat, 1 g saturated fat, 0 mg cholesterol, 2 g dietary fiber, 87 mg sodium

Grilled Chicken Pasta Salad with Oranges

If you like, grill the chicken and cook the pasta a day ahead.

Prep time: 15 minutes   Cook time: 40 minutes

CHICKEN

1 pound boneless, skinless chicken breast halves

1 teaspoon olive oil

1 teaspoon grated orange peel (reserve oranges)

⅛ teaspoon salt

⅛ teaspoon ground black pepper

PASTA SALAD

Pinch of salt + ½ teaspoon

6 ounces whole grain medium pasta shells, 2 cups

3 or 4 navel oranges

2 tablespoons olive oil

1 teaspoon balsamic vinegar

½ teaspoon sugar

¼ teaspoon ground black pepper

1 medium red bell pepper, cut into thin strips, strips cut in half

3 tender inner ribs celery with leaves, thinly sliced

¾ cup halved seedless red grapes

1. *To make the chicken:* Heat an outdoor grill to medium-hot or preheat the broiler. Rub the chicken with the oil, orange peel, salt, and pepper. Grill or broil for about 10 minutes, turning once, until no longer pink in the thickest part. Transfer to a clean plate and let cool, or cover and refrigerate.

2. *To make the pasta salad:* Bring a large covered pot of water to a boil. Add a pinch of salt and the pasta. Cook according to package directions until tender. Drain in a colander and cool under cold running water. Drain again. Cover loosely and let stand, or refrigerate until ready to use.

3. From the oranges, squeeze ¼ cup juice. Using the remaining oranges, with a serrated knife, cut off the peel and white pith. Cut each orange in half lengthwise and place cut side down on a cutting board. Cut the orange half in half again, and then cut the wedges crosswise into ½" chunks. Cut the chicken on an angle into thin slices; cut the slices in half.

4. In a large bowl, with a fork, mix the oil, vinegar, sugar, the remaining ½ teaspoon salt, the black pepper, and the reserved ¼ cup orange juice. Add the pasta, bell pepper, celery, grapes, orange pieces, and chicken. Toss to mix well. Serve soon, or cover and chill until ready to serve.

MAKES 4 SERVINGS

Per serving: 440 calories, 34 g protein, 55 g carbohydrates, 10 g total fat, 2 g saturated fat, 66 mg cholesterol, 5 g dietary fiber, 226 mg sodium

Sesame-Citrus Chicken and Broccoli Salad

Keeping essential seasonings on hand makes it easy to create great-tasting dishes; so with a jar of minced garlic in oil in the refrigerator and a knob of fresh ginger in the freezer, you're always set. No need to thaw the ginger before grating.

Prep time: 15 minutes

12 ounces cooked chicken, cubed, 2¾ cups

3 cups broccoli florets, broken into 1" pieces, steamed to crisp-tender, rinsed, and drained

1 cup sliced carrots, cut thinly on the diagonal

½ cup sliced scallions, cut in long diagonal slivers

½ red bell pepper, cut in thin slivers, ½ cup

1 tablespoon vegetable oil

1 tablespoon lemon juice

1 tablespoon orange juice

1 clove garlic, minced

1 teaspoon grated ginger

½ teaspoon soy sauce

½ teaspoon Asian toasted sesame oil

½ teaspoon salt

⅛ teaspoon Oriental hot-pepper oil (optional)

1 teaspoon sesame seeds

1. In a large bowl, place the chicken, broccoli, carrots, scallions, and bell pepper.

2. In a small bowl, mix together the oil, lemon juice, orange juice, garlic, ginger, soy sauce, sesame oil, salt, and hot-pepper oil. Pour over the chicken and vegetables. Toss gently, sprinkle with the sesame seeds, and serve.

MAKES 4 SERVINGS

Per serving: 176 calories, 22 g protein, 9 g carbohydrates, 6 g total fat, 1 g saturated fat, 49 mg cholesterol, 3 g dietary fiber, 440 mg sodium

Mango Pineapple Noodle Salad

Guests will definitely sit up and pay attention when you serve them a spaghetti salad studded with tropical fruit, rich cashew nuts, and aromatic basil. This dish is especially cooling on a humid summer day.

Prep time: 10 minutes   Cook time: 20 minutes

6 ounces whole wheat or multigrain spaghetti, broken in half

1 large mango, pitted and cut into matchsticks

1½ cups cubed fresh pineapple

1 red bell pepper, chopped

1 cucumber, peeled, seeded, and chopped

2 scallions, chopped

¼ cup salted roasted cashews, coarsely chopped

¼ cup thinly sliced fresh basil

2 tablespoons lime juice

1 tablespoon seasoned rice vinegar

1 tablespoon sugar

2 teaspoons fish sauce

1. Bring a large pot of lightly salted water to a boil over high heat. Add the spaghetti and cook according to package directions. Drain and rinse under cold water to stop the cooking; drain again.

2. In a large bowl, combine the spaghetti, mango, pineapple, pepper, cucumber, scallions, cashews, and basil; toss well. In a separate bowl, combine the lime juice, vinegar, sugar, and fish sauce. Pour over the spaghetti mixture and toss to combine.

MAKES 4 SERVINGS

Per serving: 293 calories, 9 g protein, 59 g carbohydrates, 5 g total fat, 1 g saturated fat, 0 mg cholesterol, 9 g dietary fiber, 440 mg sodium

Tuna and White Bean Parsley Lemon Salad

Select the freshest tuna for this distinctive salad. Steaks should look firm and glistening, with no sunken spots or discoloration.

Prep time: 10 minutes   Cook time: 4 minutes   Chill time: 1 hour

2 tablespoons lemon juice

1 teaspoon grated fresh lemon peel

1 tablespoon + 1 teaspoon extra virgin olive oil

1 can (15 ounces) small white beans, rinsed and drained

½ cup thinly sliced scallions

2 tablespoons chopped fresh parsley

2 skinless tuna steaks (each 8 ounces and about 1" thick)

⅛ teaspoon salt

⅛ teaspoon ground black pepper

2 cups shredded romaine lettuce

1. In a medium bowl, whisk together the lemon juice, lemon peel, and 1 tablespoon of the oil. Add the beans, scallions, and parsley and refrigerate for at least 1 hour.

2. Place a skillet over medium-high heat and coat with the remaining 1 teaspoon oil. Season the tuna with the salt and pepper. Lay the tuna in the hot oil and sear for 2 minutes on each side to form a slight crust. Remove from the skillet and let stand for 2 to 3 minutes.

3. Add the lettuce to the beans and spoon the bean salad onto 4 plates. Slice the tuna into ¼" slices and arrange on top of the bean salad. Drizzle with any remaining dressing from the bowl.

MAKES 4 SERVINGS

Per serving: 266 calories, 31 g protein,
14 g carbohydrates, 11 g total fat, 2 g saturated fat,
43 mg cholesterol, 5 g dietary fiber, 391 mg sodium

Mediterranean Shrimp and Brown Rice Salad

The tang of feta cheese and the freshness of dill lend Greek flair to this light yet substantial main dish.

Prep time: 15 minutes

1½ tablespoons extra virgin olive oil

1½ tablespoons lemon juice

1 clove garlic, crushed through a press

Pinch of salt

3 cups cooked brown rice

¾ cup halved cherry tomatoes

¾ cup peeled, seeded, and diced cucumber

⅓ cup thinly sliced red onion

¼ cup diced roasted red pepper

3 tablespoons chopped fresh dill

½ pound cooked peeled shrimp

¾ cup crumbled feta cheese, 1½ ounces

1. In a large bowl, combine the oil, lemon juice, garlic, and salt. Mix well.

2. Stir in the rice, tomatoes, cucumber, onion, pepper, and dill. Add the shrimp and cheese and gently stir again.

MAKES 4 SERVINGS

Per serving: 360 calories, 20 g protein,
39 g carbohydrates, 13 g total fat, 5 g saturated fat,
136 mg cholesterol, 4 g dietary fiber, 524 mg sodium

Thanksgiving Salad

You won't have to dread dried-out turkey leftovers anymore. Bathed in a honey mustard dressing and tossed with sweet potatoes, red onion, and dried cranberries, this fresh take on turkey is terrific.

Prep time: 10 minutes   Cook time: 30 minutes

---

3 medium-size sweet potatoes, peeled, halved, and sliced into ¼" half-moons

1 teaspoon + 1 tablespoon olive oil

⅓ cup pearl barley

3 tablespoons cider vinegar

2 teaspoons chopped fresh rosemary

2 teaspoons honey

1 teaspoon Dijon mustard

½ teaspoon salt

2 cups shredded cooked turkey breast, 12 ounces

⅔ cup thinly sliced red onions

⅓ cup dried cranberries

1. Heat the oven to 425°F. In a roasting pan, combine the sweet potatoes and 1 teaspoon of the oil and bake until fork-tender, about 25 to 30 minutes.

2. Meanwhile, in a small saucepan, cook the barley in plenty of boiling water until tender, about 30 minutes. Drain, rinse under cold water, and drain well.

3. In a large bowl, combine the vinegar, rosemary, honey, mustard, salt, and the remaining 1 tablespoon oil. Stir well. Add the sweet potatoes, barley, turkey, onions, and cranberries. Mix gently.

MAKES 4 SERVINGS

Per serving: 394 calories, 29 g protein, 51 g carbohydrates, 8 g total fat, 2 g saturated fat, 59 mg cholesterol, 7 g dietary fiber, 414 mg sodium

CHAPTER 7

DINNER

Many people describe the time between dinner and bedtime as their dieting danger zone. They come home from work or school feeling ravenous. They open the fridge, peer inside, and remove the first palatable food they see. This initial snack uncorks a ferocious desire to eat, leading to nibbling during dinner preparation, second and third helpings at dinner, and various desserts and snacks after dinner. People caught in this pattern know they are not necessarily "stomach hungry," but they seem to have lost control.

If this sounds all too familiar, try thinking about your own nighttime eating during the last few weeks. Since you've had more fiber during the day, has anything changed at night? Hopefully by day's end you are feeling more in control, so you don't feel as compelled to walk in the door and head straight for the fridge or pantry. If you've noticed some improvement, credit the fact that you are three-quarters of the way through your 4-week fiber makeover. The gradual changes you've made during the past few weeks should make the final week easier to implement. For instance, you might notice that overpowering between-meal hunger and cravings have subsided. You may already notice a difference in your energy and focus during the afternoon, and you may even find that you've started to make smarter, high-fiber dinner choices ahead of schedule.

Adding 5 or more grams of fiber to dinner will strengthen your sense of control even more. It will fill you up so that you don't want seconds and so that you are satisfied when you are done. If you still want a dessert a couple of times a week, go ahead and read Chapter 8.

FIBER BENEFIT #4

BEAT CANCER

Cancer is the second leading cause of death, next to heart disease, and excess pounds increase your risk of many types of cancer, including breast, endometrial (cancer that affects the lining of the uterus), colon, kidney, and esophageal. Here's how fiber reduces risk for some of these weight-related cancers.

Breast cancer: When researchers at the University of Leeds looked at the food records of more than 600 pre- and postmenopausal women, they determined that fiber intake reduced breast cancer risk for premenopausal women, with fiber from cereal and folate-rich foods being most protective. The news is also good for women who already have breast cancer. In one study, researchers determined that women with breast cancer lived longer if they ate more fiber, micronutrients, fruit, and vegetables and less fat.

A high-fiber diet may reduce cancer risk by normalizing levels of female sex hormones such as estrogen. Although all women need the hormone estrogen, too much of it can lead to cancer, especially of the uterus and breast. Fiber drops estrogen the same way it drops cholesterol. It soaks it up, increasing the rate at which it is excreted from the body. A high-fiber diet also helps to drop insulin levels, another hormone that has been implicated in breast cancer risk.

Colon cancer: Fiber drops risk for this deadly cancer by up to 40 percent. It may improve colon health through a number of mechanisms. First, fiber binds to bile acids, which otherwise would produce carcinogens during metabolism. Second, when friendly colon bacteria feed on fiber, they reduce the pH of the intestine, which may in turn reduce the incidence of colon polyps. This fermentation process also produces a fatty acid called butyric acid. This acid is the main energy source of colon cells and keeps them healthy. It's also a natural anti-inflammatory. In test-tube studies, it inhibits or kills tumor cells. Finally, fiber speeds the transit of stool through the colon. This may reduce the amount of time toxins in stool spend in contact with the lining of the colon. Water-packed stool also acts like a scrub brush as it passes through the colon, removing debris caught along the sides and ushering potential toxins out of the body.

Endometrial cancer: The fourth most common cancer that affects women, endometrial cancer affects the lining of the uterus (called the endometrium). A long-term study of 332 women determined that a high-fiber diet could reduce risk for this cancer by 29 to 46 percent. Fiber probably reduces this cancer in the same way it drops breast cancer risk, by normalizing levels of the hormone estrogen.

Most of the time, an entire day of high-fiber eating should have you feeling content enough to put a mental "closed" sign on the kitchen at dinner's end.

Once you make over dinner and complete your daily cycle of high-fiber eating, you'll find that each high-fiber meal or snack you eat has residual rewards—the fiber in your previous meal can actually help you to eat less at your next meal. Starting the day with a high-fiber breakfast, for example, keeps you satisfied throughout the morning, so it's easier to choose high-fiber options at lunch. Later, that high-fiber lunch will help keep blood sugar steady in the afternoon, so you have the wherewithal to reach for a healthy high-fiber midafternoon snack rather than a cola or sugary, starchy, or fatty snack food. That midafternoon snack keeps the munchies under control until dinner, and a high-fiber dinner helps you to eat less at breakfast and lunch the following day.

That's right. It's hard to believe what you eat in the evening can affect how you feel in the morning, but it does. In a study done at the University of Toronto, participants ate dinners that were either low or high on the glycemic index (GI). Low-glycemic foods tend to be rich in fiber and protein, whereas high-glycemic foods tend to be rich in sugar and starch. The next morning, participants who had the fiber-rich, low-GI dinner saw a lower and steadier blood sugar rise after breakfast, compared with a faster, more pronounced rise in the high-GI eaters. Steady blood sugar levels help to keep a lid on appetite.

So with all of the amazing benefits fiber has to offer, why wait until the 4th week of the plan to make over dinner? As mentioned earlier, there was a natural progression to each week's changes that started with the easiest meals to change—breakfast and snacks—and saved the most challenging—dinner—for last. If you dine alone at dinner, you probably will be able to switch over to high-fiber eating rather easily. If you eat with a finicky spouse or teenage children, you might encounter some resistance. Dinner also may present some new culinary challenges if you must get used to preparing new fiber-rich foods. The good news, however, is that all of these challenges are surmountable, and the rewards definitely achievable.

HOW TO DINE

On pages 181 to 253 you'll find 55 quick and easy high-fiber dinner recipes. These recipes provide you with complete meals. To put together your own high-fiber dinners using existing recipes, just follow this simple three-part rule. At every dinner, try to include one serving of lean protein, one serving of a high-fiber starch (potato, brown rice, quinoa, wild rice, etc.), and 2 or more cups of vegetables.

Whenever possible, try to get in the habit of starting dinner either with a salad or with a vegetable-rich broth-based soup. Both will help to fill you up, while providing little in the way of calories. Salads, in particular, require a lot of chewing, so they slow down eating. Research shows that munching on a salad before your meal may cut your calorie intake by up to 12 percent, or about 100 calories, depending on the size of your dinner. Use prebagged mixes for convenience, and add raw broccoli and cauliflower to pump up the fiber grams.

Also, keep your freezer stocked with an assortment of frozen vegetables. This will ensure that you always have veggies on hand, even if the fresh ones in the crisper have seen better days. You can steam many varieties of frozen veggies in the bag in your microwave. Keep at least three different colors of frozen veggies in the freezer, to ensure that you get a variety of antioxidants.

In the pantry, make sure you always have some sort of whole grain on hand. Boxes of whole grain pasta, wild or brown rice, and quinoa and other grains should be regular staples. Keep baking and sweet potatoes on hand, too. Just make sure to eat the skin, which houses most of the fiber.

FIBER TIP

Once a week, make a quadruple serving of brown rice, bulgur, or any other slow-cooking grain. Store in the fridge and reheat as needed.

Finicky spouse? Have a family meeting. Make sure everyone knows why high-fiber eating is so critical to your weight loss success. Explain why you are trying to lose weight. You might mention that high-fiber foods will help the entire family slim down and get healthy. Finally, request that they just *try* your way of eating for a week. If they are still resistant, then move into stealth chef mode. Try the following high-fiber family favorites.

Pizza. Few teens are ever caught complaining, "Pizza *again?*" Most are willing to eat it for breakfast, lunch, and dinner for 7 days straight. To bump up the fiber, make or purchase whole wheat crust. Boboli brand premade whole wheat crust, for example, provides 3 grams of fiber per serving. Top it with veggies, but dice them extremely small, so finicky eaters will be less likely to notice them. Spinach, in particular, is an easy veggie to dice into tiny pieces and hide underneath sauce. For meat, use a mixture of ground soy and ground beef or chicken. Finally, if your stealthiest cooking efforts fail and your pizza creation is met with crinkled noses, just compromise. Fill your portion with high-fiber toppings and let the rest of the family choose whatever they want for theirs.

Pasta. Many years ago, the only available whole grain pastas were a tough sell. They were so gummy that they almost made you lose your taste for pasta. During the past 10 years, however, food manufacturers have found a way to make fiber-rich pasta without sacrificing the soft texture people enjoy. In addition to grains, these newer pastas generally contain other high-fiber ingredients such as lentils, chickpeas, and/or flaxseed. The Barilla Plus brand, in particular, is generally a big hit with families. Consult the Appendix for recommended high-fiber pasta brands.

If your spouse or children give you a thumbs-down for every single high-fiber brand you try, then resort to a compromise. Create a half-and-half blend, pouring equal amounts refined pasta and whole grain pasta into the pot. Don't fret if your fussiest of eaters methodically pick through the bowl of cooked pasta in search of the refined shapes. That leaves more whole grain pasta for you.

Corn on the cob or sweet corn kernels. This family favorite is both high in fiber and high in overall nutrition. Corn is a rich source of folate, a B vitamin that protects against heart disease. It's also a rich source of the antioxidant beta-cryptoxanthin, which has been shown to protect against cancer. Plus, it contains more protective phenolic anti-oxidants than broccoli or spinach. Just don't tell them that it's good for them.

Potatoes. If your family has a lot of meat-and-potatoes fans, then baked sweet and regular potatoes are the perfect side dish. Both are high in fiber, as long as you eat the skin. Use the skins in potato salad and mashed potatoes to increase fiber in those family favorites as well. For mashed potatoes, try to sneak in more fiber by mixing cooked and pureed cauliflower into the potatoes.

Baked beans. Again, few people complain about this typical picnic dish, even though it supplies as much as 16 grams of fiber per cup!

Burgers and other ground beef foods. Add fiber by substituting ground soy for half of the beef in your burger, sloppy joe, meatball, and meat loaf recipes. Try to sneak in diced veggies as well to add even more fiber. (See Open-Faced Grilled Vegetable Sandwiches on page 127, Mom's Turkey Meat Loaf on page 200, Turkey Meatballs and Linguine on page 188, and Turkey Burgers with Chili-Beans on page 201.) If all else fails, make yourself a soy burger and everyone else a beef or turkey burger.

Getting more fiber at dinner can be as simple as making the following switches and substitutions.

IF YOU NORMALLY EAT ...	SWITCH TO THIS HIGH-FIBER ALTERNATIVE ...
All-beef burgers	Beef, ground soy, and chopped veggie burgers on whole grain buns and topped with lettuce, tomato, onion, and guacamole
Refined pasta	Whole grain pasta
White rice	Brown or wild rice
Refined dinner roll	Whole grain dinner roll
Mashed potatoes	Mashed potatoes with skins and pureed cauliflower
Shepherd's pie	Sweet Potato Shepherd's Pie (page 212)
Traditional baked ziti	Spicy Beef Baked Penne (page 210)
Refined pasta with Alfredo sauce	Whole grain pasta primavera or Orecchiette with White Beans, Sausage, and Peppers (page 215)
Chicken stir-fry with white rice	Chicken, veggie, and cashew stir-fry with brown rice. See Brown Rice and Chicken Stir-Fry (page 181).
Traditional lasagna	Grilled Vegetable and Bean Lasagna (page 232)

Dinner Recipes

(continued)

Brown Rice and Chicken Stir-Fry

As convenient to cook as boneless, skinless breasts, thighs are a much more flavorful cut of chicken. They work especially well in this dish with intense flavors like toasted sesame oil, ginger, and brown rice.

Prep time: 15 minutes   **Chill time: 30 minutes**   **Cook time: 20 minutes**

12 ounces boneless, skinless chicken thighs, cut into ¾" pieces

2 tablespoons lower-sodium soy sauce

2 tablespoons hoisin sauce

1 tablespoon honey

½ cup lower-sodium fat-free chicken broth

2 teaspoons cornstarch

¾ cup quick-cooking brown rice (cooks in 10 minutes), such as Uncle Ben's

1 teaspoon dark sesame oil

1 onion, chopped, 1 cup

1 tablespoon peeled, grated fresh ginger

½ pound snow peas, trimmed

1 can (8 ounces) sliced water chestnuts, drained

1. In a bowl, combine the chicken, 1 tablespoon of the soy sauce, 1 tablespoon of the hoisin, and 1 teaspoon of the honey; refrigerate for 30 minutes. In another bowl, combine the remaining 1 tablespoon soy sauce, 1 tablespoon hoisin, 2 teaspoons honey, broth, and cornstarch.

2. Cook the rice according to package directions.

3. Heat the oil in a large nonstick skillet and add the chicken; cook, stirring often, until the chicken is no longer pink inside, about 4 to 5 minutes. Transfer the chicken to a plate and set aside. Return the skillet to the heat and add the onion; cook for 1 minute. Stir in the ginger and cook until fragrant, about 30 seconds. Stir in the snow peas and cook until bright green, 1 to 2 minutes. Add the water chestnuts and cook until hot, 1 to 2 minutes. Stir in the reserved chicken and cook for 1 minute. Add the broth mixture, bring to a boil, and cook, stirring occasionally, until thickened, about 2 minutes. Serve over rice.

MAKES 4 SERVINGS

Per serving: 281 calories, 24 g protein, 40 g carbohydrates, 3 g total fat, 1 g saturated fat, 49 mg cholesterol, 6 g dietary fiber, 605 mg sodium

Chicken-Apricot Kebabs with Brown Rice

To speed prep time on this already quick dish, cut the chicken and vegetables up to 12 hours before cooking. Refrigerate them in separate zipper-lock plastic storage bags. You can also combine the marinade ingredients in a small glass jar and refrigerate until cooking time.

Prep time: 30 minutes   Cook time: 18 minutes

2 tablespoons olive oil

1 tablespoon grated fresh orange peel

3 tablespoons fresh orange juice

1½ teaspoons ground cumin

¼ teaspoon salt

¼–½ teaspoon crushed red-pepper flakes

1 pound boneless, skinless chicken breasts, cut into twenty-four 1" chunks

16 dried apricot halves

1 medium red bell pepper, cut into 12 squares

1 medium sweet white onion, cut into 12 squares

¾ cup quick-cooking brown rice (cooks in 10 minutes), such as Uncle Ben's

2 tablespoons chopped parsley or snipped fresh chives

4 pineapple slices

1. Soak four 12" bamboo skewers in water for 30 minutes. Heat an outdoor grill to medium.

2. In a large bowl, mix the oil, orange peel, orange juice, cumin, salt, and red-pepper flakes. Add the chicken, apricots, bell pepper, and onion and toss to mix well. Thread evenly on skewers; each skewer will get 6 pieces of chicken, 4 apricots, and 3 pieces each bell pepper and onion.

3. Cook the rice according to package directions. Fluff with a fork and stir in the parsley or chives.

4. Grill the skewers for 10 to 12 minutes, turning once (using 2 tongs will make this easier), until the chicken is no longer pink in the thickest part. Grill the pineapple slices until heated through. Serve kebabs on top of the pineapple and rice.

MAKES 4 SERVINGS

Per serving: 360 calories, 30 g protein,
65 g carbohydrates, 9 g total fat, 1 g saturated fat,
66 mg cholesterol, 4 g dietary fiber, 310 mg sodium

Spicy Grilled Chicken with Hoppin' John Rice

The complex spicing of the Louisiana seasoning mix really revs up the bean salad. If you like more fire, sprinkle with a few drops of hot sauce just before serving.

Prep time: 8 minutes **Cook time: 30 minutes**

RICE

1 tablespoon olive oil

1 medium onion, chopped

1 medium green bell pepper, chopped

1 stalk celery, thinly sliced

1 teaspoon Creole or Cajun seasoning

1 cup instant brown rice

1 can (15–16 ounces) salt-free black-eyed peas, rinsed and drained

1 can (11 ounces) 50% less sodium corn kernels

1 cup boiling water

CHICKEN

4 boneless, skinless chicken breast halves (5 ounces each)

1 tablespoon olive oil

1 teaspoon Creole or Cajun seasoning

1. *To make the rice:* Warm the oil in a large, deep nonstick skillet over medium heat. Add the onion, pepper, and celery and cook, stirring often, until tender, about 8 minutes. Stir in the seasoning.

2. Add the rice and stir until well mixed with the vegetables. Stir in the black-eyed peas, corn, and water. Bring to a boil. Reduce the heat to low, cover, and simmer for 10 to 15 minutes, or until all the liquid has been absorbed. Set aside, covered.

3. *To make the chicken:* Meanwhile, heat an outdoor grill to medium-hot or preheat the broiler. Rub the chicken with the oil and sprinkle with the seasoning. Grill or broil, turning once, about 10 minutes, or until a thermometer inserted in the thickest portion registers 160°F and the juices run clear.

4. Fluff the rice. Serve the chicken with the rice.

MAKES 4 SERVINGS

Per serving: 417 calories, 40 g protein, 41 g carbohydrates, 10 g total fat, 1 g saturated fat, 82 mg cholesterol, 5 g dietary fiber, 515 mg sodium

Chicken and Sweet Corn Succotash

Smoky bacon seems nearly irresistible with beans and corn. Also adding appeal to this sophisticated version of succotash are mustard, rosemary, and lemon peel.

Prep time: 15 minutes   Chill time: 1 hour   Cook time: 30 minutes

---

4 boneless, skinless chicken breast halves (4 ounces each)

3 cloves garlic, minced

1 tablespoon Dijon mustard

2 teaspoons chopped fresh rosemary

1 teaspoon grated lemon peel

¼ teaspoon ground black pepper

1 cup frozen baby lima beans

2 slices center-cut (30% less fat) bacon, such as Oscar Mayer, chopped

1 onion, chopped, 1 cup

1 cup chopped tomato

1½ cups fresh corn kernels, cut from 3 medium ears

½ teaspoon salt

1. Combine the chicken, 2 cloves of the garlic, mustard, rosemary, lemon peel, and ⅛ teaspoon of the pepper in a bowl; mix well to coat. Refrigerate for 1 hour.

2. Meanwhile, cook the lima beans according to package directions; drain. Heat a large nonstick skillet over medium-high heat. Add the bacon and cook, stirring occasionally, until crisp, about 4 to 5 minutes. Stir in the onion and remaining 1 clove of garlic; cook until beginning to soften, 2 to 3 minutes. Add the lima beans and cook for 2 minutes. Stir in the tomato and cook until starting to wilt, 1 to 2 minutes. Add the corn, ¼ teaspoon of the salt, and the remaining ⅛ teaspoon of the pepper; cook until hot, 1 to 2 minutes. Keep warm.

3. Preheat the grill. Sprinkle the chicken with the remaining ¼ teaspoon salt. Grill for 5 to 6 minutes per side, or until a thermometer inserted in the thickest portion registers 160°F and the juices run clear.

MAKES 4 SERVINGS

Per serving: 281 calories, 33 g protein, 31 g carbohydrates, 4 g total fat, 1 g saturated fat, 69 mg cholesterol, 6 g dietary fiber, 549 mg sodium

Penne with Chicken, Broccoli, and Cherry Tomatoes

Italian blue cheese, named after a village near Milan, is the central flavoring of this divine pasta dinner. *Gorgonzola dolce* is a younger cheese with a milder flavor. *Gorgonzola picante* is aged longer and so has a more assertive tang. If you can't get Gorgonzola, choose the best blue you can find in your market.

Prep time: 10 minutes   Cook time: 35 minutes

1 pound boneless, skinless chicken breasts, gently pounded

¼ teaspoon salt

¼ teaspoon ground black pepper

2 teaspoons olive oil

12 ounces multigrain penne (about 4 cups cooked)

3 cups broccoli florets

¾ cup low-sodium chicken broth

3 cloves garlic, minced

1 pint very small, whole cherry tomatoes

3 ounces crumbly Gorgonzola, crumbled

2 tablespoons chopped fresh parsley leaves

1. Sprinkle the chicken on both sides with the salt and pepper. In a large nonstick skillet over medium heat, cook the chicken in the oil until no longer pink inside, 10 to 12 minutes, turning once. Remove from heat. Cool, thinly slice, and set aside.

2. Cook the pasta according to package directions. After 7 minutes, add the broccoli to the cooking water. Cook for an additional 3 minutes, until the broccoli is tender and bright green. Drain the pasta and broccoli.

3. Add the broth and garlic to the skillet and boil until reduced to ½ cup (or by one-quarter of the total volume), about 5 minutes. Add the tomatoes, lower the heat to medium, and cook until the color of the tomatoes brightens and they're just soft to the touch but haven't burst their skins yet, about 8 minutes.

4. Add the cheese to the broth. Stir until well blended. Add the pasta and broccoli and the chicken to the pan and stir to combine. Top with the parsley and serve right away.

MAKES 4 SERVINGS

Per serving: 577 calories, 45 g protein,
71 g carbohydrates, 13 g total fat, 5 g saturated fat,
86 mg cholesterol, 11 g dietary fiber, 569 mg sodium

Turkey Meatballs and Linguine

Meatballs have to be one of the most-liked foods in the world. Turkey stands in here for the traditional ground beef, with wonderful results.

Prep time: 20 minutes   Cook time: 25 minutes

1 pound 7% fat or less lean ground turkey

3 cloves garlic, minced

1 egg white

⅓ cup seasoned dry bread crumbs

½ teaspoon salt

½ teaspoon black pepper

1 tablespoon extra virgin olive oil

1 onion, chopped, about 1 cup

1 teaspoon dried basil

1 teaspoon dried oregano

1 can (28 ounces) whole peeled tomatoes, chopped, juice reserved

2 tablespoons tomato paste

12 ounces whole wheat linguine

1. Preheat the oven to 400°F. Coat a baking sheet with cooking spray.

2. In a bowl, combine the turkey, 1 clove of the garlic, the egg white, bread crumbs, ¼ teaspoon of the salt, and ¼ teaspoon of the pepper. With slightly damp hands, form the mixture into eighteen 1½" balls and set them about 1" apart on the prepared baking sheet. Bake, turning once, until the meatballs are browned, firm, and no longer pink inside, 23 to 25 minutes.

3. Meanwhile, heat the oil in a large saucepan over medium-high heat. Add the remaining 2 cloves of garlic, the onion, basil, and oregano; cook, stirring occasionally, until the onion begins to soften, 2 to 3 minutes. Stir in the tomatoes and their juice, the tomato paste, and the remaining ¼ teaspoon salt and ¼ teaspoon pepper. Bring to a boil; reduce the heat to medium-low and simmer, partially covered, until the sauce starts to thicken, 12 to 15 minutes. Stir in the meatballs and simmer until the sauce has thickened and the meatballs are hot, 5 minutes.

4. Meanwhile, cook the linguine according to package directions; drain. To serve, divide the linguine among 6 shallow bowls and top each with 3 meatballs and some sauce.

MAKES 6 SERVINGS (3 MEATBALLS AND ⅓ CUP SAUCE PER SERVING)

Per serving: 369 calories, 31 g protein, 53 g carbohydrates, 5 g total fat, 1 g saturated fat, 30 mg cholesterol, 12 g dietary fiber, 534 mg sodium

Chicken Thighs with Bacon-Braised Beans

Braising, the slow-simmering cooking method that magically transforms a potful of disparate flavors into a harmonious feast, is put to good use in this dish. The creamy texture of the beans belies the fact that this meal offers more fiber than fat.

Prep time: 15 minutes   Cook time: 35 minutes

4 skinless chicken thighs

1 teaspoon chopped fresh thyme

¼ cup diced pancetta or thick-cut bacon (about 1 ounce)

1 medium onion, diced

3 cups quartered mushrooms

3 cloves garlic, chopped

1 sprig thyme

1 sprig sage

¼ teaspoon whole black peppercorns

2½ cups canned pinto beans, rinsed and drained (1½ cans)

½ cup low-sodium chicken broth

½ cup diced plum tomato

2 tablespoons chopped fresh parsley

1. Heat the oven to 375°F. Sprinkle the chicken thighs with chopped thyme. Place in a small baking dish just big enough to hold the thighs snugly and roast for 35 minutes, or until a thermometer inserted in the thickest portion registers 160°F.

2. Cook the bacon in a deep skillet over medium-low heat. Drain fat and add the onion and cook until translucent, about 5 minutes. Add the mushrooms, garlic, thyme sprig, sage sprig, and peppercorns. Raise the heat to medium and cook until the onion starts to brown, 5 minutes. Add the beans and broth. Cook for 8 minutes. Add the tomato and continue cooking 8 minutes longer.

3. To serve, place the chicken thighs in the bottom of 4 shallow bowls. Spoon the bean mixture over the top and sprinkle with the parsley.

MAKES 4 SERVINGS

Per serving: 244 calories, 23 g protein, 24 g carbohydrates, 6 g total fat, 2 g saturated fat, 57 mg cholesterol, 7 g dietary fiber, 548 mg sodium

Lemony Chicken and Olive Tagine

In the cooking of Morocco, a "tagine" refers to a slow-cooked stew and also to the earthenware pot in which it simmers. A Dutch oven or any other heavy pot with a lid works just fine for this sumptuous dish.

Prep time: 20 minutes   Cook time: 45 minutes

---

1 pound boneless, skinless chicken thighs, trimmed, cut into 1" chunks

1 onion, chopped, about 1 cup

1 small red bell pepper, chopped, about ¾ cup

3 cloves garlic, minced

⅛ teaspoon saffron threads, lightly crushed

¼ teaspoon ground ginger

½ cup lower-sodium fat-free chicken broth

½ cup orange juice

½ cup dried apricots, halved

1 can (15 ounces) chickpeas, drained and rinsed

3 oranges, cut between the membranes into segments, ¾ cup

15 stuffed manzanilla olives, halved

⅓ cup chopped fresh cilantro

1 tablespoon lemon juice

¼ teaspoon salt

1¼ cups water

1 cup whole wheat couscous

1. Coat a Dutch oven with cooking spray and heat over medium-high heat. Add the chicken and cook, turning occasionally, until browned, 5 to 6 minutes. Stir in the onion, bell pepper, and garlic; cook, stirring occasionally, until the vegetables soften, 5 to 6 minutes. Add the saffron and ginger and cook 30 seconds, or until fragrant. Add the broth, orange juice, apricots, and chickpeas. Bring to a boil, reduce the heat to medium, cover, and simmer for 30 minutes, or until the chicken is no longer pink inside and the flavors have blended. Remove from the heat and stir in the oranges, olives, cilantro, and lemon juice.

2. Meanwhile, combine the salt and water in a small saucepan over medium-high heat. Stir in the couscous; remove from the heat and let stand for 5 minutes. Serve the tagine over the couscous.

MAKES 6 SERVINGS

Per serving: 303 calories, 21 g protein, 44 g carbohydrates, 6 g total fat, 1 g saturated fat, 57 mg cholesterol, 7 g dietary fiber, 560 mg sodium

Tandoori Chicken with Brown Rice and Peas

Make sure to allow time to marinate the chicken. The spicy yogurt mixture creates grilled chicken that is moist and mouthwatering.

Prep time: 10 minutes   **Marinating time: 30 minutes**   **Cook time: 60 minutes**

RICE

2 teaspoons olive oil

1 large onion, sliced

1 cup brown rice

2 cups reduced-sodium, fat-free chicken broth, boiling

¼ teaspoon salt

1 cup frozen peas

CHICKEN

¾ cup plain nonfat yogurt

2 tablespoons fresh lemon juice

1 large clove garlic, crushed

2 teaspoons ground cumin

½ teaspoon ground ginger

¼ teaspoon ground turmeric

¾ teaspoon ground black pepper

¼ teaspoon ground red pepper

4 boneless, skinless chicken breast halves (5 ounces each), each cut in half on an angle

1. *To make the rice:* Warm the oil in a large, heavy saucepan over medium heat. Add the onion and cook, stirring often, until tender, about 5 minutes. Add the rice and cook, stirring, for 1 minute. Stir in the broth and salt and return to a boil. Reduce the heat to low, cover, and simmer for 50 to 55 minutes, or until the rice is tender and the liquid has been absorbed.

2. Remove the rice from the heat and stir in the peas with a fork. Cover and let stand until ready to serve.

3. *To make the chicken:* Meanwhile, in a large bowl, stir together the yogurt, lemon juice, garlic, cumin, ginger, turmeric, black pepper, and red pepper. Add the chicken and turn to coat. Cover and refrigerate for 30 minutes.

4. Preheat the broiler. Coat a broiler-pan rack with cooking spray. Place the chicken skinned side down on the prepared broiler pan and spoon the remaining marinade over it. Broil 3" to 4" from the heat, turning once, until a thermometer inserted in the thickest part registers 160°F and juices run clear, about 12 minutes.

5. Fluff the rice again and serve with the chicken.

MAKES 4 SERVINGS

Per serving: 421 calories, 41 g protein, 50 g carbohydrates, 6 g total fat, 1 g saturated fat, 83 mg cholesterol, 4 g dietary fiber, 535 mg sodium

Stove Top Arroz con Pollo

There was a time when brown rice for dinner meant at least 40 minutes of cooking time. Thankfully, those days are gone. With the advent of brown rice that cooks in 10 minutes, there's no excuse for not serving up all those wonderful nutrients.

Prep time: 20 minutes   Cook time: 40 minutes   Stand time: 5 minutes

1 pound boneless, skinless chicken thighs, cut into ½"-wide strips

¼ teaspoon salt

¼ teaspoon ground black pepper

1 teaspoon olive oil

1 large onion, chopped, 1½ cups

2 cloves garlic, minced

1 green bell pepper, chopped, 1 cup

1 cup quick-cooking brown rice (cooks in 10 minutes), such as Uncle Ben's

2 teaspoons ground cumin

½ teaspoon ground turmeric

1 can (14.5 ounces) diced tomatoes

1 can (14.5 ounces) lower-sodium fat-free chicken broth

8 manzanilla olives, halved

1 cup frozen peas

¼ cup drained sliced pimientos

1. Sprinkle the chicken with the salt and ⅛ teaspoon of the black pepper. Heat the oil in a nonstick Dutch oven over medium-high heat. Add the chicken and cook until browned, about 2 minutes per side. Transfer to a plate and set aside.

2. Return the Dutch oven to the stove and add the onion, garlic, and bell pepper; cook, stirring occasionally, until the vegetables start to soften, about 4 to 5 minutes. Stir in the rice, cumin, and turmeric and cook, stirring, 1 minute. Add the reserved chicken, the tomatoes, broth, and olives; bring to a boil, reduce heat to medium-low, cover, and simmer until the liquid has been absorbed and the rice is tender, about 30 minutes. Stir in the peas, pimientos, and remaining ⅛ teaspoon black pepper; cook for 2 minutes or until heated through. Remove from the heat and let stand for 5 minutes.

MAKES 4 SERVINGS

Per serving: 313 calories, 30 g protein,
30 g carbohydrates, 9 g total fat, 2 g saturated fat,
94 mg cholesterol, 4 g dietary fiber, 483 mg sodium

Turkey Gumbo

Gumbo—said to be an African derivation of the word for okra—is a fun word to say. But packed with just enough spice for some jazzy flavor, the dish is even more enjoyable to eat.

Prep time: 15 minutes   Cook time: 55 minutes

½ cup brown rice

5 teaspoons olive oil

1 cup frozen cut okra

12 ounces turkey breast cutlets, cut into ½" pieces

2 tablespoons whole wheat flour

1 onion, chopped, about 1 cup

2 ribs celery, chopped, about ¾ cup

1 medium green bell pepper, chopped, about ¾ cup

4 cloves garlic, minced

4 ounces turkey kielbasa, thinly sliced

½ teaspoon dried thyme

⅛ teaspoon ground red pepper

2 cups lower-sodium fat-free chicken broth

1 can (14.5 ounces) salt-free diced tomatoes

1. Cook the rice according to package directions, omitting any fat.

2. Heat 1 teaspoon of the oil in a nonstick Dutch oven over medium-high heat. Add the okra and cook, stirring often, until tender, about 5 to 6 minutes; transfer to a bowl and set aside. Return the Dutch oven to the stove and add the turkey breast; cook until no longer pink inside, about 4 to 5 minutes. Transfer the turkey to a separate bowl.

3. Reduce the heat to medium and add the remaining 4 teaspoons oil and the flour to the pan; cook, stirring with a wooden spoon, until the flour takes on a reddish hue, about 3 to 4 minutes. Stir in the onion, celery, bell pepper, and garlic; cook, stirring occasionally, until the vegetables start to soften, about 4 to 5 minutes. Add the kielbasa, thyme, and red pepper; cook 1 minute. Stir in the broth, tomatoes, and reserved okra; increase heat to medium-high and bring to a boil. Reduce the heat to medium and simmer, uncovered, until slightly thickened, about 30 minutes. Stir in the reserved turkey and simmer until warmed through, about 5 to 7 minutes. Serve the gumbo over the rice.

MAKES 4 SERVINGS

Per serving: 352 calories, 32 g protein, 34 g carbohydrates, 9 g total fat, 2 g saturated fat, 55 mg cholesterol, 5 g dietary fiber, 464 mg sodium

Instant Chicken and White Bean Stew

You have to love a recipe with the word *instant* in the title and *pesto* in the ingredients list. On a night when you feel too tuckered out to cook, this dish practically makes itself with a little leftover chicken and some pantry items.

Prep time: 10 minutes   Cook time: 10 minutes

---

1 onion, chopped

2 cloves garlic, minced

2 teaspoons olive oil

2 cups reduced-sodium chicken broth

2 medium zucchini, halved lengthwise and thinly sliced

1 can (19 ounces) cannellini beans, rinsed and drained

⅛ teaspoon ground black pepper

1½ cups cooked diced chicken

2 tablespoons prepared pesto

1. In a nonstick skillet over medium heat, cook the onion and garlic in the oil until soft. Add the broth, zucchini, beans, and pepper. Heat just to boiling. Boil for 2 minutes.

2. Add the chicken, return just to boiling, and remove from the heat. Add the pesto. Let stand for 2 to 3 minutes to blend the flavors.

MAKES 4 SERVINGS

Per serving: 275 calories, 25 g protein, 21 g carbohydrates, 10 g total fat, 2 g saturated fat, 48 mg cholesterol, 6 g dietary fiber, 580 mg sodium

North African Spiced Chicken and Sweet Potato Stew

If it fits better into your schedule, prepare this dish ahead of time. The intricate flavorings actually improve in the refrigerator for a day or two. Reheat gently in a pot and add the fresh basil just before serving.

Prep time: 20 minutes **Cook time: 40 minutes**

1 pound boneless, skinless chicken breasts, cut into 1½" pieces

2 tablespoons whole wheat flour

1 teaspoon salt

2 tablespoons extra virgin olive oil

1 onion, chopped, 1 cup

5 cloves garlic, minced

12 ounces sweet potato, peeled and cut into ½"–¾" pieces

4 carrots, cut into ½"–¾" pieces

2 white turnips, cut into ½"–¾" pieces

1 tablespoon ground cumin

2 teaspoons ground coriander

¼ teaspoon ground cinnamon

1 can (14.5 ounces) lower-sodium fat-free chicken broth

½ cup orange juice

½ cup currants

3 tablespoons chopped basil

1. In a bowl, combine the chicken, flour, and ½ teaspoon of the salt. Heat 1 tablespoon of the oil in a nonstick Dutch oven over medium-high heat. Add the chicken and cook, turning once, until no longer pink inside, 3 to 4 minutes; transfer to a plate.

2. Heat the remaining 1 tablespoon oil and add the onion; cook, stirring often, until starting to brown, 3 to 4 minutes. Add the garlic and cook for 30 seconds. Stir in the sweet potato, carrots, and turnips and cook for 2 minutes. Add the cumin, coriander, and cinnamon and cook for 30 seconds. Add the broth, orange juice, and currants; bring to a boil, reduce heat to medium-low, cover, and simmer until the vegetables are tender, 22 to 24 minutes. Stir in the chicken and the remaining ½ teaspoon salt and simmer until the chicken is cooked through, about 5 minutes. Remove from the heat and stir in the basil.

MAKES 6 SERVINGS

Per serving: 276 calories, 22 g protein, 34 g carbohydrates, 7 g total fat, 1 g saturated fat, 44 mg cholesterol, 5 g dietary fiber, 544 mg sodium

Home-Style Turkey Pot Pie

Savory meat and vegetable pies are a standard of American cookery. By using a purchased pie crust, you can enjoy all of the satisfaction of this old-fashioned meal with a fraction of the work. Sweet potatoes and a dash of whole wheat flour lend fiber that is otherwise missing from this family favorite. If you prefer to make individual pot pies, like those in the photo at right, cut the pie crust into six equal pieces, gather each into a ball, and roll on a lightly floured surface. Drape over individual, ovenproof dishes and proceed with Step 3.

Prep time: 20 minutes   Cook time: 45 minutes

1 onion, chopped, about 1 cup

2 cloves garlic, minced

2 teaspoons dried tarragon

1 can (14½ ounces) lower-sodium fat-free chicken broth

3 tablespoons whole wheat flour

12 ounces sweet potato, peeled and cut into ½" pieces

1 tablespoon Dijon mustard

2½ cups cubed cooked turkey breast, about 12 ounces

1 cup frozen peas and carrots

½ cup frozen corn

¼ cup chopped fresh parsley

½ teaspoon salt

1 (7½-ounce) refrigerated pie crust

1. Coat a nonstick skillet with cooking spray and heat over medium-high heat. Add the onion, garlic, and tarragon; cook, stirring occasionally, until starting to soften, 3 to 4 minutes. Combine the broth and flour and pour into the skillet. Add the sweet potato and mustard; bring to a boil, reduce the heat to medium-low, cover, and simmer until the sweet potato is tender, about 15 minutes. Stir in the turkey, peas and carrots, corn, parsley, and salt.

2. Preheat the oven to 375°F. Coat a 9" deep-dish pie pan with cooking spray.

3. Pour the filling into the prepared pie pan. Unroll the refrigerator crust and top the pie pan. Roll up any excess dough that hangs over the edge and crimp. Cut a decorative opening in crust, and bake until the top is browned and the filling is hot and bubbly, 23 to 25 minutes.

MAKES 6 SERVINGS

Per serving: 360 calories, 23 g protein,
40 g carbohydrates, 12 g total fat, 5 g saturated fat,
45 mg cholesterol, 4 g dietary fiber, 500 mg sodium

Mom's Turkey Meat Loaf

Beef up the taste and texture of mild ground turkey with nutty grains, some fresh minced veggies, and savory seasonings.

Prep time: 20 minutes   Cook time: 1 hour 10 minutes

8 ounces sweet potato, peeled and cut into ¼" cubes

3 slices multigrain bread

½ cup quick-cooking oats

½ cup fat-free milk

1½ pounds 7% fat lean ground turkey

1 small onion, chopped, about ½ cup

½ cup ketchup

¼ cup chopped fresh parsley

1 teaspoon dried oregano

1 teaspoon Worcestershire sauce

¼ teaspoon salt

¼ teaspoon ground black pepper

1. Preheat the oven to 350°F. Coat a baking sheet with cooking spray.

2. Place the sweet potato in a small saucepan with enough water to cover by 2". Bring to a boil and cook until fork-tender but still firm, about 5 to 6 minutes; drain and let cool for 5 minutes. Meanwhile, place the bread into the bowl of a food processor and pulse into bread crumbs. Transfer to a bowl and stir in the oats and milk; let stand for 5 minutes, or until softened.

3. In a large bowl, combine the turkey, sweet potato, bread crumb mixture, onion, 3 tablespoons of the ketchup, parsley, oregano, Worcestershire sauce, salt, and pepper. Transfer the mixture to the prepared baking sheet and form into a 9" × 4" loaf. Spread the top with the remaining 5 tablespoons of ketchup. Bake until a thermometer inserted into the thickest part of the loaf registers 165°F and the meat is no longer pink, about 1 hour. Remove from the oven and let stand for 10 minutes before slicing.

MAKES 6 SERVINGS

Per serving: 248 calories, 32 g protein, 26 g carbohydrates, 3 g total fat, 0 g saturated fat, 45 mg cholesterol, 4 g dietary fiber, 519 mg sodium

Turkey Burgers with Chili-Beans

Satisfy your hankering for diner fare with this smart burger and chili.
All that's gone is the grease.

Prep time: 20 minutes   Cook time: 30 minutes

CHILI-BEANS

1 large onion, chopped

1 teaspoon olive oil

2–2½ teaspoons chili powder

½ teaspoon whole cumin seeds

⅛–¼ teaspoon ground red pepper

½ cup chopped and drained roasted, jarred red peppers

1 can (15–16 ounces) navy beans, rinsed and drained

1 can (15–16 ounces) red kidney beans, rinsed and drained

1 can (8 ounces) tomato sauce, plus ½ can water

TURKEY BURGERS

1¼ pounds ground turkey breast

¼ cup chopped and drained roasted, jarred red peppers (blot dry)

2 scallions, chopped

2 tablespoons plain dry bread crumbs

2 tablespoons chopped fresh parsley

1 tablespoon Dijon mustard

½ teaspoon coarse-ground black pepper

1. *To make the beans:* In a large nonstick skillet, stir together the onion and oil. Cook over medium heat, stirring often, for 5 to 6 minutes, or until tender. Add the chili powder, cumin seeds, and red pepper; cook and stir for 30 seconds. Stir in the roasted peppers, the navy and kidney beans, and the tomato sauce and water and bring to a boil. Reduce the heat to low, cover, and simmer for 10 minutes to blend the flavors. Remove from the heat. Cover and keep warm while grilling the turkey burgers.

2. *To make the burgers:* Heat an outdoor grill to medium or preheat the broiler. Oil the grill grids or coat a broiler-pan rack with cooking spray. In a large bowl, combine the ground turkey, roasted peppers, scallions, bread crumbs, parsley, mustard, and black pepper. Mix gently but thoroughly until blended. Shape into four 1"-thick patties. Place on the prepared grill or broiler pan and grill or broil for 10 to 12 minutes, turning once, or until a thermometer inserted in the thickest part registers 165°F and the meat is no longer pink. Serve with the beans.

MAKES 4 SERVINGS (1 CUP BEANS + 1 BURGER PER SERVING)

Per serving: 369 calories, 47 g protein,
39 g carbohydrates, 4 g total fat, 0.5 g saturated fat,
56 mg cholesterol, 12 g dietary fiber, 667 mg sodium

Beef, Broccoli, and Cashew Stir-Fry with Brown Rice

Freezing the beef for 20 minutes will make it easier to slice. The beef then marinates while you prepare the remaining ingredients, steam the broccoli, and make the rice.

Prep time: 15 minutes   **Marinating time: 30 minutes**   **Cook time: 25 minutes**

3 tablespoons reduced-sodium soy sauce

1 tablespoon rice wine vinegar

¼ teaspoon crushed red-pepper flakes

12 ounces trimmed boneless beef top round, cut across the grain into thin slices, slices cut into 1" bite-size pieces

2 whole stalks broccoli, cut into small florets, stems halved lengthwise and very thinly sliced crosswise (about 5 cups)

⅓ cup reduced-sodium, fat-free chicken broth

1 tablespoon cornstarch

2 tablespoons peanut or canola oil

3 cloves garlic, thinly sliced

2 tablespoons thin matchstick strips peeled fresh ginger

1 large red bell pepper, cut into thin strips

2 tablespoons unsalted cashews

2 cups prepared instant brown rice (without butter)

1. In a medium bowl, combine the soy sauce, vinegar, and red-pepper flakes. Add the beef and toss to mix. Let stand at room temperature for 30 minutes.

2. Meanwhile, place a steamer basket in a large pot with 2" of water. Bring to a boil over high heat. Place the broccoli in the basket, cover, and steam for 6 to 8 minutes, or until crisp-tender. Remove the broccoli from the steamer and rinse briefly under cold running water. Set aside.

3. Drain the beef, reserving the marinade. Mix the broth and cornstarch in a cup.

4. In a large, deep nonstick skillet, warm 1 tablespoon of the oil over medium-high heat until hot but not smoking. Add the garlic and ginger and stir-fry for 30 seconds, just until fragrant; do not brown. Add half the drained beef strips and stir-fry about 2 minutes, or just until no longer pink; transfer to a clean plate. Repeat with the remaining beef strips.

5. Add the remaining 1 tablespoon oil to the skillet. Add the bell pepper and stir-fry until just crisp-tender, about 2 minutes. Return the beef and any juices, the reserved marinade, and the steamed broccoli to the skillet. Toss to mix. Stir-fry about 2 minutes, or until heated through. Stir the cornstarch mixture again; add to the skillet and cook, stirring, until the mixture boils and thickens. Remove from the heat and sprinkle with the cashews. Serve over the rice.

MAKES 4 SERVINGS

Per serving: 375 calories, 24 g protein, 34 g carbohydrates, 15 g total fat, 4 g saturated fat, 34 mg cholesterol, 3 g dietary fiber, 534 mg sodium

Curried Beef with Pineapple, Coconut, and Brown Basmati Rice

Canned coconut milk is one of the stellar additions to the modern American supermarket. With its fruity essence and creamy consistency, it pulls together sauces in a host of Asian and Hispanic dishes. Be sure to purchase coconut milk, not cream of coconut, which contains a great deal of sugar.

Prep time: 15 minutes   Cook time: 40 minutes

½ cup brown basmati rice

2 teaspoons olive oil

12 ounces beef top round steak, trimmed of all visible fat, thinly sliced

½ teaspoon salt

1 onion, chopped, about 1 cup

1 tablespoon peeled, grated fresh ginger

2 cloves garlic, minced

2 cups pineapple cubes

1 medium apple, cored and chopped, about 1 cup

1 teaspoon curry powder

½ teaspoon ground cumin

¾ cup light coconut milk

2 tablespoons lower-sodium soy sauce

1 tablespoon sugar

1. Cook the rice according to package directions, omitting any fat.

2. Heat 1 teaspoon of the oil in a large nonstick skillet over medium-high heat. Sprinkle the beef with the salt and add half to the skillet; cook, turning once, until no longer pink, 45 seconds per side. Remove from the skillet. Repeat with the remaining beef; set beef aside.

3. Wipe out the skillet and heat the remaining 1 teaspoon oil. Add the onion, ginger, and garlic; cook, stirring occasionally, for 1 minute. Add the pineapple and cook for 2 to 3 minutes, or until starting to brown slightly. Stir in the apple and cook until heated through, 2 minutes. Add the curry and cumin; cook until fragrant, 30 seconds. Add the coconut milk, soy sauce, and sugar; reduce heat to medium and simmer 2 minutes. Add the beef and cook until hot, 1 to 2 minutes. Serve over the rice.

MAKES 4 SERVINGS

Per serving: 361 calories, 23 g protein, 40 g carbohydrates, 13 g total fat, 5 g saturated fat, 34 mg cholesterol, 4 g dietary fiber, 478 mg sodium

Beef and Bean Chili

Ancho chile peppers—dried poblanos—can become addictive. Their color is ruddy and the taste is rich and fruity. They make this stew something special.

Prep time: 15 minutes   **Stand time: 15 minutes**   **Cook time: 38 minutes**

2 ancho chile peppers, seeded and chopped

1 cup lower-sodium fat-free chicken broth

12 ounces 93% lean ground beef

1 large onion, chopped, about 1½ cups

4 cloves garlic, minced

1 tablespoon chili powder

2 teaspoons ground cumin

1 teaspoon dried oregano

1 can (28 ounces) whole peeled tomatoes, chopped, juices reserved

1 can (15 ounces) cannellini beans, rinsed and drained

½ ounce semisweet chocolate

1 cup quick-cooking brown rice

6 tablespoons shredded reduced-fat sharp Cheddar cheese

1. Bring 2 cups of water to a boil in a small saucepan over high heat. Add the chile peppers, remove from the heat, and let stand 15 minutes. Remove the peppers with a slotted spoon and transfer to a blender, add the chicken broth, and puree; set aside.

2. Heat a large nonstick pot over medium-high heat and add the beef; cook, stirring with a wooden spoon to break up any chunks, until no longer pink, 3 to 4 minutes. Stir in the onion and garlic; cook until the beef begins to brown, 4 to 5 minutes. Add the chili powder, cumin, and oregano and cook for 1 minute. Add the reserved chile broth mixture, the tomatoes and juice, and the beans; bring to a boil, reduce the heat to medium, and simmer uncovered until thickened and the flavors blend, about 30 minutes. Remove from the heat and stir in the chocolate.

3. Meanwhile, cook the rice according to package directions, omitting any fat. Divide the rice among 6 bowls and top each with chili and 1 tablespoon of the cheese.

MAKES 6 SERVINGS

Per serving: 254 calories, 20 g protein, 31 g carbohydrates, 6 g total fat, 3 g saturated fat, 40 mg cholesterol, 6 g dietary fiber, 469 mg sodium

Spiced Beef and Lentil Stew

For those transitioning to meals with increased amounts of grains and vegetables, dishes like this one make it easy. The succulent beef chuck delivers lots of meaty satisfaction, while the lentils bring on the fiber. If you like, every time you make it, you can gradually decrease the beef and increase the lentils.

Prep time: 15 minutes   Cook time: 1 hour 50 minutes

1 tablespoon olive oil

1 large onion, sliced

4 cloves garlic, minced

1 teaspoon paprika

½ teaspoon dried thyme

½ teaspoon ground cumin

¼ teaspoon salt

½ teaspoon ground black pepper

⅛ teaspoon ground allspice

⅛ teaspoon ground red pepper

1 pound lean, well-trimmed boneless beef chuck, cut into ½" cubes

2 tablespoons all-purpose unbleached flour

1½ cups reduced-sodium, fat-free chicken broth

¾ cup water

¾ cup lentils, picked over and rinsed

2 large carrots, sliced

1. Preheat the oven to 325°F. In a large, heavy oven-proof Dutch oven, warm the oil over medium heat. Add the onion and garlic and cook, stirring often, until tender, about 5 minutes (add a tablespoon of water if the pan gets dry). Stir in the paprika, thyme, cumin, salt, black pepper, allspice, and red pepper. Cook and stir for 1 minute.

2. Toss the beef with the flour. Add the floured beef to the Dutch oven and stir to coat well with the spices and onion. Pour in the broth and water and bring to a boil.

3. Cover and transfer to the oven. Bake for 45 minutes (the meat will start to get tender). Add the lentils and carrots; cover and bake for 40 to 50 minutes more, or until the beef and lentils are tender.

MAKES 4 SERVINGS

Per serving: 283 calories, 28 g protein, 26 g carbohydrates, 7 g total fat, 2 g saturated fat, 57 mg cholesterol, 9 g dietary fiber, 452 mg sodium

Tuscan-Style Stuffed Peppers

If you should be so lucky to have any leftover peppers, they taste fabulous drizzled with a bit of balsamic vinegar for a room-temperature lunch.

Prep time: 15 minutes   Cook time: 45 minutes

½ cup quick-cooking brown rice

12 ounces 93% lean ground beef

1 small onion, chopped, ½ cup

2 cloves garlic, minced

½ cup packed golden raisins

1 tablespoon drained capers

1 teaspoon dried oregano

¼ teaspoon salt

¼ teaspoon ground black pepper

¼ cup grated Pecorino Romano cheese

4 medium red bell peppers, crowns cut off and seeded

2 cups tomato juice

1. Cook the rice according to package directions.

2. Heat a large nonstick skillet over medium-high heat. Add the beef and cook, stirring with a wooden spoon to break up any chunks, until no longer pink, 3 to 4 minutes. Add the onion, garlic, raisins, capers, and oregano; cook, stirring occasionally, until the onion begins to soften, 4 to 5 minutes. Stir in the rice, salt, and black pepper; cook 1 minute. Remove from the heat and stir in the cheese.

3. Spoon the filling into the bell peppers and set them in a saucepan or small pot just large enough to hold them snugly. Pour the tomato juice into the pot, cover, and bring to a boil over medium-high heat. Reduce the heat to medium-low, cover, and simmer until the peppers are tender, 32 to 34 minutes. Transfer to serving bowls and spoon the sauce from the pot over the peppers.

MAKES 4 SERVINGS

Per serving: 320 calories, 25 g protein,
39 g carbohydrates, 7 g total fat, 4 g saturated fat,
60 mg cholesterol, 5 g dietary fiber, 579 mg sodium

Beef, Corn, and Refried Bean Enchiladas

Like opening presents at Christmas, digging into foods that are wrapped in bundles brings plenty of joyous surprises. Meaty, cheesy, and spicy, these stuffed tortillas are a gift to everyone who eats them.

Prep time: 30 minutes   Cook time: 25–30 minutes

8 ounces 93% lean ground beef

1 onion, chopped, about 1 cup

1 tomato, chopped

½ cup frozen corn kernels

2 cloves garlic, minced

2 teaspoons chili powder

1 teaspoon dried oregano

1 tablespoon whole wheat flour

1 can (15 to 16 ounces) black beans, rinsed and drained

6 multigrain tortillas (7–8" diameter)

1 can (10 ounces) mild red enchilada sauce

⅓ cup shredded reduced-fat Mexican cheese blend

Chopped cilantro or parsley (optional)

1. Preheat the oven to 350°F. Coat a 13" × 9" baking dish with cooking spray.

2. Heat a large nonstick skillet over medium-high heat and add the beef; cook, stirring with a wooden spoon to break up any chunks, until no longer pink, 3 to 4 minutes. Stir in the onion, tomato, corn, and garlic; cook until the onion starts to soften, 1 to 2 minutes. Stir in the chili powder and oregano and cook, stirring, for 30 seconds. Sprinkle with flour and cook, stirring occasionally, until thickened, about 1 to 2 minutes. Remove from the heat and stir in the beans.

3. Wrap the tortillas in between damp paper towels and microwave until warm, 20 to 40 seconds. Working one at a time, place a tortilla on a work surface and top with ½ cup of the beef mixture spread in a line across the center, parallel to the edge of the counter closest to you. Roll up jelly roll–style and place seam side down in the prepared baking dish. Repeat with the remaining tortillas and filling. Pour the sauce over the enchiladas and sprinkle with the cheese. Bake until hot and the cheese has melted, 18 to 20 minutes. Sprinkle with cilantro or parsley, if desired. Serve immediately.

MAKES 6 SERVINGS

Per serving: 260 calories, 15 g protein,
42 g carbohydrates, 7 g total fat, 2 g saturated fat,
30 mg cholesterol, 7 g dietary fiber, 660 mg sodium

Spicy Beef Baked Penne

A cheesy, meaty tomato sauce pasta bake is a dish that few people could resist. If you don't have penne pasta, any short shape of dried macaroni-style pasta will do. Choose among shells, farfalle, or rotini.

Prep time: 20 minutes   Cook time: 50 minutes

12 ounces multigrain penne

12 ounces 93% lean ground beef

1 onion, chopped, about 1 cup

3 cloves garlic, minced

1 teaspoon dried basil

⅛ teaspoon red-pepper flakes

1 can (28 ounces) salt-free diced tomatoes

1 tablespoon tomato paste

½ teaspoon salt

1 container (15 ounces) fat-free ricotta cheese

1 cup shredded reduced-fat mozzarella cheese

3 tablespoons grated Parmesan cheese

1. Preheat the oven to 350°F. Coat an 11" × 7" baking dish with cooking spray.

2. Bring a large pot of lightly salted water to a boil. Add the penne and cook according to package directions, but stopping when the pasta is still slightly underdone; drain and rinse under cold water.

3. Heat a large nonstick skillet over medium-high heat and add the beef; cook, stirring with a wooden spoon to break up any chunks, until no longer pink, 3 to 4 minutes. Stir in the onion, garlic, basil, and red-pepper flakes; cook until the onion is starting to soften, 3 to 4 minutes. Add the tomatoes, tomato paste, and salt; reduce the heat to medium and simmer, uncovered, until slightly thickened, about 9 to 10 minutes. Meanwhile, combine the ricotta cheese, ½ cup of the mozzarella, and the Parmesan cheese in a bowl.

4. Pour half of the penne into the bottom of the prepared baking dish. Top with half of the sauce, then spread with the cheese mixture and top with the remaining penne. Spread the top of the penne with the remaining sauce and sprinkle with the remaining ½ cup mozzarella. Bake until the penne is bubbling and the cheese has completely melted, about 30 minutes. Let stand for 5 minutes before serving.

MAKES 4 SERVINGS

Per serving: 437 calories, 33 g protein,
57 g carbohydrates, 7 g total fat, 3 g saturated fat,
59 mg cholesterol, 4 g dietary fiber, 548 mg sodium

Sweet Potato Shepherd's Pie

Like Dorothy arriving in the land of Oz, you'll rub your eyes in wonder when you see the technicolor topping of this popular oven meal.

Prep time: 15 minutes   Cook time: 45 minutes

---

2 pounds sweet potatoes, peeled and cut into 1" pieces

¾ cup 1% milk

1 teaspoon salt

¼ teaspoon ground black pepper

1½ pounds 93% lean ground beef

1 onion, chopped, about 1 cup

2 cloves garlic, minced

¼ cup lower-sodium fat-free beef broth or water

¼ cup tomato paste

1 package (10 ounces) frozen peas and carrots

1 teaspoon Worcestershire sauce

1 teaspoon Dijon mustard

1. Preheat the oven to 350°F. Coat an 8-cup baking dish with cooking spray.

2. Place the potatoes in a large saucepan over high heat with enough cold water to cover by 2". Bring to a boil and cook until the potatoes are tender, 15 to 18 minutes. Drain and return the potatoes to the pot. Add the milk, ½ teaspoon of the salt, and ⅛ teaspoon of the pepper and mash until smooth; set aside.

3. Meanwhile, heat a large nonstick skillet over medium-high heat. Add the beef and cook, stirring with a wooden spoon to break up any chunks, until no longer pink, 4 to 5 minutes; transfer to a bowl. Return the skillet to the heat and add the onion and garlic; cook, stirring occasionally, until the onion begins to brown, 4 to 5 minutes. Add the broth or water and the tomato paste; cook until the mixture is slightly thickened, 2 to 3 minutes. Add the peas and carrots; cook until thawed, 1 to 2 minutes. Add the Worcestershire sauce, mustard, and the remaining ½ teaspoon salt and ⅛ teaspoon pepper; cook 30 seconds. Stir in the beef and transfer to the prepared baking dish. Cover the beef mixture with the potatoes and smooth with a spatula.

4. Bake until the filling is bubbling up around the edges, 18 to 20 minutes. Turn on the broiler and broil until the top browns slightly, 1 to 2 minutes. Let cool for 5 minutes before serving.

MAKES 6 SERVINGS

Per serving: 325 calories, 30 g protein, 37 g carbohydrates, 6 g total fat, 3 g saturated fat, 72 mg cholesterol, 7 g dietary fiber, 499 mg sodium

Beef and Black-Bean Picadillo over Brown Rice

Black beans are truly mellow (supposedly, they're the dried bean that causes the least digestive upset) and take to so many different seasonings. Here, they get the Cuban treatment in a delicious stew over rice.

Prep time: 12 minutes   Cook time: 35 minutes

1 cup instant brown rice, cooked according to package directions

¾ pound lean ground beef

2 teaspoons olive oil

1 red bell pepper, coarsely chopped

1 cup chopped red onion (reserve 2 tablespoons for topping)

2 cloves garlic, minced

2½ teaspoons ground cumin

½ teaspoon granulated sugar

¼ teaspoon salt

½ teaspoon crushed red-pepper flakes

1 can (15–16 ounces) black beans, rinsed and drained

1 can (14½ ounces) no-salt diced tomatoes in juice

½ cup dark raisins

2 tablespoons pimiento-stuffed olives

1. Cook the rice according to package directions.

2. Mist a large nonstick skillet with olive oil spray and heat over medium-high heat. Crumble in the ground beef and cook, stirring to break up any chunks, for 5 minutes, or until no longer pink. Drain and set aside.

3. In the same skillet, heat the oil over medium heat. Add the bell pepper, remaining onion, and garlic. Cook, stirring often, until tender, about 5 minutes. Return the beef to the skillet and stir in the cumin, sugar, salt, and red-pepper flakes. Cook and stir for 1 minute. Stir in the beans, the tomatoes with their juice, and raisins; bring to a simmer. Reduce the heat to low, cover, and simmer, stirring once or twice, until the flavors have blended, 15 minutes.

4. Sprinkle the picadillo with the olives and reserved 2 tablespoons of onion and serve with the rice.

MAKES 4 SERVINGS

Per serving: 320 calories, 25 g protein, 39 g carbohydrates, 8 g total fat, 2 g saturated fat, 55 mg cholesterol, 8 g dietary fiber, 580 mg sodium

Orecchiette with White Beans, Sausage, and Peppers

Orecchiette is a pasta shape that means "little ears," and that's what they look like. If you can't find them in your supermarket, use medium-size pasta shells instead.

Prep time: 15 minutes   Cook time: 20 minutes

2 teaspoons olive oil

1 cup chopped onion

2 cups chopped bell peppers

½ pound sweet Italian sausage

3 cloves garlic, minced

½ teaspoon red-pepper flakes

1 can (28 ounces) diced tomatoes in juice

1 can (15.5 ounces) small white beans, rinsed and drained

½ cup chopped fresh basil

¼ teaspoon salt

¼ teaspoon ground black pepper

8 ounces orecchiette (scant 3 cups)

¼ cup grated Parmesan cheese

1. Heat the oil in a large nonstick skillet over medium-high heat. Add the onion and bell peppers and cook until tender, about 5 minutes. Add the sausage, garlic, and red-pepper flakes and cook until the sausage is no longer pink, breaking it up into small pieces with the side of a wooden spoon.

2. Stir in the tomatoes with their juice and bring to a boil. Reduce the heat to medium; simmer until the sauce thickens, stirring occasionally, about 10 minutes. Stir in the beans, basil, salt, and black pepper.

3. Meanwhile, cook the pasta in a large pot of boiling salted water for 12 minutes, or until the pasta is just tender but still firm to the bite. Drain the pasta and return to the cooking pot.

4. Add the tomato sauce to the pasta and toss to blend. Transfer the pasta to a bowl. Sprinkle with the cheese and serve.

MAKES 6 SERVINGS

Per serving: 309 calories, 17 g protein, 47 g carbohydrates, 7 g total fat, 2 g saturated fat, 14 mg cholesterol, 6 g dietary fiber, 596 mg sodium

Penne with Broccoli Rabe, Sausage, and Garlic

The Italian vegetable broccoli rabe is particularly good in this dish because its pungency counters the richness of the sausage. When choosing broccoli rabe, look for bunches with fresh-looking dark green leaves crowned with tiny broccoli-like florets.

Prep time: 10 minutes   Cook time: 15 minutes

1 pound broccoli rabe, woody stems trimmed, yield about 8 ounces

8 ounces multigrain penne

1½ tablespoons extra virgin olive oil

8 ounces sweet Italian sausage, removed from the casing

6 cloves garlic, sliced

1 cup lower-sodium fat-free chicken broth

½ teaspoon salt

1 tablespoon grated Parmesan cheese

1. Bring a large pot of lightly salted water to a boil. Add the broccoli rabe and cook until bright green and crisp-tender, 2 minutes (the water does not have to come back to a full boil). With kitchen tongs or a slotted spoon, transfer the broccoli rabe to a bowl of ice water to stop the cooking. Drain well and gently squeeze to remove any excess water. Return the water in the pot to a boil, add the penne, and cook according to package directions; drain.

2. Meanwhile, heat the oil in a large nonstick skillet over medium-high heat. Add the sausage and cook, stirring and breaking it into smaller pieces with a wooden spoon, until no longer pink, 4 to 6 minutes. Add the garlic and cook until lightly golden, 1 to 2 minutes. Pour in the broth and bring to a boil; cook until reduced by about half, 3 to 4 minutes. Stir in the broccoli rabe and salt and cook, stirring, until hot, 1 to 2 minutes. Add the penne and cheese and toss well; serve immediately.

MAKES 4 SERVINGS

Per serving: 374 calories, 24 g protein, 47 g carbohydrates, 11 g total fat, 1 g saturated fat, 26 mg cholesterol, 4 g dietary fiber, 520 mg sodium

Pork Souvlaki with Yogurt Sauce

One taste of these juicy kebabs and your tastebuds will sail to the sunny Greek isles. The oregano-oil-lemon marinade is essential for seasoning and moistening the lean meat.

Prep time: 15 minutes   Chill time: 2 Hours   Cook time: 27 minutes

1 pound lean pork tenderloin, trimmed and cut into 24 pieces

1 tablespoon extra virgin olive oil

1 tablespoon lemon juice

1 teaspoon Worcestershire sauce

2 cloves garlic, minced

½ teaspoon dried oregano

¾ cup plain nonfat yogurt

¼ cup finely chopped cucumber

1 tablespoon chopped fresh dill

¼ teaspoon salt

¼ teaspoon ground black pepper

1 onion, cut into four ¼"-thick slices

4 plum tomatoes

4 multigrain pitas

4 leaves romaine lettuce

1. In a large bowl, combine the pork, oil, lemon juice, Worcestershire sauce, garlic, and oregano; refrigerate for 2 hours.

2. Meanwhile, in a bowl, combine the yogurt, cucumber, dill, and a small pinch of the salt; refrigerate until ready to use.

3. Preheat the grill. Discard the marinade from the pork. Thread 6 pieces of the pork onto each of 4 skewers. Sprinkle the pork with the pepper. Sprinkle the onion slices with the remaining salt. Grill the onion slices for 6 minutes per side, or until tender. Grill the pork for 8 minutes, turning every 2 minutes, until well marked and cooked through. Grill the tomatoes until just starting to wilt, about 6 to 8 minutes. Grill the pitas until toasted, 1 minute per side.

4. To serve, place a pita onto each of 4 plates. Top each with 1 lettuce leaf, 1 pork skewer, 1 onion slice, and 1 tomato. Top each with ¼ cup of the yogurt sauce.

MAKES 4 SERVINGS

Per serving: 392 calories, 33 g protein, 47 g carbohydrates, 9 g total fat, 2 g saturated fat, 75 mg cholesterol, 7 g dietary fiber, 588 mg sodium

Grilled Pork Tacos with Avocado-Radish Salad

This is a healthy version of the Mexican pork dish carnitas, which is simmered in its own fat. The toasted oregano adds an authentic touch. To ensure a terrific fiber boost, look for low-carb tortillas that offer about 50 calories and 8 grams fiber.

Prep time: 12 minutes   Cook time: 35 minutes

PORK

1½ teaspoons paprika

¼ teaspoon kosher salt

¼ teaspoon garlic powder

¼ teaspoon dry mustard

¼–½ teaspoon ground red pepper

1¼ pounds trimmed pork tenderloin

1 tablespoon olive oil

8 low-carb whole grain tortillas (6"–7" diameter)

SALAD

¼ teaspoon dried oregano

1 ripe medium avocado, halved, pitted, peeled, and cut into ¼" chunks

½ cup sliced radishes

2 scallions, thinly sliced

1 tablespoon fresh lime juice

1. *To make the pork:* Heat an outdoor grill to medium. In a cup, mix the paprika, salt, garlic powder, mustard, and red pepper. Rub all over the pork; drizzle with the oil. Stack the tortillas and wrap in foil to heat on the grill.

2. Grill the pork, turning 2 or 3 times, for 20 to 25 minutes, or until a meat thermometer inserted in the thickest part registers 150° to 155°F. Transfer to a cutting board and let stand for 10 minutes for easier slicing. Meanwhile, place the tortillas on a cool corner of the grill to warm for about 10 minutes.

3. *To make the salad:* In a small skillet, cook the oregano over medium heat, stirring often, for 2 to 3 minutes, until it smells toasty. Tip into a cup. In a medium bowl, mix the avocado, radishes, scallions, lime juice, and toasted oregano. Cut the pork on an angle into thin slices and cut larger slices in half. Pour the pork juices into the salad.

4. Place a tortilla on a work surface. Arrange some pork on the bottom half; top with some of the salad and roll up, folding in the sides. Repeat with the remaining tortillas, pork, and salad. Serve right away.

MAKES 4 SERVINGS (2 TACOS PER SERVING)

Per serving: 382 calories, 41 g protein, 28 g carbohydrates, 19 g total fat, 3 g saturated fat, 92 mg cholesterol, 20 g dietary fiber, 592 mg sodium

Pork Tenderloin with Brown Rice and Apricot Stuffing

This stunning dish looks like something you'd order in a fancy restaurant but is actually surprisingly easy to prepare.

Prep time: 30 minutes   Cook time: 50 minutes   Stand time: 10 minutes

½ cup quick-cooking brown rice
(cooks in 10 minutes), such as Uncle Ben's

2 teaspoons extra virgin olive oil

1 red onion, chopped, 1 cup

1 rib celery, chopped, ½ cup

⅓ cup chopped carrot

2 cloves garlic, minced

½ cup dried apricots, chopped

⅓ cup packed golden raisins

1 tablespoon chopped fresh rosemary

½ cup orange juice

2 tablespoons flaxseeds

1 egg

3 tablespoons grated Parmesan cheese

1 teaspoon salt

¼ teaspoon ground black pepper

1½ pounds lean pork tenderloin, trimmed of all visible fat

1. Preheat the oven to 400°F. Coat a baking sheet with cooking spray. Cook the rice according to package directions.

2. Heat the oil in a large nonstick skillet over medium-high heat. Add the onion, celery, carrot, and garlic; cook, stirring occasionally, until softened, 6 to 7 minutes. Stir in the apricots, raisins, and rosemary and cook until the fruit starts to soften, about 2 minutes. Add the orange juice and cook until evaporated, about 1½ to 2 minutes. Stir in the rice and flaxseeds and transfer to a bowl. When cool, stir in the egg, cheese, and half of the salt and pepper.

3. Meanwhile, with a sharp knife, carefully slice the pork tenderloin lengthwise, leaving a ½" hinge. Cover with plastic wrap and pound the meat out with a mallet to a ½" thickness. Sprinkle both sides with the remaining salt and pepper.

4. Spread 1 cup of the rice mixture over the pork, leaving a 1" border near both long edges. Starting at one long edge, roll up the pork jelly roll–style and secure with kitchen twine or toothpicks. Transfer the remaining rice mixture to a small baking dish coated with cooking spray and cover with aluminum foil.

5. Wipe out the skillet, coat with cooking spray, and heat over medium-high heat. Add the pork and cook, turning occasionally, until browned. Transfer to the prepared baking sheet and bake, along with the additional rice mixture, for 40 to 45 minutes, or until a thermometer inserted in the center reaches 155°F and the juices run clear. Let stand for 10 minutes before slicing.

MAKES 6 SERVINGS

Per serving: 273 calories, 28 g protein, 20 g carbohydrates, 8 g total fat, 2 g saturated fat, 111 mg cholesterol, 3 g dietary fiber, 512 mg sodium

Linguine with White Clam Sauce

This Italian comfort dish comes together easily with mostly pantry ingredients.

Prep time: 10 minutes   Cook time: 15 minutes

8 ounces whole wheat linguine

1 tablespoon extra virgin olive oil

2 slices center-cut (30% less fat) bacon, such as Oscar Mayer, chopped

5 cloves garlic, chopped

1 bottle (8 ounces) clam juice

2 cans (6.5 ounces each) chopped clams, drained

¼ teaspoon salt

¼ teaspoon ground black pepper

¼ cup chopped fresh parsley

3 tablespoons chopped fresh basil

1 tablespoon unsalted butter

1. Bring a large pot of lightly salted water to a boil. Add the linguine and cook according to package directions; drain.

2. Meanwhile, heat the oil in a large nonstick skillet over medium-high heat. Add the bacon and cook until crisp, about 4 to 5 minutes; remove with a slotted spoon and set aside. Stir in the garlic and cook until lightly golden, 45 seconds. Add the clam juice, clams, salt, and pepper; bring to a boil and cook until slightly reduced, about 2 minutes. Stir in the linguine, parsley, basil, butter, and reserved bacon; toss until hot and the butter melts, about 1 minute.

MAKES 4 SERVINGS

Per serving: 406 calories, 32 g protein, 45 g carbohydrates, 11 g total fat, 3 g saturated fat, 69 mg cholesterol, 9 g dietary fiber, 439 mg sodium

Fusilli Spirals with Shrimp and White Bean Sauce

This recipe gives new meaning to the phrase "surf and turf" by replacing beef with a legume. We could dub it "sea and pea"—a combination that deserves more attention. Here the sweetness of the shrimp contrasts beautifully with the earthy cannellini beans.

Prep time: 10 minutes   Cook time: 15 minutes

12 ounces fusilli pasta

1 can (15.5 ounces) cannellini beans, rinsed and drained

½ cup low-sodium chicken broth

½ pound peeled and deveined large shrimp, halved lengthwise

¾ teaspoon salt

½ teaspoon ground black pepper

2 cloves garlic, thinly sliced

1 tablespoon olive oil

3 plum tomatoes (about 12 ounces), halved and sliced in half moons

2 tablespoons chopped flat-leaf parsley

Whole parsley leaves, to garnish

1. Cook the pasta according to package directions. Puree 1 cup of the beans and the broth in a blender until smooth.

2. Sprinkle the shrimp with ⅛ teaspoon of the salt and ¼ teaspoon of the pepper. In a large skillet, cook the garlic in the oil over medium heat for 1 minute, or until golden. Add the shrimp and sear on both sides, 2 minutes per side, or until opaque. Remove. Add the tomato slices and cook for 1 minute. Return the shrimp to the skillet with the chopped parsley, the remaining salt and pepper, and the remaining beans. Heat through.

3. Toss the pasta with the bean puree and the shrimp mixture. Garnish with whole parsley leaves.

MAKES 6 CUPS

Per serving: 316 calories, 18 g protein, 52 g carbohydrates, 4 g total fat, 1 g saturated fat, 58 mg cholesterol, 4 g dietary fiber, 471 mg sodium

Creole Shrimp with Green Beans and Corn-Scallion Grits

Many Southerners assign a singular verb to their beloved ground hominy dish called grits, as in "The grits is great" as opposed to "The grits are great." One thing about which there is no debate—shrimp and green beans in a spicy tomato sauce are heavenly with cooked grits.

Prep tlme: 18 minutes   Cook time: 40 minutes

GRITS

¾ cup old-fashioned grits

4 cups cold water

½ teaspoon salt

1 can (11 ounces) low-sodium corn kernels, drained

2 tablespoons sliced scallion greens

CREOLE SHRIMP AND GREEN BEANS

1 pound fresh green beans, trimmed and cut into 1" pieces (4 cups)

2 tablespoons olive oil

1 medium leek, halved, sliced ½" thick, well rinsed of sand

1 medium stalk celery, thinly sliced

2 large cloves garlic, thinly sliced

1 teaspoon dried thyme

⅛–¼ teaspoon ground red pepper

2 cans (14 ounces each) diced no-salt-added tomatoes in juice

1 pound peeled and deveined medium or large shrimp, tails left on, thawed if frozen, rinsed and drained

1. To make the grits: Combine the grits and 1 cup of the water. Bring the remaining water and salt to a boil in a large, heavy saucepan. Add the grits, whisking until smooth. Reduce the heat to low, cover, and simmer, stirring often, until the grits have thickened and are soft, 25 to 30 minutes. Stir in the corn and scallions. Remove from the heat and cover.

2. Meanwhile, to make the shrimp and green beans: Place a steamer basket in a large pot with 2" of water. Bring to a boil over high heat. Place the green beans in the basket, cover, and steam about 8 to 9 minutes, or until tender. Drain. Rinse briefly under cold running water and drain again.

3. Warm the oil in a large, deep nonstick skillet. Stir in the leek, celery, and garlic and cook, stirring often, until tender, about 5 minutes. Stir in the thyme, salt, and red pepper, then the tomatoes with juice. Bring to a boil. Reduce the heat to low, cover, and simmer 10 minutes. Add the shrimp; increase the heat to medium, cover, and cook until they're opaque, 3 minutes. Stir in the green beans; cover, and cook 1 minute, or until heated through. Serve the shrimp over the grits.

MAKES 6 SERVINGS

Per serving: 280 calories, 19 g protein, 38 g carbohydrates, 6 g total fat, 1 g saturated fat, 101 mg cholesterol, 6 g dietary fiber, 410 mg sodium

Tomato-Feta Shrimp with Quinoa and Broccoli

Quinoa is a fooler. Although these tiny grains are very high in protein, they have a light texture and pop pleasantly when you bite into them.

Prep time: 12 minutes   Cook time : 40 minutes

1 cup quinoa

2 cups water

⅛ teaspoon + ¼ teaspoon salt

1 large bunch broccoli, cut into small florets, stems trimmed and thinly sliced

1 pound peeled and deveined medium or large shrimp, tails left on, thawed if frozen, patted dry

2 tablespoons olive oil

2 large cloves garlic, minced

1 tablespoon chopped fresh marjoram or oregano or ¼ teaspoon dried

1 teaspoon paprika

½ teaspoon ground black pepper

12 ounces cherry tomatoes, halved (2 cups)

½ cup reduced-fat crumbled feta cheese

Lemon wedges for serving

1. In a medium saucepan, combine the quinoa, water, and ⅛ teaspoon of the salt. Bring to a boil over high heat. Reduce the heat to low, cover, and simmer until the quinoa is tender and the grains have started to uncoil, 20 to 25 minutes. Remove from the heat and set aside, covered, to keep warm.

2. Meanwhile, place a steamer basket in a large pot with 2" of water. Bring to a boil over high heat. Place the broccoli in the basket, cover, and steam about 8 minutes, or until crisp-tender. Drain and transfer to a bowl. Cover to keep warm.

3. Preheat the broiler. On a rimmed baking sheet, mix the shrimp, oil, garlic, marjoram or oregano, paprika, pepper, and the remaining ¼ teaspoon salt. Add the cherry tomatoes and mix again. Broil 3 to 4" from the heat, stirring once, for 5 minutes. Sprinkle with the feta and broil 1 to 2 minutes more, until the shrimp are opaque and the cherry tomatoes are juicy.

4. Fluff the quinoa with a fork and spread on a large, rimmed platter. Arrange the broccoli around the outside edge of the platter and mound the shrimp and any pan juices in the center. Serve with lemon wedges.

MAKES 4 SERVINGS

Per serving: 396 calories, 33 g protein, 39 g carbohydrates, 13 g total fat, 3 g saturated fat, 157 mg cholesterol, 6 g dietary fiber, 499 mg sodium

Seafood Frogmore Stew

Said to be named after a town on St. Helena Island, South Carolina, this delectable concoction is a spicy treat.

Prep time: 15 minutes   Cook time: 20 minutes

1 bottle (8 ounces) clam juice

1 cup low-sodium chicken broth

1 cup chopped tomato

5 sprigs fresh parsley

2 sprigs fresh thyme

2 dried bay leaves

10 cloves garlic

2 teaspoons Old Bay seasoning

⅛ teaspoon ground red pepper

2½ quarts water

2 pounds sweet potatoes, peeled and cut into 1" chunks

4 ounces turkey kielbasa, cut into thin slices

4 ears corn, halved

2 red onions, cut into 8 wedges each, about 1 pound

1½ pounds shell-on, deveined large shrimp, about 21–25 per pound

½ pound sea scallops

1. In a large pot, combine the clam juice, broth, tomato, parsley, thyme, bay leaves, garlic, Old Bay seasoning, red pepper, and water. Bring to a boil over high heat and add the potatoes and kielbasa; cook until the potatoes are almost cooked through, about 10 to 11 minutes. Add the corn and onions and cook for 3 minutes, or until corn is bright yellow (or white). Stir in the shrimp and scallops and cook until opaque, about 3 to 4 minutes.

2. Drain the liquid and discard the bay leaves, thyme, and parsley. Serve immediately.

MAKES 8 SERVINGS

Per serving: 312 calories, 29 g protein, 37 g carbohydrates, 4 g total fat, 0.5 g saturated fat, 143 mg cholesterol, 5 g dietary fiber, 550 mg sodium

Fish Tacos

To increase your fish intake, try tucking seasoned tilapia into piping hot tortillas. These morsels are popular street food fare in Mexican seaside towns.

Prep time: 10 minutes   Cook time: 12 minutes

---

1 tablespoon unsalted butter

1 onion, thinly sliced, 1 cup

1 cup chopped tomato

1 tablespoon lime juice

2 tilapia fillets (6 ounces each), halved lengthwise

¼ teaspoon ground chipotle chile pepper

½ teaspoon salt

2 tablespoons chopped fresh cilantro

4 multigrain tortillas (7–8" diameter)

1 cup chopped romaine lettuce, 2 leaves

4 tablespoons fat-free sour cream

1. Melt 1 teaspoon of the butter in a large nonstick skillet over medium-high heat. Add the onion and cook, stirring occasionally, until starting to soften, 2 to 3 minutes. Stir in the tomato and cook until wilted, 2 minutes. Add the lime juice and transfer mixture to a bowl. Wipe out the skillet and melt the remaining 2 teaspoons butter over medium-high heat. Sprinkle the tilapia with the ground chipotle and salt. Add to the skillet and cook 3 minutes per side, or until the fish flakes easily. Add the onion mixture and cook for 1 minute. Remove from the heat and stir in the cilantro.

2. Heat the tortillas according to package directions. Fill each with ¼ of the tilapia mixture, ¼ cup lettuce, and 1 tablespoon of the sour cream. Serve immediately.

MAKES 4 SERVINGS

Per serving: 212 calories, 22 g protein,
19 g carbohydrates, 6 g total fat, 2 g saturated fat,
50 mg cholesterol, 3 g dietary fiber, 517 mg sodium

Flounder and Broccoli Roll-Ups

This elegant main dish is fancy enough for guests. Pair with Lemony White Bean Puree (page 242).

Prep time: 15 minutes   Cook time: 30 minutes

3 cups broccoli florets

2 slices multigrain bread

4 ounces fat-free cream cheese, softened

1 egg white

2 tablespoons grated Parmesan cheese

4 skinless flounder fillets (6 ounces each), rinsed and patted dry with paper towels

¼ teaspoon salt

¼ teaspoon ground black pepper

2 teaspoons extra virgin olive oil

3 cloves garlic, sliced

2 cups chopped tomatoes

2 tablespoons chopped fresh basil

1. Preheat the oven to 350°F. Coat an 8" × 8" baking dish with cooking spray.

2. Bring a large saucepan of lightly salted water to a boil. Add the broccoli, return to a boil, and cook for 2 minutes; drain, rinse under cold water, and drain well. Transfer broccoli to a cutting board, and finely chop.

3. Meanwhile, place the bread into the bowl of a food processor and pulse into bread crumbs. Transfer to a bowl and add the broccoli, cream cheese, egg white, and Parmesan.

4. Place the flounder fillets on a work surface and sprinkle with ⅛ teaspoon of the salt and ⅛ teaspoon of the pepper. Top one end of each fillet with one-quarter of the broccoli mixture. Roll up jelly roll–style and secure the ends with toothpicks. Place the fillets in the prepared dish, seam side down. Cover with aluminum foil and bake for 25 minutes, or until the fish flakes easily.

5. Meanwhile, heat the oil in a medium nonstick skillet over medium-high heat. Add the garlic and cook 45 seconds, or until starting to brown. Add the tomatoes and cook until softened, 2 to 3 minutes. Remove from the heat and stir in the basil and remaining salt and pepper. Serve over the flounder.

MAKES 4 SERVINGS

Per serving: 293 calories, 43 g protein,
16 g carbohydrates, 6 g total fat, 2 g saturated fat,
86 mg cholesterol, 5 g dietary fiber, 577 mg sodium

Garlic-Roasted Salmon
with Tomato-Basil French Lentils

This is best made with the small French lentils found in better grocery stores. They hold their shape after cooking and have a delicious, nutty flavor.

Prep time: 15 minutes   Cook time: 50 minutes

LENTILS

¾ cup lentils, preferably small French lentils, picked over and rinsed

3 cups water

1 clove garlic, minced

1 bay leaf

¼ teaspoon ground black pepper

Pinch of kosher salt

1 large tomato, chopped (8 ounces)

¼ cup slivered fresh basil leaves

2 scallions, thinly sliced

2 tablespoons fresh lemon juice

1 tablespoon olive oil

SALMON

1¼ pounds skinned salmon fillet

1 large clove garlic

½ teaspoon kosher salt

1 tablespoon fresh lemon juice

2 teaspoons olive oil

1. *To make the lentils:* In a heavy medium saucepan, combine the lentils, water, garlic, bay leaf, pepper, and salt. Bring to a boil over high heat. Reduce the heat to low, cover, and simmer until the lentils are tender, 20 to 25 minutes. Drain the lentils and transfer to a serving bowl. Remove and discard the bay leaf. Add the tomato, basil, scallions, lemon juice, and oil; stir to mix. Cover loosely and let stand while making the salmon.

2. *To make the salmon:* Preheat the oven to 425°F. Coat a baking sheet with olive oil spray. Cut the salmon into 4 equal portions. On a cutting board, chop the garlic. Sprinkle it with the salt and crush with the flat side of a chef's knife to form a paste. Mix the garlic paste with the lemon juice and oil and rub on the salmon. Place the salmon on the prepared baking sheet. Roast for 8 to 12 minutes, depending on thickness, until just opaque in the thickest part. Serve with the lentils.

MAKES 4 SERVINGS

Per serving: 438 calories, 37 g protein, 24 g carbohydrates, 21 g total fat, 4 g saturated fat, 84 mg cholesterol, 6 g dietary fiber, 374 mg sodium

Grilled Vegetable and Bean Lasagna

Grilling is one of the best things that can happen to vegetables. As they brown, their natural sugars caramelize to produce wonderful, rich flavors.

Prep time: 20 minutes   **Cook time: 45 minutes**   **Cool time: 20 minutes**

8 ounces whole wheat lasagna noodles

1½ pounds eggplant, trimmed, cut into ¼"-thick slices

3 medium zucchini, 1½ pounds total, trimmed and cut lengthwise into ¼"-thick slices

1 tablespoon extra virgin olive oil

Pinch of salt

¼ teaspoon ground black pepper

2 containers (15 ounces) fat-free ricotta cheese

2 cups shredded carrots

1 can (15 ounces) cannellini beans, drained and rinsed

1 cup shredded reduced-fat mozzarella cheese

¼ cup grated Romano cheese

2 egg whites

2 cups prepared fat-free tomato basil sauce

1. Bring a large pot of lightly salted water to a boil. Add the lasagna noodles and cook according to package directions. Drain and rinse under cold water.

2. Preheat the grill. Brush the eggplant and zucchini slices with the oil and sprinkle with the salt and pepper. Grill the eggplant and zucchini slices until tender and well marked, about 4 to 6 minutes per side. Transfer to a baking sheet and cool for 10 minutes. Meanwhile, combine the ricotta, carrots, beans, ½ cup of the mozzarella, the Romano, and egg whites in a bowl.

3. Preheat the oven to 375°F. Coat a 13" × 9" baking dish with cooking spray. Spread ½ cup of the tomato sauce in the bottom of the prepared dish. Top with 3 lasagna noodles. Spread with one-half of the ricotta mixture; arrange the eggplant slices in a single layer over the ricotta mixture. Spread the eggplant with ½ cup of the tomato sauce and top with 3 noodles. Spread with the remaining ricotta mixture and the zucchini slices. Top with ½ cup of the tomato sauce and 3 noodles. Spread the top noodles with the remaining ½ cup of the tomato sauce and sprinkle with the remaining ½ cup mozzarella. Coat a sheet of aluminum foil with cooking spray and cover the lasagna.

4. Bake for 35 minutes. Uncover and bake for 20 minutes longer, or until the cheese has melted and started to brown slightly. Cool for 10 minutes before cutting.

MAKES 8 SERVINGS

Per serving: 387 calories, 33 g protein,
53 g carbohydrates, 7 g total fat, 3 g saturated fat,
18 mg cholesterol, 11 g dietary fiber, 619 mg sodium

Green Bean Burritos

To ensure that the flavors mingle properly, the rice should be added warm; if it is not warm, heat it separately in a microwave. You can also use the oven to heat the burritos.

Prep time: 10 minutes   Cook time: 20 minutes

---

1 can (15 ounces) salt-free pinto beans, rinsed and drained

¾ cup green salsa

2½ cups cooked brown rice

2 tablespoons lime juice

¼ cup chopped cilantro

4 whole wheat tortillas (8" diameter)

1 cup (4 ounces) shredded Monterey Jack cheese

½ avocado, sliced

1. Heat the oven to 350°F.

2. In a saucepan or skillet over medium heat, combine the beans and salsa and heat until warmed through, about 3 minutes. Remove from the heat. Add the rice, lime juice, and cilantro.

3. Heat the tortillas according to package directions and place on a work surface. Sprinkle ¼ cup of the cheese in the center of a tortilla. Top with one-quarter of the avocado slices. Mound a scant 1 cup of the rice and bean mixture on top. Fold the sides of the tortilla over the filling and roll up. Place on a baking sheet, seam side down, and prepare the remaining burritos.

4. Heat the burritos until golden and heated through, 15 minutes, turning once.

MAKES 4 SERVINGS

Per serving: 512 calories, 20 g protein, 69 g carbohydrates, 16 g total fat, 6 g saturated fat, 25 mg cholesterol, 11 g dietary fiber, 605 mg sodium

Whole Wheat Orzo with Peas, Asparagus, and Toasted Pine Nuts

If you've never eaten orzo before, you might be tempted to think it's the most tender, flavorful rice you've ever tasted. It's actually dried pasta shaped like plump grains of rice.

Prep time: 12 minutes   **Cook time: 25 minutes**

Salt

8 ounces whole wheat orzo (1⅓ cups)

1 pound asparagus, tough ends trimmed, sliced ½" thick (about 2½ cups)

1½ cups frozen peas

2 tablespoons olive oil

3 large cloves garlic, cut into thin slivers

2 tablespoons chopped fresh thyme leaves

½ cup reduced-sodium, fat-free chicken or vegetable broth

½ teaspoon ground black pepper

¼ cup grated Parmesan cheese

2 tablespoons pine nuts, toasted

1. Bring a large, heavy, covered pot of water to a boil over high heat. Add the salt and the orzo. Cook, stirring often, for 6 minutes. Add the asparagus and peas and cook, stirring often, for 4 to 6 minutes more, until the pasta and vegetables are tender. Drain in a colander.

2. In the pasta cooking pot, combine the oil, garlic, and thyme. Cook and stir over medium heat until the garlic just starts to turn golden, about 3 minutes. Add the pasta and vegetables, the broth, pepper, and ½ teaspoon salt. Toss the pasta until well coated with the garlic mixture and the broth starts to get absorbed. Remove from the heat; stir in the cheese and sprinkle with the pine nuts.

MAKES 4 SERVINGS

Per serving: 385 calories, 17 g protein, 56 g carbohydrates, 12 g total fat, 2 g saturated fat, 4 mg cholesterol, 10 g dietary fiber, 214 mg sodium

Baked Macaroni and Cheese

Life is good when you can have your gooey macaroni and cheese and healthy fiber, too.

Prep time: 15 minutes   Cook time: 45 minutes

8 ounces whole wheat elbow macaroni

3 slices multigrain bread

3 tablespoons unsalted butter

1 onion, chopped, about 1 cup

2 cups 1% milk

2 tablespoons whole wheat flour

½ teaspoon dried mustard

¼ teaspoon salt

1½ cups shredded reduced-fat mozzarella cheese

1 cup shredded reduced-fat sharp Cheddar cheese

¼ cup grated Romano cheese

1 can (14.5 ounces) salt-free diced tomatoes, drained

1. Preheat the oven to 350°F. Coat an 11" × 7" baking dish with cooking spray.

2. Bring a large pot of lightly salted water to a boil. Add the pasta and cook according to package directions; drain and rinse under cold water to stop the cooking, then drain again. Return to the pot. Meanwhile, place the bread into the bowl of a food processor and pulse into bread crumbs.

3. Melt 1 tablespoon of the butter in a medium saucepan over medium heat. Add the onion and cook until softened, about 6 to 7 minutes. Meanwhile, whisk together the milk, flour, mustard, and salt. Pour into the saucepan and cook, whisking, until the mixture begins to thicken, about 3 to 4 minutes. Stir in the mozzarella, Cheddar, and Romano and cook until melted, about 2 minutes. Pour over the macaroni, add the tomatoes, and mix well to coat. Immediately pour into the prepared baking dish. Melt the remaining 2 tablespoons butter in a medium nonstick skillet over medium heat. Add the bread crumbs and cook, stirring, until they're coated with the butter, about 1 minute. Sprinkle over the macaroni and cheese.

4. Bake until bubbly and the top is golden, about 20 to 22 minutes.

MAKES 8 SERVINGS

Per serving: 323 calories, 19 g protein,
36 g carbohydrates, 13 g total fat, 7 g saturated fat,
38 mg cholesterol, 5 g dietary fiber, 494 mg sodium

Wild and Brown Rice Pilaf with Cranberries, Pearl Onions, and Apricots

So many vibrant colors, toothsome textures, and tantalizing flavors converge in this dish. It's a dream date for roast turkey.

Prep time: 15 minutes   Cook time: 40 minutes

---

2 cups lower-sodium fat-free chicken broth

1¼ cups wild and whole grain brown rice blend, such as Lundberg

½ cup water

4 teaspoons unsalted butter

2 cups frozen pearl onions

½ cup chopped carrots

½ cup chopped celery

½ teaspoon dried thyme

½ cup dried cranberries

⅓ cup dried apricots, chopped

½ cup orange juice

½ teaspoon salt

¼ teaspoon ground black pepper

1. Combine the broth, rice, and water in a medium saucepan and cook according to package directions.

2. Meanwhile, melt the butter in a large nonstick skillet over medium-high heat. Add the onions and cook, stirring occasionally, until beginning to brown slightly, about 5 to 6 minutes. Stir in the carrots, celery, and thyme and cook until beginning to soften, about 3 to 4 minutes. Add the cranberries and apricots and cook for 1 minute. Stir in the orange juice and cook until evaporated, 1 to 1½ minutes. Add the rice, salt, and pepper and cook until hot, 1 to 2 minutes.

MAKES 6 SERVINGS

Per serving: 282 calories, 6 g protein, 55 g carbohydrates, 4 g total fat, 2 g saturated fat, 7 mg cholesterol, 4 g dietary fiber, 250 mg sodium

Penne with Broccoli, Brown Butter, and Pecorino

Not all pasta dishes have to swim in sauce. Think of this oh-so-easy meal as an Italian pasta stir-fry.

Prep time: 10 minutes   Cook time: 16 minutes

8 ounces multigrain penne

4 cups broccoli florets

3 tablespoons unsalted butter

1 tablespoon lemon juice

2 tablespoons chopped fresh basil

½ teaspoon salt

⅛ teaspoon ground black pepper

3 tablespoons grated Pecorino Romano cheese

1. Bring a large pot of lightly salted water to a boil. Add the penne and cook according to package directions. Stir in the broccoli during the last 2 minutes the pasta cooks; drain.

2. Melt the butter in a large nonstick skillet over medium-high heat. Cook until the butter starts to brown and smells nutty, about 2 to 3 minutes. Stir in the lemon juice, basil, salt, and pepper. Add the penne mixture and cook, tossing, until hot, 1 minute. Add the cheese and toss for 1 minute. Divide among 6 plates.

MAKES 6 SERVINGS

Per serving: 218 calories, 8 g protein, 31 g carbohydrates, 8 g total fat, 4 g saturated fat, 19 mg cholesterol, 3 g dietary fiber, 267 mg sodium

Simmered Chickpeas in Tomato Sauce

Capitalize on the Mediterranean themes in this hearty entrée by serving it with toasted whole wheat pita, a cucumber salad, and a sprinkling of feta cheese.

Prep time: 8 minutes   Cook time: 20 minutes

1 tablespoon olive oil

1 medium onion, sliced

2 large cloves garlic, thinly sliced

1 small zucchini (6 ounces), cut into rough ¼" chunks

¼ teaspoon salt

¼ teaspoon ground black pepper

1 can (14½ ounces) diced no-salt-added tomatoes in juice

1 can (15–16 ounces) chickpeas, rinsed and drained

2 tablespoons chopped fresh basil or parsley

1. Warm the oil in a large nonstick skillet over medium heat. Add the onion and garlic and cook, stirring often, until tender, about 5 minutes. Add the zucchini and sprinkle with the salt and pepper. Stir to blend well with the onion.

2. Add the tomatoes and their juice and bring to a simmer. Cook, uncovered, stirring occasionally, until the zucchini is crisp-tender, 6 to 8 minutes. Add the chickpeas; cover and cook just until heated through. Sprinkle with the basil or parsley and serve.

MAKES 4 SERVINGS

Per serving: 162 calories, 5 g protein, 25 g carbohydrates, 4 g total fat, 1 g saturated fat, 0 mg cholesterol, 5 g dietary fiber, 420 mg sodium

Lemony White Bean Puree

You can puree these beans without leaving the stove top or dirtying the food processor by using a hand blender. Just be sure to turn off the heat before beginning. Enjoy the bright flavor and creamy texture of this dish as an alternative to mashed potatoes.

Prep time: 5 minutes   **Cook time: 15 minutes**

½ cup chicken broth

2 large cloves garlic, sliced

2 cans (15.5 ounces each) cannellini beans

Grated peel of one lemon

1 tablespoon unsalted butter

3 tablespoons lemon juice

½ teaspoon salt

1. In a medium saucepan, combine the broth and garlic. Heat to boiling, reduce the heat, and simmer until the garlic is tender, 10 minutes.

2. Combine the beans, lemon peel, and broth mixture in a food processor until smooth. Return to the saucepan and heat over medium-high heat, stirring until thick and hot. Stir in the butter until melted and add the lemon juice and salt.

MAKES 4 SERVINGS

Per serving: 107 calories, 5 g protein, 16 g carbohydrates, 2 g total fat, 1 g saturated fat, 5 mg cholesterol, 4 g dietary fiber, 426 mg sodium

Mashed Sweet Potatoes with Apples

You can vary the sweetness of this dish by making it with different types of sweet potatoes. Orange-fleshed sweet potatoes, such as Beauregard, Jewel, and Garnet, are the sweetest. Boniato sweet potatoes, found in Latin American and Asian food markets, are less sweet and fluffier.

Prep time: 12 minutes   Cook time: 25 minutes

1¼ pounds sweet potatoes (about 2 medium), peeled and sliced ¼" thick (4 cups)

2 large Granny Smith apples (about 1 pound), peeled, cored, and sliced (3 cups)

½ cup sliced onion

¼ cup water

2 tablespoons frozen apple juice concentrate

1 tablespoon unsalted butter, cut up

Pinch each salt and ground black pepper

1. In a 12" × 8" glass baking dish, place the sweet potatoes, apples, onion, water, apple juice concentrate, and butter. Toss to mix. Cover with waxed paper and microwave on high, stirring 2 or 3 times, until everything is very tender, 15 to 18 minutes.

2. Transfer to a food processor and whirl until smooth. Scrape into a serving dish and stir in the salt and pepper.

MAKES 4 SERVINGS

Per serving: 150 calories, 3 g protein, 29 g carbohydrates, 3 g total fat, 2 g saturated fat, 8 mg cholesterol, 4 g dietary fiber, 81 mg sodium

Broccoli Cauliflower Puree

Rather than straining the yogurt yourself, you can use nonfat or low-fat Greek strained yogurt, available in many supermarkets. Serve with roasted carrots and grilled chicken.

Prep time: 10 minutes   Cook time: 15 minutes   Drain time: 1 hour

---

1½ **cups low-fat yogurt**

½ **pound broccoli**

½ **cup chicken broth**

1 **clove garlic, coarsely chopped**

½ **pound cauliflower florets, chopped (3 cups)**

½ **teaspoon salt**

⅛ **teaspoon ground black pepper**

1. Place a coffee filter in a mesh strainer placed over a bowl. Fill with the yogurt and refrigerate until the yogurt is thickened, 1 to 2 hours.

2. Cut off the dark green broccoli tops and set aside. Cut the broccoli stalks into ¾" pieces.

3. In a medium saucepan over medium-high heat, combine the broth and garlic. Add the broccoli stalks and cauliflower and cook, covered, for 10 minutes, or until tender. Add the broccoli tops, cover, and continue cooking until they are bright green, about 5 minutes. Drain off the liquid.

4. Combine the broccoli mixture, yogurt, salt, and pepper in a food processor. Puree until smooth.

MAKES 4 SERVINGS

Per serving: 104 calories, 8 g protein, 18 g carbohydrates, 1 g total fat, 1 g saturated fat, 6 mg cholesterol, 3 g dietary fiber, 373 mg sodium

Roasted Broccoli and Cauliflower with Lemon and Orange

If childhood memories of smelly boiled broccoli have kept you from enjoying cruciferous vegetables, this cooking method may very well change your mind. Baking lightly oiled broccoli and cauliflower until crisp-tender inhibits the release of any unpleasant sulphur aromas. Tossed with sweet citrus just before serving, the vegetable mellows even more.

Prep time: 10 minutes   Cook time: 20 minutes

4 cups broccoli florets

4 cups cauliflower florets

5 teaspoons extra virgin olive oil

½ teaspoon salt

⅛ teaspoon ground black pepper

1 teaspoon grated lemon peel

1 teaspoon grated orange peel

1. Preheat the oven to 450°F. Coat a large baking sheet with cooking spray.

2. Combine the broccoli and cauliflower in a large bowl. Toss with the oil, salt, and pepper. Spread over the prepared baking sheet and cook, stirring occasionally, until crisp-tender and slightly browned, 20 to 22 minutes. Return to the bowl and toss with the lemon and orange peels.

MAKES 4 SERVINGS

Per serving: 98 calories, 4 g protein, 9 g carbohydrates, 6 g total fat, 1 g saturated fat, 0 mg cholesterol, 5 g dietary fiber, 340 mg sodium

Garlic-Roasted Asparagus

Could there be an easier way than roasting to prepare asparagus? Toss the spears with a few vivid flavorings and pop them into the oven. This dish puts limp boiled asparagus to shame.

Prep time: 5 minutes   Cook time: 10 minutes

---

1 bunch asparagus, trimmed

1 tablespoon olive oil

3 cloves garlic, minced

⅛ teaspoon salt

⅛ teaspoon ground black pepper

1. Heat the oven to 425°F. On a baking sheet or shallow baking dish, combine the asparagus, oil, garlic, salt, and pepper. Toss well. Arrange the asparagus side by side in a single layer.

2. Roast the asparagus for 10 to 15 minutes, or until tender, tossing once.

MAKES 4 SERVINGS

Per serving: 46 calories, 1 g protein, 3 g carbohydrates, 3 g total fat, 1 g saturated fat, 0 mg cholesterol, 1 g dietary fiber, 73 mg sodium

Roasted Brussels Sprouts and Onions with Thyme

Even if you think you're not a brussels sprouts fan, you'll fall in love with them here. Quartering the sprouts exposes more surface area to browning, and baking them sweetens their sharpness. This is sure to be a big hit as a side dish for a holiday meal.

Prep time: 14 minutes   Cook time: 20–25 minutes

1½ pounds fresh brussels sprouts

1 large sweet white onion, quartered and cut into ½"-thick slices

1 tablespoon olive oil

4 teaspoons fresh thyme leaves or ½ teaspoon dried thyme

¼ teaspoon salt

⅛ teaspoon ground black pepper

1. Preheat the oven to 400°F. Set out a rimmed baking sheet.

2. Trim the yellowed leaves and the ends from the sprouts. Cut each into quarters or into halves, if small. Place on the baking sheet and toss with the onion, oil, thyme, salt, and pepper.

3. Roast for 20 to 25 minutes, stirring 2 or 3 times, until the vegetables are tender and lightly browned.

MAKES 4 SERVINGS

Per serving: 120 calories, 6 g protein, 19 g carbohydrates, 4 g total fat, 1 g saturated fat, 0 mg cholesterol, 7 g dietary fiber, 192 mg sodium

Honey-Baked Squash

Acorn squash can have orange, dark green, or tan skin. To pick a good-tasting one, press it all around to make sure it's devoid of soft spots. Don't refrigerate—just store the squash in an airy dry spot for up to 3 weeks.

Prep time: 5 minutes   Cook time: 60 minutes

---

1 large acorn squash (1½ pounds), cut into quarters, seeds removed

⅛ teaspoon ground cinnamon

⅛ teaspoon salt

⅛ teaspoon ground black pepper

1 tablespoon honey

1. Preheat the oven to 400°F. Arrange the squash skin side down in a baking dish.

2. Sprinkle the squash with the cinnamon, salt, and pepper and drizzle with the honey. Bake, uncovered, for 50 to 60 minutes, or until browned at the edges and very tender when pierced with a fork.

MAKES 4 SERVINGS

Per serving: 66 calories, 1 g protein, 17 g carbohydrates, 0 g total fat, 0 g saturated fat, 0 mg cholesterol, 2 g dietary fiber, 77 mg sodium

Two Potato and Turnip Gratin

Turnips are pleasantly sharp, and it's that quality that heightens the sweet, starchy savor of the other root vegetables in this comforting side dish. Serve with roast beef or pork for a perfect autumn celebration.

Prep time: 15 minutes   Cook time: 1 hour 15 minutes

2 sweet potatoes, 1½ pounds

1 large russet potato, 1 pound

3 white turnips, 12 ounces

2 slices multigrain bread

¼ cup grated Parmesan cheese

1 teaspoon salt

⅛ teaspoon ground black pepper

⅛ teaspoon ground nutmeg

½ cup milk

3 tablespoons unsalted butter

1. Place the sweet potatoes, potato, and turnips in a large pot with enough cold water to cover by 2". Bring to a boil over high heat and cook until just tender, 18 to 20 minutes. Drain, transfer to a bowl, and let stand until cool enough to handle, about 15 minutes. Peel the sweet potatoes, potato, and turnips.

2. Meanwhile, place the bread into the bowl of a food processor and pulse into bread crumbs; set aside. Combine the cheese, salt, pepper, and nutmeg in a bowl.

3. Preheat the oven to 350°F. Coat a 6-cup baking dish, preferably an oval gratin, with cooking spray. Cut the potatoes and turnips into scant ¼"-thick slices and arrange in a single layer in the bottom of the prepared pan, filling in any spaces with smaller pieces if necessary. Sprinkle with one-third of the cheese mixture. Top with a slightly overlapping layer of vegetables and sprinkle with one-third of the cheese mixture. Repeat with the remaining vegetables, and then pour the milk into the dish. Sprinkle with the remaining cheese mixture. Cut 2 tablespoons of the butter into small pieces and dot the top of the sweet potatoes. Melt the remaining 1 tablespoon butter in a medium nonstick skillet over medium heat. Add the bread crumbs and cook until well combined, 1 to 2 minutes. Sprinkle over the sweet potatoes.

4. Cover the dish with foil and bake for 40 minutes. Uncover and bake until the top is golden and the vegetables are tender, about 15 to 20 minutes longer.

MAKES 8 SERVINGS

Per serving: 208 calories, 5 g protein, 34 g carbohydrates, 6 g total fat, 3 g saturated fat, 15 mg cholesterol, 5 g dietary fiber, 422 mg sodium

Cider-Glazed Sweet Potatoes

This robust side dish is especially welcome in the fall, when you can make it with freshly pressed apple cider. Pair it with pan-seared pork chops.

Prep time: 10 minutes   Cook time: 37 minutes

1 cup apple cider

2 tablespoons maple syrup

2 pounds sweet potatoes, peeled and cut into 1½" chunks

1 tablespoon olive oil

¾ teaspoon salt

¼ teaspoon ground black pepper

⅛ teaspoon ground cinnamon

1. Preheat the oven to 425°F. Coat a large baking sheet with cooking spray.

2. In a small saucepan over medium-high heat, combine the cider and syrup. Bring to a boil and reduce the mixture until a light syrup forms, about 12 to 13 minutes.

3. Meanwhile, toss the sweet potatoes with the oil, salt, pepper, and cinnamon. Spread in a single layer on the baking sheet; bake until tender, about 25 minutes. Remove from the oven; transfer the sweet potatoes to a bowl, add the cider syrup, and toss well. Return the sweet potatoes to the baking sheet and bake for 5 minutes longer, until glazed.

MAKES 6 SERVINGS

Per serving: 162 calories, 2 g protein, 34 g carbohydrates, 2 g total fat, 0.5 g saturated fat, 0 mg cholesterol, 4 g dietary fiber, 362 mg sodium

Buttermilk Sweet Potato Cornbread

Mashed cooked sweet potatoes naturally sweeten this southern classic quick bread. Serve it steaming from the oven alongside Chicken Thighs with Bacon-Braised Beans (see page 189).

Prep time: 12 minutes   Cook time: 45 minutes

12 ounces sweet potato, peeled and cut into 1" pieces

1¾ cups low-fat buttermilk

2 eggs

2 egg whites

¼ cup corn oil

1¾ cups yellow cornmeal

1½ cups whole wheat flour

½ cup sugar

1 tablespoon baking powder

1 teaspoon baking soda

1 teaspoon salt

¼ teaspoon ground cinnamon

1. Preheat the oven to 400°F. Spray a 9" × 9" baking pan with cooking spray.

2. Place the sweet potato in a medium saucepan with enough cold water to cover by 2". Bring to a boil over high heat and cook until very tender, 12 to 14 minutes; drain and return to the saucepan. Mash the potato until smooth. Let cool for 5 minutes, then stir in the buttermilk, eggs, egg whites, and oil.

3. In a bowl, combine the cornmeal, flour, sugar, baking powder, baking soda, salt, and cinnamon. Stir in the potato mixture until just moistened. Pour the batter into the prepared baking pan. Bake until a toothpick inserted into the center of the bread comes out clean, about 30 minutes.

MAKES 12 SERVINGS

Per serving: 246 calories, 7 g protein, 43 g carbohydrates, 6 g total fat, 1 g saturated fat, 37 mg cholesterol, 4 g dietary fiber, 460 mg sodium

BONUS EATING

The 4-week plan in this book provides a detailed prescription of what to eat for breakfast, lunch, and dinner each day. However, most successful dieters find it helps to add a personal touch to how they eat to lose weight. Rather than following a menu verbatim, they make small tweaks here and there. These little changes often make all the difference between being able to turn a way of eating into a lasting lifestyle and backsliding into old eating habits.

That's where bonus eating comes in. While you should follow the 4-week menus as closely as possible for your main meals and your afternoon snack, if you look closely, you'll see that there are some choices as well. On select days of your 4-week plan, you have the option of a bonus food. You can choose from the following bonus items:

1. An appetizer before dinner

2. Dessert after dinner

3. An extra snack that you can have at any time of day

It's your choice. Eat the same bonus foods or alternate between the three types. The only rule is that your bonus food should be about 200 calories or less, and—you probably guessed it—it must contribute to your fiber goals. You'll find 27 recipes for appetizers and desserts in this chapter that fit the bill. With appetizers like bruschettas and dolmades and sweet potato pancakes, you'll find something to suit every taste and every ethnic occasion. You'll also find fiber-rich desserts, including puddings, crisps, pies, cheesecake, cookies, and cakes. No matter the appetizer or dessert, we found a way to add fiber, often sneaking it in with pureed sweet potato, fruit, oats, flaxseed, and brown rice. But you'd never guess it—these recipes taste out of this world.

GUILTLESS PLEASURE

Each of this chapter's recipes provides roughly 200 calories or less per serving, *so don't feel guilty about your bonus foods*. If you follow the high-fiber recommendations in this plan, you will have space for the occasional dessert. These sweet treats will not block your weight loss. If anything, they'll probably help.

You can't go the rest of your life without ever having another dessert or a seemingly decadent appetizer or snack. Dieting shouldn't be about deprivation. It should be about fueling your body with fiber and other nutrients and your tastebuds with the foods you most love. Nothing you love should ever be totally off-limits, no matter how much fat or sugar it contains.

In fact, there's evidence that people who feel guilty and try to mentally restrain themselves from eating dessert actually end up eating more than people who savor the experience without guilt. Guilty feelings override your natural sense of hunger and fullness, and they provide emotional fuel to eat even more. By including these treats from Day 1, you'll never feel so deprived that you end up polishing off an entire pie or chocolate frosted cake. To help turn these guilty pleasures into guiltless pleasures, pay attention to your body as you eat. Are you tasting your dessert or zoning out? Interestingly, many people who associate guilt with eating certain foods rarely taste

the foods they most crave. They feel so guilty about eating that they read a book, watch TV, or surf the Internet as they indulge. They can easily polish off a dozen cookies without tasting a single bite. When the bag is empty, they wonder, "Where did all the cookies go?"

In addition to your tastebuds, pay attention to your stomach hunger. Is your stomach still yearning for more, or are you comfortably satisfied? You may find that it helps to rate your hunger on a scale from 1 to 10, with 1 being the hungriest you've ever been and 10 being the most stuffed you've ever been. Your goal is to put down your fork when you're between a 7 and an 8.

Using the dessert recipes in this chapter will also help to satisfy you, as all are rich both in fiber and overall nutrition. By using fruit, whole wheat flour, bran, oats, flaxseed, and chopped nuts, they all are as high in vitamins, minerals, and antioxidants as they are in taste.

FIBER BENEFIT #5

STAY REGULAR

Digestion affects how we feel. When you're not regular, you may not feel energetic enough to exercise. You may in fact feel so distracted by discomfort that you have a hard time motivating yourself to stick with dietary changes.

Constipation is the most common GI complaint in the United States, and excess pounds generally make it worse. Fortunately, a high-fiber diet will get things moving. As fiber travels through the digestive tract, it absorbs water and softens and adds bulk, helping waste move efficiently through the digestive tract. Fiber may also trigger muscles along the sides of the intestines to contract and relax—an action called peristalsis—which moves things along more quickly.

For simple bag-to-table dessert and snack options, consider the following high-fiber options.

Dark chocolate. The darker and purer the chocolate, the more fiber it contains, with some bars offering as much as 4 grams per serving. Plus, 1/2 ounce of dark chocolate contains more antioxidants than a glass of OJ. Melt it over another high-fiber food such as nuts or fruit, and you have an incredibly high-fiber dessert. Chocolate-covered espresso beans and chocolate-covered raisins or peanuts make great fiber treats, too.

Fruit. It's nature's original sweet treat. Place any fruit you enjoy in a bowl and top with a dollop of whipped cream or vanilla-flavored yogurt. For extra texture, add any of the following fiber-rich toppings: shaved coconut, ground flaxseed, or honey-flavored wheat germ. Also, look for ways to incorporate fruit into desserts. Add it to ice cream. Dip it in pudding. Use it to top angel food cake. For just one example of a refreshing fruit desert, see Berries and Melon with Lime and Mint on page 276.

THE REST OF YOUR LIFE

What do you do once you reach the end of the 4-week plan? You embark on the rest of your life, and you do it by continuing to pile the fiber into every meal and snack. Of course, the rest of your life will be filled with holidays, special occasions, and lots of eating out. In this section, you'll find advice for maximizing the fiber, no matter where you find yourself.

Special Occasions

You don't have to wake up the day after a party feeling bloated and exhausted. Whether you are throwing the party at home or going to one held somewhere else, use the following advice to keep the fiber in the celebration.

- Take a walk before your party. The exercise will put you in a healthy mind-set, encouraging you to reach for the veggies and dip rather than the Brie and fried ravioli.

- Have a high-fiber snack before the party. Munch on some raw veggies, a handful of almonds, or a piece of fruit. This will take the edge off your hunger, so you are less likely to arrive famished and head straight to the buffet table.

- Serve high-fiber finger foods or bring them with you to the party, using the recipes in this chapter for inspiration. In addition to the ones in this chapter, consult Chapter 5 for great party dip and snack options.

- Come up with an eating strategy before the party starts. Just how many low-fiber options will you allow yourself? It's much easier to make these decisions when tasty food isn't right in front of you.

Holidays and Special Days

Starting with candy at Halloween in October and sometimes not ending until the Super Bowl in February, fall and early winter provide one eating challenge after another. It's no wonder that most people gain 2 or more pounds over the holidays. But it doesn't have to be this way. Switching to a high-fiber holiday plan can help turn down your appetite, so you avoid the overeating that leads to weight gain. Below is a holiday-by-holiday guide for high-fiber eating.

Halloween. Hand out candy apples, chocolate-covered raisins, or individual servings of dark chocolate or trail mix. Then you won't have an overload of no-fiber candy bars left over to tempt you.

Thanksgiving and winter holidays. Serve mashed potatoes mixed with pureed cauliflower, whole sweet potatoes, or steamed spinach or broccoli as side dishes. Use whole grain bread in your stuffing recipe. For dessert, think pumpkin pie with a whole grain crust. Canned pumpkin is surprisingly high in fiber, with 7 grams per cup. For other side

---

FIBER FACT

The GI tract is 35 feet long. That's seven people who are 5 feet tall lying feet to head and head to feet in a row. That's a lot of tubing coiled up inside the body, and what you eat has to pass through all of it. Once you chew and swallow, it takes roughly 39 hours for your food to pass through your stomach, small intestine, and colon, and then exit the body.

dish ideas, see Thanksgiving Salad (page 171) and Roasted Sweet and Russet Potato Salad (page 156).

Fourth of July and other picnics. Bring along this fiber-packed bean and whole grain pasta salad: Combine one 15-ounce can of rinsed and drained beans of your choice with 4 cups of cooked whole grain pasta of your choice, 1 cup of thawed frozen peas, and 2 tablespoons of chopped onion. Mix with ½ cup low-fat Italian dressing and ¼ cup reduced-fat mayo. Other great high-fiber picnic options: Fresh Corn and Tomato Bruschetta Salad (page 151), Whole Wheat Orzo with Peas, Asparagus, and Toasted Pine Nuts (page 235), Roasted Sweet and Russet Potato Salad (page 156), Barley, Asparagus, and Cucumber Salad with Yogurt-Dill Dressing (page 161), Mango Pineapple Noodle Salad (page 167), and Buttermilk Sweet Potato Corn Bread (page 253).

Cinco de Mayo. Think guacamole, but use whole grain bread or whole grain crackers as dippers instead of chips. For a more substantial offering, serve Fish Tacos (page 228), Green Bean Burritos (page 233), Beef, Corn, and Refried Bean Enchiladas (page 208), or Mexican Chicken and Avocado Soup (page 144).

Super Bowl and other bowl games. Put out a bowl of popcorn, a small bowl of nuts, and lots of dips with veggies or whole grain bread or crackers as dippers. At halftime, serve some bruschetta. See Edamame, Tomato, and Pecorino Bruschetta (page 262), White Bean and Olive Bruschetta (page 264), and Broccoli Cheese Bruschetta (page 265). For a more substantial offering, try Beef and Bean Chili (page 205).

Saint Patrick's Day. Think cabbage, such as corned beef and cabbage. Savoy cabbage offers the most fiber with 4 grams per cup, but other cabbages also have good amounts. As an added bonus, cabbage boasts cancer-fighting antioxidants such as beta carotene and sulforaphane.

Eating Out

Most restaurants provide many high-fiber options. Use the following guide to order up more fiber at any type of restaurant.

Indian. Choose vegetarian dishes that feature chickpeas (chole bhatura), lentils (dal, dahi vada, dhokla, or amti), or other beans (rajma).

Middle Eastern. Choose dips (hummus, baba ghannouj), falafel (fried chickpea balls), or tabbouleh (cracked wheat salad).

Japanese. Start with edamame (steamed soybeans) or seaweed salad. If ordering hibachi, make sure veggies come with the main course. If ordering sushi, get a few rolls that contain avocado or veggies.

Mexican. Get a dish that includes beans, such as a bean and beef burrito or a bean and chicken quesadilla. Pile on the salsa and/or guacamole.

Family restaurants. Start with a salad and order a side of steamed veggies with your main course. If you order a pasta dish, pay extra and get the vegetable side dish.

Italian. Start with roasted red peppers, bruschetta, minestrone soup, or a salad. If ordering fish or pasta, get a side of steamed veggies. Look for pasta dishes that include vegetables, such as pasta primavera or spinach lasagna.

Pizza. Ask if whole wheat crust is available. Top your pizza with your choice of veggies.

Southern barbecue. Start with a salad, and get a side of collards, corn on the cob, or baked beans with your main course.

EASY FIBER SWAPS

Getting more fiber at dessert can be as simple as making the following switches and substitutions.

IF YOU NORMALLY EAT ...	SWITCH TO THIS HIGH-FIBER ALTERNATIVE ...
Ice cream	Berry and Peach Sundaes (page 279)
Rice pudding	Tropical Rice Pudding (page 277)
Pie	Mixed Berry, Lemon, and Thyme Pie (page 285), Apricot, Nectarine, and Raspberry Crisp (page 283), Sweet Potato Pie with Oat-Pecan Streusel (page 284)
Cheesecake	Ginger–Sweet Potato Cheesecake (page 287)
Cake	Lemon-Cornmeal Cake with Berry Sauce (page 288), Apricot-Blueberry Bundt Cake (page 291)
Cookies	Add oats, flaxseed, nuts, raisins, and other high-fiber ingredients. See Oatmeal-Flax Cranberry Cookies (page 293) and Banana–Brown Sugar Cookies (page 296).
Milk or white chocolate	Dark chocolate that contains at least 60 percent cacao solids. The higher the percentage of cacao, the higher the fiber. Bonus points if you get a bar that contains nuts or fruit.

Bonus Eating Recipes

Edamame, Tomato, and Pecorino Bruschetta

Edamame lend a delicious, nutty flavor to this summer-fresh bruschetta combo, as well as 8 grams of fiber per cup. If you can't find fresh edamame, frozen works just as well.

Prep time: 5 minutes   Cook time: 15 minutes

1 cup shelled edamame

1 cup grape tomatoes, quartered

4 teaspoons extra virgin olive oil

1½ teaspoons balsamic vinegar

2 tablespoons shredded Pecorino Romano cheese

¼ teaspoon salt

⅛ teaspoon ground black pepper

6 slices country style multigrain bread

1. Bring ¾ cup water to a boil in a small saucepan over medium-high heat. Add the edamame and cook for 5 minutes; drain and transfer to a bowl. Stir in the tomatoes, 3 teaspoons of the oil, vinegar, cheese, salt, and pepper.

2. Heat a grill pan over medium-high heat. Brush 1 side of each slice of bread with the remaining 1 teaspoon oil. Grill the bread until well marked and toasted, about 1 minute per side. Transfer to a serving platter and top each slice with ¼ cup of the edamame mixture.

MAKES 6 SERVINGS

Per serving: 123 calories, 6 g protein, 14 g carbohydrates, 5 g total fat, 1 g saturated fat, 5 mg cholesterol, 4 g dietary fiber, 230 mg sodium

White Bean and Olive Bruschetta

The bean mixture will gain flavor if you let it stand for an hour or so before serving.

Prep time: 10 minutes   Cook time: 4 minutes

½ cup quartered cherry tomatoes

1 tablespoon + 1 teaspoon extra virgin olive oil

1 clove garlic, crushed

⅛ teaspoon salt

⅛ teaspoon ground black pepper

1¼ cups white beans, rinsed and drained

⅛ cup whole parsley leaves

6 kalamata olives, sliced

4 slices crusty whole grain bread

1. In a medium bowl, combine the tomatoes, oil, garlic, salt, and pepper. Stir vigorously until the tomatoes release their juice. Add the beans, parsley, and olives.

2. Toast or grill the bread until lightly brown and crisp. Top with the bean mixture and any juices. Cut in half and serve.

MAKES 4 SERVINGS

Per serving: 217 calories, 8 g protein, 33 g carbohydrates, 7 g total fat, 1 g saturated fat, 0 mg cholesterol, 9 g dietary fiber, 251 mg sodium

Broccoli Cheese Bruschetta

These garlicky crusty toasts are like fancy little pizzas—lots of cheese and flavor melted over crunchy bread. Healthy never tasted so decadent. If you don't need to make 4 servings at once, the broccoli mixture will keep up to 4 days if covered in the refrigerator.

Prep time: 15 minutes   **Cook time: 15 minutes**

4 slices crusty whole grain bread

1½ cups broccoli florets, broken into ½" pieces, steamed to crisp-tender

½ cup shredded part-skim mozzarella cheese

¼ cup grated Parmesan cheese

3 tablespoons chopped fresh basil

2 cloves garlic, crushed in a press

1 teaspoon fresh thyme leaves

¼ teaspoon ground black pepper

1. Heat the oven to 350°F. Toast the bread until golden.

2. In a medium bowl, combine the broccoli, mozzarella, Parmesan, basil, garlic, thyme, and pepper and toss well. Spoon about ½ cup of the broccoli mixture over each slice of toasted bread and place on a baking sheet. Bake until the cheese is melted and warm, 12 to 15 minutes.

MAKES 4 SERVINGS

Per serving: 130 calories, 9 g protein, 17 g carbohydrates, 4 g total fat, 2 g saturated fat, 13 mg cholesterol, 6 g dietary fiber, 250 mg sodium

Poached Salmon on Toast Points with Dill-Dijonaise

These elegant toasts are swanky enough to serve at a dinner party.

Prep time: 10 minutes   Cook time: 15 minutes   Cooling Time: 10 minutes

1 small yellow onion, halved
+ 8 teaspoons finely chopped onion

1 bay leaf

8 ounces skinless salmon fillet, pin bones removed

2 tablespoons low-fat mayonnaise

2 teaspoons chopped fresh dill

1 teaspoon Dijon mustard

½ teaspoon grated lemon peel

4 slices multigrain bread

32 watercress leaves

4 cherry tomatoes, cut into 4 slices each

1. In a medium skillet, combine the onion halves, bay leaf, and 3 cups of water over medium-high heat. Bring to a slow boil; add the salmon, reduce the heat to medium, and gently simmer for 12 to 14 minutes, or until the fish is opaque. Remove the salmon from the liquid and let it cool for 10 minutes. Discard the cooking liquid and remaining contents. Carefully flake or cut the fish into 16 pieces.

2. Meanwhile, in a small bowl, combine the mayonnaise, dill, mustard, and lemon peel. Toast the bread slices and cut each slice twice on a diagonal into 4 triangles.

3. To assemble, place the bread triangles on a work surface. Top each with 2 watercress leaves, 1 tomato slice, 1 piece of the salmon, ½ teaspoon of the mayonnaise mixture, and ½ teaspoon of the chopped onion.

MAKES 4 SERVINGS

Per serving: 170 calories, 14 g protein, 13 g carbohydrates, 8 g total fat, 2 g saturated fat, 35 mg cholesterol, 3 g dietary fiber, 260 mg sodium

Turkish Leaves

As the lentils cook, the water becomes a little dark and will color the bulgur, but it's not a problem. The finished salad, studded with flecks of tomatoes, apples, and walnuts, is very pretty.

Prep time: 20 minutes   Cook time: 35 minutes   Chill time: 30 minutes

½ cup French green lentils, picked over and rinsed

3 cups water

¾ teaspoon salt

⅓ cup medium-grain bulgur

2 medium tomatoes, about 12 ounces

¼ cup chopped fresh flat-leaf parsley

1 tablespoon olive oil

2 teaspoons red wine vinegar

1 small clove garlic, minced

⅛ teaspoon ground black pepper

1 medium Granny Smith apple

⅓ cup finely chopped walnuts

3 hearts of romaine, cored, leaves separated, rinsed, and dried

1. In a medium, heavy saucepan, combine the lentils, water, and ¼ teaspoon of the salt. Bring to a boil over high heat. Reduce the heat to low, cover, and simmer for 10 minutes.

2. Stir in the bulgur. Cover and simmer for 10 to 15 minutes more, until the lentils and bulgur are tender, yet the lentils hold their shape. Drain well, shaking off any cooking liquid.

3. Meanwhile, finely chop the tomatoes so they almost become a sauce, or core, chunk, and whirl in the food processor just until saucy. Transfer to a large serving bowl. Stir in the parsley, oil, vinegar, garlic, ½ teaspoon salt, and the pepper. Add the lentil mixture and stir to mix. Cover loosely and refrigerate for at least 30 minutes, or until chilled. The lentils and bulgur should absorb most of the juice from the tomatoes. If the mixture is very soupy, discard some liquid.

4. Finely chop the apple. Stir the apple and walnuts into the lentils.

5. Place the bowl of salad on a platter and surround with the romaine leaves. Diners should spoon the mixture into the leaves.

MAKES 6 SERVINGS

Per serving: 172 calories, 7 g protein, 24 g carbohydrates, 7 g total fat, 1 g saturated fat, 0 mg cholesterol, 6 g dietary fiber, 39 mg sodium

Greek-Style Dolmades

These tasty bundles offer an amazing combination of salty and sweet flavors. This recipe makes 8 servings, so if you're not planning on serving them at a dinner party, refrigerate extras in the cooled cooking broth for up to a week.

Prep time: 40 minutes   Cook time: 55 minutes

---

2 teaspoons extra virgin olive oil

1 small onion, chopped, about ½ cup

½ medium fennel bulb, chopped, about ½ cup

¼ cup pine nuts

⅓ cup packed golden raisins

¼ cup currants

3 cups cooked brown rice

¼ cup chopped fresh parsley

3 tablespoons flaxseeds

2 tablespoons chopped fresh dill

½ teaspoon salt

⅛ teaspoon ground black pepper

32 grape leaves, rinsed several times with cold water

2 cups lower-sodium fat-free chicken broth

2 tablespoons lemon juice

1. Heat the oil in a large nonstick skillet over medium-high heat. Add the onion and fennel; cook, stirring occasionally, until lightly golden, 5 to 6 minutes. Stir in the pine nuts and cook for 1 minute. Add the raisins and currants and cook for 1 minute. Transfer to a bowl and stir in the rice, parsley, flaxseeds, dill, salt, and pepper.

2. Lay a grape leaf on a work surface with the smooth side down. Place a scant 2 tablespoons of the filling near the stem and fold the stem end over the filling. Fold both sides into the middle and roll up jelly roll–style so that it looks like a short cylinder. Repeat with the remaining leaves and filling.

3. Set the dolmades in a large nonstick pot, seam side down. Pour in the broth, lemon juice, and enough water to make the liquid come halfway up the dolmades. Bring to a simmer over medium heat. Cover and simmer until the grape leaves are tender, 40 to 45 minutes. Remove from the heat and serve at room temperature or chilled.

MAKES 8 SERVINGS (4 DOLMADES PER SERVING)

Per serving: 190 calories, 5 g protein, 31 g carbohydrates, 6 g total fat, 1 g saturated fat, 0 mg cholesterol, 5 g dietary fiber, 270 mg sodium

Sweet Potato Pancakes
with Apple Horseradish Cream

Savory and slightly sweet, these griddle cakes are sure to leave you smiling. For a party, arrange on a festive platter and pass as finger food.

Prep time: 15 minutes   Cook time: 15 minutes

---

12 ounces sweet potato, peeled and shredded

12 ounces russet potato, peeled and shredded

1 medium onion, grated, excess liquid squeezed out

1 egg

¼ cup whole wheat flour

½ teaspoon salt

¼ teaspoon ground black pepper

3 tablespoons olive oil

¼ cup light sour cream

¼ cup low-fat mayonnaise

¼ cup finely chopped apple

1 tablespoon prepared horseradish, squeezed dry

1. Preheat the oven to 200°F.

2. In a large bowl, combine the sweet potato, russet potato, onion, egg, flour, salt, and pepper. Form the mixture into 24 patties, approximately 2 tablespoons each and about 1½ inches in diameter.

3. Heat 2 tablespoons of the oil in a large nonstick skillet over medium heat. Add 12 pancakes and cook, turning once, for 7 minutes, or until golden and cooked through. Transfer to a baking sheet and keep warm in the oven. Heat the remaining 1 tablespoon oil and repeat.

4. Meanwhile, in a small bowl, combine the sour cream, mayonnaise, apple, and horseradish; mix well. Serve with the pancakes.

MAKES 12 SERVINGS (2 PANCAKES PER SERVING)

Per serving: 120 calories, 2 g protein, 14 g carbohydrates, 6 g total fat, 1.5 g saturated fat, 25 mg cholesterol, 2 g dietary fiber, 160 mg sodium

Roasted Butternut Squash Skewers with Rosemary Dip

The rosemary flavor in this dish will increase over time. If you are planning to serve the skewers right away, you might want to add a bit more rosemary, but if you are making it ahead of time, the flavors will be just right.

Prep time: 10 minutes   Cook time: 35 minutes

2½ **pounds butternut squash**

1 **tablespoon olive oil**

¼ **teaspoon salt**

¼ **teaspoon ground black pepper**

½ **cup low-fat yogurt**

½ **teaspoon dried rosemary**

1. Heat the oven to 425°F. Cut the squash in half lengthwise and scoop out the seeds. Peel and cut the squash halves into 1" to 1½" cubes. Place on a baking sheet, toss with 2 teaspoons of the oil, and sprinkle with the salt and ⅛ teaspoon of the pepper.

2. Roast the squash for 30 to 35 minutes, or until tender and lightly browned, stirring once or twice. Cool slightly. Thread about 3 squash cubes onto each of 12 small wooden skewers.

3. In a small bowl, combine the yogurt, rosemary, the remaining 1 teaspoon oil, and the remaining ⅛ teaspoon pepper. Serve alongside the skewers.

MAKES 4 SERVINGS (3 SKEWERS PER SERVING)

Per serving: 132 calories, 2 g protein, 27 g carbohydrates, 4 g total fat, 1 g saturated fat, 0 mg cholesterol, 5 g dietary fiber, 140 mg sodium

Berry Soup

Rather than using a food processor, you can puree the strawberry mixture right in the pan using a stick blender. Just be very careful not to splash the hot mixture anywhere.

Prep time: 5 minutes   Cook time: 13 minutes

2½ cups sliced strawberries, about 1 pound

1 cup fruity red wine, preferably Beaujolais

¾ cup + 2 tablespoons water

¼ cup sugar

2½ teaspoons cornstarch

1 tablespoon lemon juice

1 pint raspberries, 6 ounces

1 pint blackberries, 6 ounces

6 tablespoons low-fat vanilla yogurt

1. In a medium saucepan, combine the strawberries, wine, ¾ cup of the water, and the sugar. Bring the mixture just to a boil. Reduce the heat and simmer for 10 minutes. In a small bowl, mix the cornstarch with the remaining 2 tablespoons water and stir it into the strawberry mixture. Continue stirring until slightly thickened, 2 to 3 minutes.

2. Transfer the mixture to the bowl of a food processor. Puree until smooth. Transfer the mixture to a bowl and chill until cold.

3. Just before serving, stir in lemon juice. Pour the soup into 6 serving bowls and top each with raspberries, blackberries, and 1 tablespoon of yogurt.

MAKES 6 SERVINGS

Per serving: 143 calories, 2 g protein, 26 g carbohydrates, 1 g total fat, 0.5 g saturated fat, 1 mg cholesterol, 7 g dietary fiber, 14 mg sodium

Chocolate Fondue with Fresh Fruit Dippers

While dark chocolate does offer some fiber, when weight loss is the goal, it's best put it to good use paired with fresh fruit. If you're a chocolate fan, this luscious dessert will have you swooning.

Prep time: 12 minutes   Cook time: 4 minutes

FONDUE

5 ounces dark or semisweet chocolate chips, heaping ¾ cup

½ cup evaporated nonfat milk

1 tablespoon dark brown sugar

DIPPERS

3 long peeled fresh pineapple spears, each cut in half

½ pound medium-size strawberries, rinsed and patted dry, hulls left on

2 bananas, peeled and cut on an angle into 2"-thick slices

1. *To make the fondue:* In a small, heavy saucepan, place the chocolate chips, evaporated milk, and sugar. Cook over low heat, stirring often with a heat-proof spatula or wooden spoon, until the chocolate has melted and the sauce is smooth. Remove from the heat. Cover to keep warm.

2. *To make the dippers:* On a large platter, arrange the pineapple, strawberries, and bananas.

3. Pour a scant 3 tablespoons fondue into 6 rame-kins or custard cups. Provide toothpicks or wooden skewers or fondue forks. Diners will spear a piece of fruit and dip it into their own pot of fondue.

MAKES 6 SERVINGS

Per serving: 200 calories, 4 g protein, 33 g carbohydrates, 7 g total fat, 5 g saturated fat, 0 mg cholesterol, 4 g dietary fiber, 75 mg sodium

Berries and Melon with Lime and Mint

When the summer humidity is thick enough to cut with a knife, this cool concoction will soothe and satisfy you.

Prep time: 15 minutes   Standing time: 10 minutes

---

2 cups thinly sliced strawberries

1 container (6 ounces) fresh raspberries (1½ cups), or 1½ cups frozen unsweetened raspberries, thawed for 10 minutes

2 tablespoons sugar

1½ cups honeydew balls

1½ cups cantaloupe balls

¼ cup fresh lime juice

2 tablespoons slivered fresh mint leaves

1. In a large serving bowl, place the strawberries and raspberries. Sprinkle with the sugar and mix gently with a rubber spatula. Let stand for 10 minutes to allow the juices to flow.

2. Add the honeydew, cantaloupe, lime juice, and mint and mix gently.

MAKES 4 SERVINGS

Per serving: 124 calories, 2 g protein, 31 g carbohydrates, 1 g total fat, 0 g saturated fat, 0 mg cholesterol, 6 g dietary fiber, 24 mg sodium

Tropical Rice Pudding

Rice pudding with cinnamon and raisins is standard diner fare, but you'd have to travel to a diner in Bali to sample rice pudding this exotic.

Prep time: 10 minutes   Cook time: 10 minutes   Standing time: 25 minutes

---

2 cups fat-free milk

1 cup quick-cooking brown rice (cooks in 10 minutes), such as Uncle Ben's

⅓ cup sugar

¼ cup golden raisins

1 teaspoon vanilla extract

¼ teaspoon salt

½ cup sweetened coconut flakes

¼ cup sliced almonds

1 cup banana slices

½ cup finely chopped mango

1. In a medium saucepan over medium-high heat, combine the milk, 1 cup water, rice, sugar, raisins, vanilla extract, and salt. Bring to a boil, reduce the heat to medium-low, and simmer, covered, until the rice is tender and most of the liquid has been absorbed. Remove from the heat and let stand for 10 minutes. Transfer to a bowl and cool for 15 minutes.

2. Meanwhile, heat a small nonstick skillet over medium heat. Add the coconut and cook, stirring often, until lightly browned, about 5 minutes; transfer to a bowl and cool. Return the skillet to the heat and add the almonds; cook, stirring occasionally, until lightly browned, about 6 to 7 minutes. Transfer to a separate bowl and cool.

3. Stir ¼ cup of the coconut, the almonds, banana, and mango into the cooled rice pudding. Divide among 6 bowls and sprinkle with the remaining ¼ cup coconut. Serve warm or refrigerate and serve chilled.

MAKES 8 SERVINGS

Per serving: 170 calories, 5 g protein, 36 g carbohydrates, 4 g total fat, 2 g saturated fat, 36 mg cholesterol, 2 g dietary fiber, 120 mg sodium

Berry and Peach Sundaes

The true fruit flavors, simply dressed with just a hint of sugar, really shine in this exquisite dessert.

Prep time: 10 minutes   Refrigeration time: 1 hour

½ cup fresh raspberries

½ cup fresh blueberries

½ cup fresh peach slices, about 1 medium

1 tablespoon sugar

2 cups low-fat vanilla ice cream

¼ cup seedless strawberry jam, warmed

2 tablespoons walnuts, coarsely chopped

4 maraschino cherries

1. In a medium bowl, combine the raspberries, blueberries, peach, and sugar; refrigerate for 1 to 2 hours, stirring occasionally.

2. Scoop ½ cup of the ice cream into each of 4 small sundae cups. Top each with one-quarter of the fruit mixture, 1 tablespoon of the jam, ½ tablespoon of the walnuts, and 1 cherry.

MAKES 4 SERVINGS

Per serving: 220 calories, 4 g protein, 43 g carbohydrates, 3.5 g total fat, 1 g saturated fat, 5 mg cholesterol, 3 g dietary fiber, 45 mg sodium

Roasted Pears with Lemon Yogurt

To boost your fiber intake even more, look for yogurt with added fiber.

Prep time: 15 minutes   Bake time: 20–30 minutes

2 tablespoons unsalted butter

3 tablespoons sugar

2 teaspoons grated fresh lemon peel

1 tablespoon fresh lemon juice

4 large ripe pears, about 10 ounces each, unpeeled

1 cup fat-free lemon or vanilla yogurt

Curls of lemon peel and mint sprigs, optional

1. Preheat the oven to 450°F. While the oven is heating, place the butter in a 13" × 9" glass baking dish and put in the oven to melt, about 5 minutes.

2. Remove the dish from the oven and stir in the sugar, lemon peel, and lemon juice.

3. Meanwhile, halve the pears and remove the cores with a melon baller or small spoon. Make a V-shaped cut at the bottom of each to remove the blossom end.

4. Place the pears in the baking dish and turn in the butter-sugar mixture until coated. Turn the pears cut side up, making sure some of the butter is in the cavities. Roast for 20 to 30 minutes, or until the pears are very tender when pierced with a fork.

5. Allow the pears to cool in the pan for about 10 minutes before serving. To serve, transfer 2 halves to each of 4 dessert dishes, and spoon some of the pan juices and ¼ cup of the yogurt over each. If desired, garnish with lemon peel and a mint sprig.

MAKES 4 SERVINGS

Per serving: 209 calories, 3 g protein, 40 g carbohydrates, 6 g total fat, 4 g saturated fat, 16 mg cholesterol, 5 g dietary fiber, 35 mg sodium

Baked Apples with Raisins

You can refrigerate these apples if you like for several days. To reheat, place a cooked apple on a work surface and cut into slices or wedges. Place in a microwaveable bowl and drizzle with some of the cooking liquid. Microwave on medium power for 2 to 3 minutes, or until warmed through.

Prep time: 8 minutes   Bake time: 40–50 minutes   Stand time: 30 minutes

4 large Granny Smith apples, about 8 ounces each

¼ cup dark raisins

3 tablespoons sugar

2 tablespoons unsalted butter, diced

½ teaspoon ground cinnamon

1. Preheat the oven to 350°F. Set out a 13" × 9" glass baking dish.

2. Cut each apple in half through the stem end and remove the core with a melon baller. With a small paring knife, make V-shaped cuts in the stem and blossom ends to remove them. Place the apples skin side down in the baking dish.

3. In a small bowl, with your fingers, mix the raisins, sugar, butter, and cinnamon until crumbly. Spoon the mixture evenly into the cavity of each apple. Pour 1 cup water into the baking dish.

4. Bake for 40 to 50 minutes, or until the apples are very tender when pierced with a fork. Let them stand in the baking dish for 30 minutes before serving. Spoon some cooking juices over each serving.

MAKES 4 SERVINGS (2 HALVES PER SERVING)

Per serving: 175 calories, 1 g protein, 34 g carbohydrates, 6 g total fat, 4 g saturated fat, 15 mg cholesterol, 3 g dietary fiber, 3 mg sodium

Bananas Foster Bread Pudding

This decadent creation combines two of the South's best-loved desserts into one dish of pure unabashed pleasure.

Prep time: 10 minutes　　**Cook time: 35 minutes**　　**Standing time: 45 minutes**

1½ cups 1% milk

4 eggs, lightly beaten

½ cup + 3 tablespoons sugar

1 teaspoon vanilla extract

½ teaspoon ground cinnamon

10 slices multigrain bread, cut into 1" pieces

1 tablespoon unsalted butter

½ cup orange juice

1 tablespoon lemon juice

3 medium bananas, sliced, about 3 cups

1. Preheat the oven to 350°F.

2. Meanwhile, spray a 6-cup baking dish with cooking spray. In a large bowl, combine the milk, eggs, ½ cup of the sugar, vanilla extract, and cinnamon. Stir in the bread; let stand for 30 minutes, stirring occasionally. Pour the mixture into the prepared baking dish.

3. Bake the bread pudding for 30 to 35 minutes, or until puffed and set. Remove from the oven and let cool for 15 minutes. Meanwhile, melt the butter in a large nonstick skillet over medium-high heat. Add the remaining 3 tablespoons sugar and cook for 1 minute, or until beginning to turn golden in color. Stir in the orange juice and cook for 1 minute. Add the lemon juice; stir until slightly thickened, about 1 minute. Add the bananas and stir to coat with the thickened sauce. Spoon over individual servings of bread pudding.

MAKES 8 SERVINGS

Per serving: 216 calories, 8 g protein, 40 g carbohydrates, 5 g total fat, 2 g saturated fat, 115 mg cholesterol, 5 g dietary fiber, 203 mg sodium

Apricot, Nectarine, and Raspberry Crisp

When tree fruits like apricots and nectarines are baked with berries, alchemy occurs. The resulting blend of flavors is greater than the sum of the parts.

Prep time: 20 minutes   Cook time: 40 minutes

1½ pounds apricots, pitted and sliced

1½ pounds nectarines, pitted and sliced

1 cup frozen raspberries, thawed

¾ cup sugar

1 tablespoon cornstarch

½ teaspoon almond extract

⅛ teaspoon ground ginger

½ cup quick-cooking oats

½ cup whole wheat flour

3 tablespoons sliced almonds

¼ teaspoon salt

3 tablespoons unsalted butter, diced

1. Preheat the oven to 375°F. Coat an 11" × 7" baking dish with cooking spray.

2. In a large bowl, combine the apricots, nectarines, raspberries, ½ cup of the sugar, cornstarch, almond extract, and ginger; toss well and pour into the prepared baking dish.

3. In a separate bowl, combine the remaining ¼ cup sugar, oats, flour, almonds, and salt. Rub in the butter with your fingertips until the mixture resembles coarse crumbs. Rub in 2 teaspoons of water and firmly press the mixture into clumps. Break the clumps into smaller pieces and scatter them over the apricot mixture to cover. Bake for 38 to 40 minutes, until the filling is bubbling and thick and the top is golden. Serve warm or at room temperature.

MAKES 12 SERVINGS

Per serving: 170 calories, 4 g protein, 32 g carbohydrates, 4 g total fat, 2 g saturated fat, 10 mg cholesterol, 4 g dietary fiber, 50 mg sodium

Sweet Potato Pie with Oat-Pecan Streusel

Roasting the potatoes really heightens their natural sweetness. Roast double the amount if you like, and freeze half of the mash for your next pie. This pie is relatively calorie dense, so portion sizes are small; fortunately, it's packed with fiber *and* flavor, so a small slice is extremely satisfying.

Prep time: 20 minutes   Cook time: 1 hour 40 minutes   Cool time: 30 minutes

1½ pounds sweet potatoes

5 low-fat honey graham crackers

½ cup ground flaxseed

2 tablespoons + ¾ cup packed brown sugar

5 tablespoons unsalted butter

¾ cup fat-free evaporated milk

2 eggs, lightly beaten

1 egg white, lightly beaten

¼ cup whole wheat flour

1 teaspoon vanilla extract

¾ teaspoon ground cinnamon

¼ teaspoon ground ginger

½ cup quick-cooking oats

¼ cup pecan halves, coarsely chopped

1. Preheat the oven to 375°F. Coat a 9" pie pan with cooking spray.

2. Prick the sweet potatoes with a fork in several places. Set on a baking sheet and roast until tender, 45 to 50 minutes. Allow to cool for 15 minutes. Halve and scoop out the potato with a spoon, discarding the skin. Transfer the potato to a bowl and mash until smooth.

3. Reduce the oven to 350°F. In the bowl of a food processor, place the graham crackers, flaxseed, and 2 tablespoons of the sugar. Process into coarse crumbs and transfer to a bowl. Melt 2 tablespoons of the butter and pour into the crumb mixture; mix until well combined. Pour into the prepared pie dish and press into the bottom and up the sides. Bake for 8 minutes, or until lightly browned. Cool.

4. Meanwhile, in a large bowl, combine the potatoes, ½ cup of the sugar, the milk, eggs, egg white, 2 tablespoons of the flour, vanilla extract, cinnamon, and ginger and whisk until smooth. Pour into the cooled crust and bake for 25 minutes.

5. While the pie bakes, in a small bowl, combine the remaining ¼ cup sugar, 2 tablespoons flour, oats, and pecan halves. Add the remaining 3 tablespoons butter and rub in with your fingertips until the mixture holds clumps when pressed. Remove the pie from the oven and sprinkle the top with the oat mixture. Return to the oven and bake until the filling is set and the top is browned, 18 to 20 minutes. Cool for 30 minutes before slicing.

MAKES 16 SERVINGS

Per serving: 190 calories, 4 g protein, 27 g carbohydrates, 8 g total fat, 3 g saturated fat, 35 mg cholesterol, 3 g dietary fiber, 50 mg sodium

Mixed Berry, Lemon, and Thyme Pie

You might be surprised to see fresh thyme in a pie, but this common herb is actually a member of the mint family, an ideal accent for berries.

Prep time: 15 minutes   **Cook time: 1 hour**   **Cool time: 30 minutes**

1 refrigerated pie crust, 7½ ounces

2 cups frozen raspberries

1¾ cups frozen blueberries

1½ cups frozen strawberries

1¼ cups + ⅓ cup sugar

2 teaspoons grated lemon peel

1 teaspoon chopped fresh thyme

3 tablespoons cornstarch

⅓ cup whole wheat flour

⅓ cup all-purpose flour

⅓ cup Fiber One cereal, lightly crushed

4 tablespoons unsalted butter

1. Preheat the oven to 375°F.

2. On a lightly floured surface, roll out the pie crust to a 12"-diameter circle. Line a 9" pie dish with the crust and roll up any overhang to form a rim; flute between your thumb and index finger.

3. In a large bowl, combine the raspberries, blueberries, strawberries, 1¼ cups of the sugar, lemon peel, thyme, and cornstarch; mix well. Pour into the pie crust. In another bowl, combine the remaining ⅓ cup sugar, whole wheat flour, all-purpose flour, and cereal. Add the butter and rub it in with your fingers until the mixture holds clumps when pressed. Sprinkle the topping over the berry mixture to cover (don't worry if the filling is not completely covered).

4. Bake for 55 to 60 minutes, until the filling is thick and bubbly and the top is golden. If the crust starts to brown too much, tent it loosely with aluminum foil. Cool for at least 30 minutes before slicing.

MAKES 16 SERVINGS

Per serving: 220 calories, 2 g protein, 41 g carbohydrates, 2 g total fat, 4 g saturated fat, 10 mg cholesterol, 3 g dietary fiber, 55 mg sodium

Ginger–Sweet Potato Cheesecake

Silken and spicy, this dreamy dessert encapsulates the flavors of fall. For a cheesecake, it's surprisingly low in calories and fat. In addition to sweet potato, it draws extra fiber from the cereal crust.

Prep time: 15 minutes   **Cook time: 1 hour 10 minutes**   **Chill time: 3 hours**

12 ounces sweet potatoes, peeled and cut into 1" pieces

1 cup dried apricots, chopped

15 gingersnap cookies

¾ cup Fiber One cereal

2 tablespoons unsalted butter, melted

8 ounces fat-free cream cheese, softened

8 ounces Neufchâtel cheese, softened

1 cup plain nonfat yogurt

3 egg whites

⅔ cup packed brown sugar

3 tablespoons finely chopped crystallized ginger

1 tablespoon whole wheat flour

2 teaspoons pumpkin pie spice

2 teaspoons vanilla extract

¼ teaspoon salt

1. Preheat the oven to 350°F. Coat a 9" springform pan with cooking spray.

2. Combine the potatoes in a large saucepan over high heat with enough cold water to cover by 2". Bring to a boil; cook until the potatoes are tender, 12 to 15 minutes. Drain and mash; cool. Meanwhile, bring 1 cup water to a boil in a small saucepan over high heat. Remove from the heat, add the apricots and let stand for 10 minutes; drain.

3. In the bowl of a food processor, combine the cookies and cereal; process until finely ground. Transfer to a bowl and add the butter; mix well. Firmly press the mixture into the bottom and 1" up the sides of the prepared pan. Bake for 10 minutes; cool on a wire rack. Reduce the oven temperature to 325°F.

4. In the bowl of an electric mixer, place the mashed sweet potatoes, cream cheese, and Neufchâtel cheese and beat on high speed until smooth, about 1 to 2 minutes. Add the yogurt, egg whites, sugar, ginger, flour, pumpkin pie spice, vanilla extract, and salt and beat well. Sprinkle the apricots over the bottom of the prepared crust. Pour the potato mixture over the apricots. Bake until the cheesecake is almost set, about 42 to 45 minutes. Turn the oven off and let stand for 1 hour. Remove from the oven and allow to cool to room temperature. Cover with plastic wrap and chill for at least 3 hours before serving.

MAKES 16 SERVINGS

Per serving: 160 calories, 6 g protein, 24 g carbohydrates, 5 g total fat, 3 g saturated fat, 15 mg cholesterol, 2 g dietary fiber, 260 mg sodium

Lemon-Cornmeal Cake with Berry Sauce

The cake will sink just a little in the center, making a natural cup to hold the juicy berry sauce.

Prep time: 23 minutes   Bake time: 20–25 minutes

CAKE

1 cup yellow cornmeal

½ cup whole grain pastry flour

1 teaspoon baking powder

½ teaspoon baking soda

¼ teaspoon salt

2 large eggs

⅔ cup sugar

¾ cup plain nonfat yogurt

4 tablespoons unsalted butter, melted

1 tablespoon grated fresh lemon peel

2 teaspoons vanilla extract

BERRY SAUCE

1 pound strawberries, hulled and cut into quarters or sixths, if large

1 package (5.6 ounces) fresh blackberries (about 1½ cups), cut in half if large, or frozen blackberries thawed for 10 minutes

2 tablespoons sugar

1. *To make the cake:* Preheat the oven to 350°F. Coat an 8" × 8" cake pan with cooking spray.

2. In a large bowl, stir together the cornmeal, flour, baking powder, baking soda, and salt. In a medium bowl, whisk the eggs, sugar, yogurt, butter, lemon peel, and vanilla extract until well blended.

3. Pour the egg mixture into the dry ingredients and stir just until blended. Scrape the batter into the prepared pan. Bake for 20 to 25 minutes, or until browned, firm, and a wooden pick inserted just off-center comes out clean. Let the cake cool on a wire rack in the pan.

4. *To make the sauce:* Just before serving the cake, in a medium serving bowl, mix the strawberries, blackberries, and sugar. Let stand for 10 minutes to allow the juices to flow. Cut the cake into 12 pieces and serve with the sauce.

MAKES 12 SERVINGS

Per serving: 180 calories, 4 g protein, 30 g carbohydrates, 5 g total fat, 3 g saturated fat, 45 mg cholesterol, 3 g dietary fiber, 160 mg sodium

Glazed Pumpkin Fruitcake

Feel free to soak the fruit the night before. The longer it macerates, the plumper it will become.

Prep time: 20 minutes   Soaking time: 2 hours   Bake time: 45–55 minutes

FRUITCAKE

½ cup dark raisins

½ cup chopped dried apricots

¼ cup dried cherries

2 tablespoons brandy or rum or orange juice

1¼ cups whole grain pastry flour

¾ cup unbleached all-purpose flour

1½ teaspoons baking powder

½ teaspoon baking soda

¼ teaspoon salt

½ teaspoon ground cinnamon

½ teaspoon ground nutmeg

½ teaspoon ground ginger

⅛ teaspoon ground cloves

½ cup packed dark brown sugar

2 large eggs

¼ cup canola oil

1 cup plain canned pumpkin

ORANGE GLAZE

½ cup confectioners' sugar

2 teaspoons orange juice

1. In a medium bowl, mix the raisins, apricots, and cherries with the brandy, rum, or orange juice and let soak for 2 hours or overnight.

2. Preheat the oven to 350°F. Coat a 9" × 5" loaf pan with cooking spray. Line the pan with foil, letting the edges hang over. Spray the foil.

3. In a large bowl, stir together the pastry flour, all-purpose flour, baking powder, baking soda, salt, cinnamon, nutmeg, ginger, and cloves.

4. In a medium bowl, whisk the brown sugar, eggs, and oil. Whisk in the pumpkin and stir in the fruit with any juices. Stir the pumpkin mixture into the dry ingredients just until blended. Scrape the batter into the prepared pan.

5. Bake for 45 to 55 minutes, or until the top is golden brown and a toothpick inserted into the center comes out clean. Transfer to a wire rack to cool for 30 minutes. Using the foil as a lifter, remove the cake from the pan. Carefully peel off the foil and set the cake upright on the rack. Allow to cool completely. To serve, halve lengthwise and then slice into 1" pieces.

6. *To make the glaze:* Put the confectioners' sugar in a small bowl. Stir in the orange juice until smooth. Drizzle the glaze decoratively over the cooled cake. Cut the cake into slices with a serrated knife.

MAKES 18 SERVINGS

Per serving: 140 calories, 3 g protein, 25 g carbohydrates, 4 g total fat, 0 g saturated fat, 25 mg cholesterol, 2 g dietary fiber, 110 mg sodium

Apricot-Blueberry Bundt Cake

Apricots and blueberries ripen at just about the same time in early summer, so this pairing is a natural. Whole wheat flour and ground flaxseed lend an important fiber boost.

Prep time: 15 minutes   Bake time: 50 minutes

1½ cups whole wheat flour

1½ cups all-purpose flour

1½ cups sugar

½ cup ground flaxseed

1 tablespoon baking powder

1 teaspoon baking soda

¼ teaspoon salt

1⅓ cups low-fat buttermilk

6 tablespoons canola oil

4 large eggs

1 teaspoon vanilla extract

2 cups fresh blueberries or frozen and thawed blueberries

4 apricots, pitted and chopped, 2 cups

1 cup confectioners' sugar

5–6 teaspoons lemon juice

1. Preheat the oven to 350°F. Coat a 12-cup tube or Bundt pan with cooking spray and sprinkle lightly with flour to coat.

2. In the bowl of an electric mixer, combine the whole wheat flour, all-purpose flour, sugar, flaxseed, baking powder, baking soda, and salt. In a separate bowl, combine the buttermilk, oil, eggs, and vanilla extract and mix well. Pour the buttermilk mixture into the flour mixture and beat on medium speed until well combined, about 1 minute. With a rubber spatula or wooden spoon, gently fold in the blueberries and apricots. Pour into the prepared pan.

3. Bake in the center of the oven for 45 to 50 minutes, or until a toothpick inserted into the center of the cake comes out clean. Cool in the pan on a wire rack for 15 minutes. Carefully remove the cake from the pan and cool on the rack for 30 minutes longer.

4. Transfer the cake to a serving platter. Combine the confectioners' sugar and lemon juice in a small bowl. Drizzle the glaze over the top of the cake and let stand for 5 minutes to set before slicing.

MAKES 24 SERVINGS

Per serving: 200 calories, 4 g protein, 34 g carbohydrates, 6 g total fat, 1 g saturated fat, 35 mg cholesterol, 2 g dietary fiber, 150 mg sodium

Apricot-Honey Spice Bars

Dense and sweet and chewy, these bars keep well in an airtight tin.

Prep time: 20 minutes   **Bake time: 20–25 minutes**

---

1 cup whole grain pastry flour

¾ teaspoon baking powder

¼ teaspoon baking soda

¼ teaspoon ground cinnamon

¼ teaspoon ground cardamom

¼ teaspoon salt

¾ cup coarsely chopped dried apricots

¼ cup golden raisins

1 large egg

1 egg white

¼ cup + 1 tablespoon honey

¼ cup canola oil

¼ cup cooled strong tea

1. Preheat the oven to 350°F. Coat an 8" × 8" baking pan with cooking spray.

2. In a large bowl, stir together the flour, baking powder, baking soda, cinnamon, cardamom, and salt. Stir in the apricots and raisins. In a medium bowl, whisk the egg, egg white, ¼ cup of the honey, the oil, and tea. Pour the egg mixture into the dry ingredients. Stir just to mix.

3. Scrape the batter into the prepared pan and bake for 20 to 25 minutes, or until golden brown and a toothpick inserted into the center comes out clean. Transfer to a wire rack and let cool for about 30 minutes. Brush with the remaining 1 tablespoon honey and let cool completely.

4. Cut into twelve 2" × 2½" bars.

MAKES 12

Per bar: 116 calories, 2 g protein, 16 g carbohydrates,
5 g total fat, 1 g saturated fat, 18 mg cholesterol,
1 g dietary fiber, 111 mg sodium

Oatmeal-Flax Cranberry Cookies

Few sweet treats are as satisfying as old-fashioned oatmeal cookies. If you can find them, dried tart cherries make a fitting substitute for the cranberries.

Prep time: 15 minutes   Bake time: 15 minutes per batch

1¼ cups quick-cooking oats

1 cup whole wheat flour

6 tablespoons ground flaxseed

1 teaspoon baking powder

¼ teaspoon baking soda

¼ teaspoon ground cinnamon

¼ teaspoon salt

¾ cup packed light brown sugar

6 tablespoons unsalted butter, softened

2 egg whites

1 teaspoon vanilla extract

¾ cup dried cranberries

1. Preheat the oven to 350°F. Coat 2 baking sheets with cooking spray.

2. In a medium bowl, combine the oats, flour, flaxseed, baking powder, baking soda, cinnamon, and salt. In a large bowl, combine the sugar and butter and beat with an electric mixer on medium speed until well combined. Beat in the egg whites and vanilla extract until well blended. Add the oat mixture and cranberries and beat on low until combined.

3. Drop level tablespoonfuls of dough 1½" apart onto the prepared baking sheets, making 36 cookies. With the heel of your hand or the bottom of a glass, press each cookie down to form a disc, about 2½" in diameter. Bake, one sheet at a time, for 14 to 16 minutes, or until the cookies are lightly browned. Transfer the cookies to a wire rack to cool.

MAKES 18 SERVINGS (2 COOKIES PER SERVING)

Per serving: 150 calories, 3 g protein, 23 g carbohydrates, 5 g total fat, 3 g saturated fat, 10 mg cholesterol, 2 g dietary fiber, 85 mg sodium

Oat Nut Brittle

Candy that's good for us—now that's a concept we can warm up to. This crunchy confection is chock-full of grains and nuts made yummy with maple syrup and just a hint of butter.

Prep time: 15 minutes   Cook time: 15 minutes   Cool time: 45 minutes

1 cup quick-cooking oats

½ cup Fiber One cereal

½ cup slivered almonds

¼ cup salted oil-roasted peanuts

1 cup sugar

¼ cup maple syrup

2 tablespoons lemon juice

1 teaspoon grated fresh lemon peel

¼ teaspoon salt

2 tablespoons unsalted butter

1. Preheat the oven to 350°F.

2. On a baking sheet, combine the oats, cereal, almonds, and peanuts. Bake, stirring occasionally, for 12 to 15 minutes, or until the oats are lightly toasted. Transfer to a bowl. Coat the baking sheet with cooking spray.

3. In a heavy saucepan over medium-high heat, combine the sugar, maple syrup, lemon juice, lemon peel, and salt. Bring the mixture to a boil and cook, stirring occasionally, for 8 to 9 minutes, or until the sugar has dissolved and turned golden (325°F on a candy thermometer). Remove from the heat and stir in the butter until melted. Pour over the oat mixture, stirring until well coated. Pour onto the prepared baking sheet, top with a piece of parchment paper, and roll the brittle out thin with a rolling pin. Peel off the parchment paper and let cool for 45 minutes. Break into pieces to serve.

MAKES 12 SERVINGS

Per serving: 160 calories, 2 g protein, 29 g carbohydrates, 5 g total fat, 2 g saturated fat, 5 mg cholesterol, 3 g dietary fiber, 60 mg sodium

Banana–Brown Sugar Cookies

Be sure to allow the banana skins to turn dark brown before you mash the fruit. Your patience will be rewarded with moist, sweet cookies.

Prep time: 15 minutes   **Bake time: 12–15 minutes**

1¼ cups whole grain pastry flour

¾ cup old-fashioned rolled oats

¼ cup wheat bran (sometimes called miller's bran)

½ teaspoon baking soda

¼ teaspoon salt

½ teaspoon ground cinnamon

½ cup dark raisins

1 large egg

⅓ cup packed brown sugar

3 tablespoons canola oil

1 teaspoon vanilla extract

1 cup mashed ripe bananas, about 3 large

1. Preheat the oven to 350°F. Coat 2 heavy baking sheets with cooking spray.

2. In a large bowl, stir together the flour, oats, bran, baking soda, salt, and cinnamon. Stir in the raisins. In a medium bowl, whisk the egg, sugar, oil, and vanilla extract. Whisk in the bananas. Stir the banana mixture into the dry ingredients and mix just until blended.

3. Drop the batter in level tablespoonfuls onto the prepared baking sheets, making 24 cookies. Flatten each cookie slightly with a rubber spatula so they bake evenly.

4. Bake for 12 to 15 minutes, or until the cookies are firm to the touch and lightly browned, switching the baking sheets from the top rack to the bottom halfway through baking. Transfer the cookies to wire racks to cool completely.

MAKES 24

Per cookie: 83 calories, 2 g protein, 15 g carbohydrates, 2 g total fat, 0.5 g saturated fat, 9 mg cholesterol, 2 g dietary fiber, 55 mg sodium

CHAPTER 9

MENU PLANS

Congratulations! After 4 weeks discovering the many delicious ways to work more fiber into your meals, you're well on your way to reaching your weight-loss goals. To help fuel your progress, we've put together the following meal plans so you can see how easy it is to maintain your fiber momentum. Each menu uses the recipes in this book along with some other simple-to-prepare dishes to provide over 30 grams of fiber per day and around 1,600 calories. And that's with three meals and two snacks! As you now know, enjoying a steady and delicious dose of fiber throughout the day is the best way to stay comfortably satisfied. Bon appétit!

SUNDAY

BREAKFAST

Yogurt All-Bran Honey Parfait (page 36)

1 cup mango chunks

LUNCH

2 slices whole grain bread filled with 3 ounces thinly sliced low-sodium deli ham, 1 slice reduced-fat Swiss cheese, lettuce, and tomato

2 cups baby greens tossed with 2 tablespoons light balsamic vinaigrette

SNACK

Cumin-Toasted Chickpeas (page 72)

1 medium Bosc pear

DINNER

Mediterranean Chicken Pasta: $^3/_4$ cup cooked whole wheat penne pasta tossed with $^1/_2$ cup low-sodium marinara sauce, $^1/_2$ cup sliced mushrooms, 3 ounces cubed grilled chicken breast, 1 tablespoon pine nuts, and 4 chopped sundried tomatoes

SNACK

1 cup grape tomatoes

1 ounce reduced-fat extra sharp Cheddar cheese

DAILY ANALYSIS

Calories: 1,502

Carbohydrates: 231 g

Protein: 89

Fat: 40 g

Saturated Fat: 10 g

Cholesterol: 149 mg

Sodium: 2,475 mg

Fiber: 46 g

MONDAY

BREAKFAST

1 slice 100% whole grain toast spread with 1 tablespoon almond butter, sprinkled with ¼ cup raisins

1 cup fat-free milk

LUNCH

California Club Sandwich (page 111)

1 cup baby carrots

1 medium Red Delicious apple

SNACK

6 ounces low-fat vanilla yogurt mixed with ½ cup sliced strawberries

DINNER

Grilled Pork Tacos with Avocado-Radish Salad (page 219)

1 tangerine

SNACK

1 cup fat-free milk

2 dried figs, each smeared with ½ tablespoon peanut butter

DAILY ANALYSIS

Calories: 1,671

Carbohydrates: 234 g

Protein: 93 g

Fat: 54 g

Saturated Fat: 10 g

Cholesterol: 113 mg

Sodium: 1,686 mg

Fiber: 46 g

TUESDAY

BREAKFAST

Banana Smoothie: 1 cup fat-free milk blended with 1 tablespoon peanut butter, 2 tablespoons wheat germ, 1 small frozen banana, 1 teaspoon honey, and a handful of ice

LUNCH

2 cups torn romaine lettuce tossed with 1 tablespoon red wine vinaigrette, topped with 2 ounces canned chunk light tuna, $\frac{1}{3}$ cup unsalted canned garbanzo beans, $\frac{1}{4}$ cup chopped carrots, 1 sliced plum tomato, and $\frac{1}{4}$ red onion

6 whole grain crackers

SNACK

Broccoli Spears with Light Cheese Fondue (page 76)

4 whole grain crackers

DINNER

3 ounces roasted turkey breast paired

1 cup red potatoes roasted with 1 teaspoon extra virgin olive oil and fresh rosemary

1 cup steamed green beans

SNACK

Oatmeal-Granola Marshmallow Treats (page 100)

1 cup fat-free milk

DAILY ANALYSIS

Calories: 1,642

Carbohydrates: 214 g

Protein: 99 g

Fat: 45 g

Saturated Fat: 11 g

Cholesterol: 125 mg

Sodium: 1,545 mg

Fiber: 30 g

WEDNESDAY

BREAKFAST

Hot Oatmeal with Blueberries, Cherries, and Brown Sugar (page 39)

1 cup fat-free milk

LUNCH

One 6" whole grain pita filled with $1/3$ cup hummus, $1/2$ sliced plum tomato, $1/2$ cup baby spinach, $1/4$ cup sprouts, and $1/4$ sliced avocado

SNACK

1 medium apple

1 reduced-fat string cheese

DINNER

Chicken-Apricot Kebabs with Brown Rice (page 183)

SNACK

1 cup blueberries mixed into $1/2$ cup ricotta cheese sprinkled with dash of cinnamon and nutmeg

DAILY ANALYSIS

Calories: 1,524

Carbohydrates: 212 g

Protein: 85 g

Fat: 41 g

Saturated Fat: 12 g

Cholesterol: 107 mg

Sodium: 1,430 mg

Fiber: 34 g

THURSDAY

BREAKFAST

Top 1 cup shredded wheat (small biscuit) cereal with 1 cup fat-free milk, 1 tablespoon slivered almonds, and $\frac{1}{2}$ cup raspberries

LUNCH

Thai Beef Salad Wraps (page 115)

1 cup red grapes

SNACK

1 cup nonfat cottage cheese mixed with $\frac{1}{2}$ cup pineapple canned in pineapple juice

DINNER

3 ounces cooked lean ham

$\frac{3}{4}$ cup cooked barley

1 cup summer squash seasoned with parsley and oregano, sautéed with 1 teaspoon minced garlic and 1 tablespoon extra virgin olive oil

SNACK

Grown-Up French Bread Pizza (page 95)

$\frac{1}{2}$ cup each red and green peppers, sliced into strips

DAILY ANALYSIS

Calories: 1,545

Carbohydrates: 186 g

Protein: 114 g

Fat: 45 g

Saturated Fat: 10 g

Cholesterol: 93 mg

Sodium: 1,960 mg

Fiber: 31 g

WEEK 1
FRIDAY

BREAKFAST

1 slice whole grain toast spread with ⅓ cup nonfat ricotta, topped with 1 tablespoon chopped pecans and slices from 1 medium peach

LUNCH

Fruited Spinach Salad with Smoked Turkey and Toasted Walnuts (page 147)

6 ounces low-fat vanilla yogurt

SNACK

6 ounces low-fat lemon yogurt mixed with ½ cup drained canned mandarin oranges sprinkled with 2 teaspoons sunflower seeds

DINNER

Linguini with White Clam Sauce (page 222)

Green Salad: 1 cup greens, 3 frozen artichoke hearts, 2 teaspoons sliced almonds, and 1 tablespoon balsamic vinaigrette

2 slices whole wheat Italian bread brushed with 1 teaspoon olive oil combined with 1 clove minced garlic

SNACK

¼ triangle whole grain pita spread with 1 wedge reduced-fat spreadable cheese

DAILY ANALYSIS

Calories: 1,650
Carbohydrates: 225 g
Protein: 87 g
Fat: 48 g
Saturated Fat: 11 g
Cholesterol: 132 mg
Sodium: 2,311 mg
Fiber: 30 g

SATURDAY

BREAKFAST

Ham and Vegetable Omelet Wrap (page 45)

1 cup fat-free milk

1 cup 100% orange juice

LUNCH

Fiesta Platter: 1/2 cup each onions and peppers sautéed in 1 tablespoon canola oil, served with 1/2 cup brown rice and 1/2 cup black beans sprinkled with 1/4 cup reduced-fat Colby jack cheese and 1/2 cup chopped tomato

SNACK

Roasted Eggplant Dip with Miso (page 80)

1/2 whole grain pita

DINNER

4 ounces tilapia drizzled with juice from 1 fresh lemon wedge, brushed with 1 tablespoon olive oil, and broiled

3/4 cup wild rice

1 1/2 cups steamed broccoli

SNACK

Very Berry Smoothie: 1 cup skim or soy milk blended with 1 cup frozen mixed berries

DAILY ANALYSIS

Calories: 1,602

Carbohydrates: 213 g

Protein: 96 g

Fat: 47 g

Saturated Fat: 10 g

Cholesterol: 196 mg

Sodium: 1,533 mg

Fiber: 37 g

WEEK 2
SUNDAY

BREAKFAST

Sweet Couscous with Pistachios, Peaches, and Figs (page 40)

¾ cup fat-free milk

LUNCH

1 whole grain English muffin open-faced, each half topped with 2 tablespoons marinara, 1.5 ounces Canadian bacon, and a total of ¼ cup part-skim mozzarella cheese

2 cups mixed baby greens, ¼ cup unsalted chickpeas, and 2 teaspoons sliced almonds tossed with 1 tablespoon balsamic vinaigrette

SNACK

Curried Snack Mix with Golden Raisins (page 96)

½ cup fat-free milk

DINNER

3 ounces grilled chicken breast

1 medium baked sweet potato dressed with 2 teaspoons brown sugar and 1 teaspoon trans fat–free margarine

1 cup steamed green beans

SNACK

1 cup whole grain cereal

1 cup fat-free milk

DAILY ANALYSIS

Calories: 1,605

Carbohydrates: 233 g

Protein: 98 g

Fat: 34 g

Saturated Fat: 8 g

Cholesterol: 144 mg

Sodium: 2,225 mg

Fiber: 30 g

WEEK 2
MONDAY

BREAKFAST

1 slice whole grain toast spread with 1 teaspoon trans fat–free margarine

1 scrambled egg made with 2 tablespoons reduced-fat shredded Cheddar cheese and 1 tablespoon each diced peppers and onion

1 cup cubed cantaloupe

LUNCH

Tex-Mex Turkey, Mango, and Pineapple Wraps (page 117)

2 cups steamed yellow wax beans tossed with 2 tablespoons artichoke tapenade

SNACK

6 ounces low-fat peach yogurt mixed with 1 fresh peach sliced into wedges and topped with ¼ cup Mixed Fruit Granola (page 37)

DINNER

Tuscan-Style Stuffed Peppers (page 207)

1 Granny Smith apple

SNACK

Chipotle Bean Nachos (page 92)

DAILY ANALYSIS

Calories: 1,533

Carbohydrates: 226 g

Protein: 90 g

Fat: 39 g

Saturated Fat: 12 g

Cholesterol: 356 mg

Sodium: 2,091 mg

Fiber: 36 g

WEEK 2
TUESDAY

BREAKFAST

Orange, Grapefruit, and Kiwi with Toasted Almonds (page 35)

$^{1}/_{2}$ cup whole grain flake cereal

$^{1}/_{2}$ cup fat-free milk

LUNCH

Veggie Pitas with Hummus Dressing (page 128)

1 stalk celery cut into 3-inch sticks with 2 tablespoons light ranch dressing

SNACK

1 reduced-fat string cheese

1 cup black grapes

DINNER

Beef Stir-Fry: 3 ounces cooked lean beef served with $^{1}/_{2}$ cup cooked brown rice and $^{1}/_{2}$ cup each broccoli, cauliflower, and snap peas stir-fried in 1 teaspoon canola oil, 1 tablespoon low-sodium soy sauce sprinkled with 1 tablespoon black sesame seeds

1 cup cubed watermelon

SNACK

4 graham cracker squares with 4 teaspoons almond butter

$^{1}/_{2}$ cup fat-free milk

DAILY ANALYSIS

Calories: 1,601

Carbohydrates: 217 g

Protein: 77 g

Fat: 54 g

Saturated Fat: 9 g

Cholesterol: 85 mg

Sodium: 2,099 mg

Fiber: 30 g

WEDNESDAY

BREAKFAST

Ricotta and Fig Breakfast Sandwich (page 44)

1 cup 100% grape juice

LUNCH

Southwest Salad: 2 cups mixed greens topped with $\frac{1}{3}$ cup black beans, $\frac{1}{4}$ cup corn, $\frac{1}{4}$ cup chopped tomato, $\frac{1}{4}$ cup shredded reduced-fat Colby jack cheese, and $\frac{1}{4}$ diced avocado topped with 2 tablespoons balsamic vinaigrette

SNACK

1 small Fuji apple sliced, with 1 tablespoon almond butter for spreading

$\frac{1}{2}$ cup fat-free milk

DINNER

Mom's Turkey Meat Loaf (page 200)

$1\frac{1}{2}$ cups steamed cauliflower

$\frac{1}{2}$ cup cooked lima beans

SNACK

1 reduced-fat string cheese

1 red pear

DAILY ANALYSIS

Calories: 1,565

Carbohydrates: 227 g

Protein: 86 g

Fat: 39 g

Saturated Fat: 9 g

Cholesterol: 69 mg

Sodium: 1,604 mg

Fiber: 42 g

WEEK 2
THURSDAY

BREAKFAST

1 cup cooked oatmeal sprinkled with 2 tablespoons ground flaxseed and topped with ½ cup pitted cherries

1 cup fat-free milk

LUNCH

Tuna and White Bean Parsley Lemon Salad (page 168)

1 medium sliced kiwi

¼ cup walnut halves

SNACK

6 ounces low-fat raspberry yogurt mixed with ½ cup raspberries and 2 tablespoons semisweet chocolate chips

DINNER

3 ounces grilled pork tenderloin

½ cup cooked quinoa

⅓ cup each zucchini, peppers, onions, and mushrooms sautéed with ½ tablespoon canola oil

SNACK

Tropical Rice Pudding (page 277)

DAILY ANALYSIS

Calories: 1,598

Carbohydrates: 209 g

Protein: 78 g

Fat: 59 g

Saturated Fat: 12 g

Cholesterol: 68 mg

Sodium: 805 mg

Fiber: 32 g

FRIDAY

BREAKFAST

6 ounces vanilla yogurt topped with ½ cup granola and ½ cup blackberries

LUNCH

Mediterranean platter: ½ cup tabouli topped with ¼ cup feta cheese

Artichoke salad: 1 cup drained artichoke hearts canned in water mixed with ¼ cup drained and rinsed canned chickpeas and 3 diced sundried tomatoes

SNACK

Brown Rice California Rolls (page 86)

DINNER

Fish Tacos (page 228)

1½ cups fresh coleslaw mix tossed with 2 tablespoons light red wine vinaigrette

SNACK

Pineapple strawberry Smoothie: 1 cup fat-free milk blended with 1 cup sliced frozen strawberries and ½ cup crushed pineapple in natural juice

DAILY ANALYSIS

Calories: 1,508

Carbohydrates: 241 g

Protein: 73 g

Fat: 33 g

Saturated Fat: 11 g

Cholesterol: 96 mg

Sodium: 2,070 mg

Fiber: 41 g

SATURDAY

BREAKFAST

Broccoli Red Pepper Frittata (page 47)

1 slice whole grain toast spread with 1 teaspoon trans fat–free margarine

¼ honeydew melon

LUNCH

Lentil Soup with Butternut Squash and Swiss Chard (page 135)

1 cup steamed asparagus

1 whole grain roll with 2 teaspoons herbed oil for dipping

SNACK

4 dried apricots

1 ounce reduced-fat extra sharp Cheddar cheese

DINNER

3 ounces grilled chicken dressed with 2 tablespoons barbecue sauce

½ cup corn, ½ cup black-eyed peas, and 1 cup spinach sautéed with 1 teaspoon chili oil

1 fresh fig

SNACK

4 cups air-popped popcorn sprinkled with 3 tablespoons Parmesan cheese

DAILY ANALYSIS

Calories: 1,528

Carbohydrates: 208 g

Protein: 77 g

Fat: 50 g

Saturated Fat: 13 g

Cholesterol: 229 mg

Sodium: 2,480 mg

Fiber: 39 g

WEEK 3
SUNDAY

Multigrain French Toast with Strawberry-Banana Topping (page 57)

6 ounces low-fat vanilla yogurt sprinkled with 1 tablespoon slivered almonds

LUNCH

2 slices whole rye bread spread with 2 teaspoons spicy brown mustard and filled with 3 ounces thinly sliced deli chicken, lettuce, sliced cucumbers, and sprouts

1 cup grape tomatoes

SNACK

$\frac{1}{2}$ cup part-skim ricotta cheese topped with wedges of 2 medium plums

DINNER

Turkey Meatballs and Linguine (page 188)

$\frac{1}{2}$ cup steamed asparagus

1 baked apple with $\frac{1}{2}$ teaspoon cinnamon and 2 teaspoons brown sugar

SNACK

$\frac{1}{2}$ toasted whole grain English muffin topped with 1 slice reduced-fat Swiss

DAILY ANALYSIS

Calories: 1,572

Carbohydrates: 226 g

Protein: 99 g

Fat: 36 g

Saturated Fat: 13 g

Cholesterol: 233 mg

Sodium: 2,405 mg

Fiber: 35 g

MONDAY

BREAKFAST

$\frac{1}{2}$ whole grain English muffin filled with 1 poached egg, 1 slice reduced-fat jalapeño cheese, and 1 tablespoon salsa

$\frac{1}{2}$ pink grapefruit

LUNCH

Corn and Green Chile Soup with Tomato-Avocado Salad (page 131)

Bite-Size Bean and Cheese Quesadillas (page 88)

1 small red pepper sliced into strips

1 nectarine

SNACK

Raisin bran muffin

$\frac{1}{2}$ cup fat-free milk

DINNER

1 small baked potato dressed with 2 tablespoons sour cream and 1 tablespoon chives

3 ounces cooked pork tenderloin

1 cup steamed carrots

SNACK

6 ounces low-fat lemon yogurt mixed with wedges from 1 medium orange

DAILY ANALYSIS

Calories: 1,615

Carbohydrates: 242 g

Protein: 83 g

Fat: 39 g

Saturated Fat: 15 g

Cholesterol: 372 mg

Sodium: 2,096 mg

Fiber: 31 g

TUESDAY

BREAKFAST

Apple Smoothie: 6 ounces low-fat vanilla yogurt blended with 1 apple, cubed; 2 tablespoons wheat germ; $\frac{1}{2}$ teaspoon apple pie spice; and a handful of ice

1 slice whole grain toast spread with 1 teaspoon trans fat–free margarine

LUNCH

Thai Beef Salad Wraps (page 115)

$\frac{1}{2}$ cup fresh pineapple wedges

SNACK

$\frac{1}{2}$ cup nonfat unsalted cottage cheese mixed with $\frac{1}{2}$ cup sliced papaya

4 whole wheat crackers

DINNER

Flatbread Pizza: 1 whole grain flatbread spread with 1 tablespoon pesto, 3 ounces canned and drained baby shrimp, $\frac{1}{2}$ cup baby spinach leaves, 1 tablespoon pine nuts, and 1 ounce feta cheese

SNACK

Stuffed Apricots (page 99)

$\frac{3}{4}$ cup fat-free milk

DAILY ANALYSIS

Calories: 1,560

Carbohydrates: 185 g

Protein: 96 g

Fat: 55 g

Saturated Fat: 15 g

Cholesterol: 297 mg

Sodium: 2,297 mg

Fiber: 31 g

WEDNESDAY

BREAKFAST

Tex-Mex Breakfast Sandwich (page 12)

1 medium banana

LUNCH

Crisp Asian Salad: 1 cup fresh baby spinach tossed with 1 tablespoon citrus vinaigrette, topped with $\frac{1}{3}$ cup cooked, shelled edamame, $\frac{1}{3}$ cup mandarin oranges, and 1 tablespoon slivered almonds

SNACK

6 ounces low-fat cherry yogurt mixed with $\frac{1}{2}$ cup pitted cherries sprinkled with 1 teaspoon chopped pecans

DINNER

Curried Beef with Pineapple, Coconut, and Brown Basmati Rice (page 204)

1 cup steamed broccoli topped with 1 tablespoon of ginger sesame salad dressing

SNACK

1 cup whole grain flake cereal

1 cup fat-free milk

DAILY ANALYSIS

Calories: 1,594

Carbohydrates: 224 g

Protein: 73 g

Fat: 53 g

Saturated Fat: 14 g

Cholesterol: 68 mg

Sodium: 1,724 mg

Fiber: 33 g

THURSDAY

BREAKFAST

$\frac{1}{2}$ whole grain bagel spread with 1 tablespoon peanut butter and 1 tablespoon dried cranberries

1 cup fat-free milk

LUNCH

Broccoli Rabe and Roasted Red Pepper Wraps (page 112)

3 ounces grilled wild salmon

$\frac{1}{3}$ cup wild rice

1 banana

SNACK

$\frac{1}{4}$ triangle whole grain pita spread with 1 wedge reduced-fat spreadable cheese

DINNER

Turkey Gumbo (page 194)

Salad: 2 cups greens, 4 cherry tomatoes, and $\frac{1}{4}$ cup shredded carrot with 1 tablespoon vinaigrette

1 tangerine

SNACK

4 cups air-popped popcorn sprinkled with 3 tablespoons Parmesan cheese

DAILY ANALYSIS

Calories: 1,525

Carbohydrates: 194 g

Protein: 102 g

Fat: 44 g

Saturated Fat: 11 g

Cholesterol: 149 mg

Sodium: 2,281 mg

Fiber: 30 g

WEEK 3
FRIDAY

BREAKFAST

1 whole wheat English muffin with 2 teaspoons trans fat–free margarine

6 ounces low-fat vanilla yogurt mixed with 2 tablespoons whole oats, ½ cup red grapes, and 1 tablespoon chopped walnuts

LUNCH

2 cups mixed baby greens tossed with 2 tablespoons red wine vinaigrette topped with 1 ounce smoked deli ham, 2 slices reduced-fat Swiss cheese cut into strips, ½ red bell pepper sliced into rings, ½ cup raw cauliflower florets, and 1 sliced plum tomato

1 whole grain roll

SNACK

Blueberry Smoothie: 1 cup fat-free milk blended with 1 cup frozen blueberries

DINNER

Grilled Vegetable and Bean Lasagna (page 232)

SNACK

Roasted Pears with Lemon Yogurt (page 280)

DAILY ANALYSIS

Calories: 1,607

Carbohydrates: 230 g

Protein: 90 g

Fat: 46 g

Saturated Fat: 14 g

Cholesterol: 75 mg

Sodium: 2,250 mg

Fiber: 35 g

SATURDAY

BREAKFAST

Artichoke, Mushroom, and Goat Cheese Omelet (page 48)

1 cup sliced melon and 1 slice whole grain toast spread with 1 teaspoon trans fat–free margarine

LUNCH

Zesty Pasta Salad: 1 cup cooked whole grain pasta spirals tossed with 1 tablespoon balsamic vinaigrette, ¼ cup chopped tomato, ¼ cup chopped cucumber, ¼ cup chopped peppers, ¼ cup sliced mushrooms, ½ cup kidney beans, and 1 tablespoon pine nuts

SNACK

4 whole grain crackers

1 ounce reduced-fat extra sharp Cheddar cheese

DINNER

Creole Shrimp with Green Beans and Corn-Scallion Grits (page 225)

1 cup steamed yellow wax beans

SNACK

2 soft corn tortillas each filled with 1 tablespoon reduced-fat shredded Cheddar cheese, warmed to melt cheese, and served with ¼ cup chunky salsa

DAILY ANALYSIS

Calories: 1,617

Carbohydrates: 216 g

Protein: 76 g

Fat: 52 g

Saturated Fat: 14 g

Cholesterol: 302 mg

Sodium: 1,920 mg

Fiber: 41 g

WEEK 4
SUNDAY

BREAKFAST

Raspberry-Oat Muffin (page 61)

1 cup fat-free milk

1 medium Golden Delicious apple

LUNCH

Chicken Burrito: 1 whole grain tortilla filled with 3 ounces cooked chicken breast, $\frac{1}{4}$ cup refried pinto beans, 2 tablespoons salsa, $\frac{1}{2}$ cup shredded carrots, torn romaine lettuce, and $\frac{1}{4}$ avocado, sliced

SNACK

1 reduced-fat string cheese

1 cup green grapes

DINNER

Home-Style Turkey Pot Pie (page 198)

Salad: 2 cups baby spinach; $\frac{1}{3}$ cup canned, drained mandarin oranges; 2 tablespoons dried cranberries; and 1 tablespoon balsamic vinaigrette

1 cup steamed cauliflower

SNACK

2 dried dates, each smeared with $\frac{1}{2}$ tablespoon almond butter

$\frac{1}{2}$ cup fat-free milk

DAILY ANALYSIS

Calories: 1,629

Carbohydrates: 238 g

Protein: 92 g

Fat: 43 g

Saturated Fat: 10 g

Cholesterol: 159 mg

Sodium: 1,833 mg

Fiber: 30 g

MONDAY

BREAKFAST

1 whole grain waffle drizzled with 1 tablespoon warmed peanut butter topped with 1 sliced banana

1 cup fat-free milk

LUNCH

Mango Pineapple Noodle Salad (page 167)

4 slices roasted deli turkey, rolled up

SNACK

Chocolate Fondue with Fresh Fruit Dippers (page 274)

DINNER

3 ounces broiled haddock

1 cup brussels sprouts

$\frac{1}{2}$ cup steamed carrots

1 cup brown rice

6 ounces low-fat vanilla yogurt topped with $\frac{1}{2}$ cup sliced strawberries

SNACK

$\frac{1}{4}$ triangle whole grain pita spread with 1 wedge reduced-fat spreadable cheese

DAILY ANALYSIS

Calories: 1,568

Carbohydrates: 250 g

Protein: 83 g

Fat: 34 g

Saturated Fat: 12 g

Cholesterol: 150 mg

Sodium: 2,032 mg

Fiber: 30 g

TUESDAY

BREAKFAST

Fruit Sandwich (page 41)

6 ounces low-fat vanilla yogurt

LUNCH

1 whole grain pita filled with 3 ounces drained chunk light tuna in water seasoned with juice from fresh wedge of lemon and ground pepper, $\frac{1}{4}$ cup sliced cucumber, 1 sliced plum tomato, $\frac{1}{4}$ cup sprouts, $\frac{1}{4}$ cup sliced avocado, and $\frac{1}{4}$ cup baby spinach leaves

SNACK

6 ounces low-fat peach yogurt mixed with wedges of 1 medium peach

DINNER

$\frac{1}{2}$ cup whole grain spaghetti tossed with 1 cup baby spinach leaves, $\frac{1}{2}$ cup chunky marinara, and 3 ounces cooked chicken breast, diced, and sprinkled with $\frac{1}{4}$ cup part-skim mozzarella cheese and 1 tablespoon Parmesan cheese

SNACK

Trail Mix (page 97)

1 Granny Smith apple

DAILY ANALYSIS

Calories: 1,591

Carbohydrates: 239 g

Protein: 97 g

Fat: 31 g

Saturated Fat: 12 g

Cholesterol: 176 mg

Sodium: 2,100 mg

Fiber: 30 g

WEDNESDAY

BREAKFAST

Muesli with Dried Fruit and Almonds (page 38)

1 cup fat-free milk

LUNCH

1 whole grain hamburger bun, toasted and spread with 2 teaspoons spicy mustard and filled with 3-ounce turkey burger, lettuce, tomato, and red onion with 2 cups baby greens, $\frac{1}{4}$ cup salt-free chickpeas, and $\frac{1}{4}$ cup shredded carrots tossed with 2 tablespoons balsamic vinaigrette

SNACK

$\frac{1}{2}$ cup cottage cheese mixed with 1 cup mixed berries sprinkled with 1 tablespoon whole oats

DINNER

Tomato-Feta Shrimp with Quinoa and Broccoli (page 226)

SNACK

6 whole grain crackers

1 ounce reduced-fat extra sharp Cheddar cheese

DAILY ANALYSIS

Calories: 1,548

Carbohydrates: 186 g

Protein: 103 g

Fat: 47 g

Saturated Fat: 13 g

Cholesterol: 252 mg

Sodium: 2,315 mg

Fiber: 30 g

THURSDAY

BREAKFAST

1 cup cooked old-fashioned oats topped with 3 prunes, 2 tablespoons chopped pecans, and 1 tablespoon maple syrup

LUNCH

Turkey, Pear, and Arugula Panini (page 119)

6 ounces nonfat vanilla yogurt with ½ cup blueberries

SNACK

Crisp Broccoli Spears with Asian Peanut Dipping Sauce (page 77)

4 whole grain crackers

DINNER

3 ounces grilled tuna steak

½ cup cooked quinoa

1 cup steamed asparagus

Salad: 2 cups greens, ¼ cup grape tomatoes, 1 thinly sliced scallion, and 2 tablespoons vinaigrette dressing

SNACK

1 reduced-fat string cheese

½ large pink grapefruit

DAILY ANALYSIS

Calories: 1,570

Carbohydrates: 201 g

Protein: 103 g

Fat: 48 g

Saturated Fat: 9 g

Cholesterol: 96 mg

Sodium: 1,437 mg

Fiber: 33 g

FRIDAY

BREAKFAST

$\frac{1}{2}$ whole grain English muffin spread with $\frac{1}{4}$ cup nonfat ricotta cheese and topped with wedges from 1 large Anjou pear

LUNCH

Red Bean and Corn Sloppy Janes (page 123)

$\frac{1}{2}$ cup cooked brown rice topped with 2 tablespoons tomato salsa

Cucumber Salad: 1 medium cucumber sliced and dressed with 2 tablespoons red wine vinaigrette

SNACK

Banana Pineapple Smoothie: 1 cup fat-free milk blended with 1 small frozen banana and $\frac{1}{4}$ cup crushed pineapple in natural juice

DINNER

Baked Macaroni and Cheese (page 236)

1 cup steamed broccoli

SNACK

4 cups air-popped popcorn sprinkled with 3 tablespoons Parmesan cheese

DAILY ANALYSIS

Calories: 1,535

Carbohydrates: 244 g

Protein: 73 g

Fat: 35 g

Saturated Fat: 12 g

Cholesterol: 83 mg

Sodium: 2,381 mg

Fiber: 40 g

WEEK 4
SATURDAY

BREAKFAST
Breakfast Strata (page 52)

1 cup green grapes

LUNCH
Havana Black Bean Soup with Oranges and Sherry (page 146)

4 whole grain crackers spread with $\frac{1}{4}$ cup mashed avocado

SNACK
2 tablespoons hummus sprinkled with 1 tablespoon feta cheese served with 1 small red pepper cut into strips

DINNER
3 ounces cooked chicken breast, diced, served with $\frac{1}{4}$ cup each red and yellow peppers and $\frac{1}{2}$ cup snow peas stir-fried in 1 teaspoon sesame oil, then topped with 1 tablespoon cashews

$\frac{1}{2}$ cup brown rice

SNACK
6 ounces low-fat vanilla yogurt mixed with $\frac{1}{2}$ cup whole grain flake cereal and $\frac{1}{2}$ cup blueberries

DAILY ANALYSIS
Calories: 1,653

Carbohydrates: 236 g

Protein: 83 g

Fat: 51 g

Saturated Fat: 13 g

Cholesterol: 233 mg

Sodium: 2,125 mg

Fiber: 43 g

APPENDIX

Use the following lists for guidance when shopping for high-fiber packaged foods. Although these lists are extensive, they are by no means exhaustive. So if you find a high-fiber bread or pasta or other product not listed here, just remember this simple advice: When choosing grains, make sure a "whole" grain is first on the list of ingredients. When choosing other foods, make sure they offer the following fiber amounts per serving:

Breakfast cereal: 4 grams per serving

Waffles: 2 grams per waffle

Bread: 2 grams per slice

Pasta: 3 grams per serving

Cereal bars: 5 grams per bar

RECOMMENDED CEREALS AND WAFFLES

COLD CEREALS

The following cereals all contain 4 grams or more of fiber per serving.

ARROWHEAD MILLS	SERVING SIZE	CALORIES	FIBER	SUGAR
Shredded Wheat	1 cup	190	6 g	2 g
Sweetened Shredded Wheat	1 cup	200	5 g	12 g
Oatbran Flakes	1 cup	140	4 g	3 g
Spelt and Cranberries Flakes	1 cup	170	4 g	9 g
BACK TO NATURE	**SERVING SIZE**	**CALORIES**	**FIBER**	**SUGAR**
Heart Basics—Flax and Fiber Crunch	¾ cup	180	9 g	13 g
BARBARA'S	**SERVING SIZE**	**CALORIES**	**FIBER**	**SUGAR**
Organic Grain Shop	½ cup	80	8 g	6 g
Shredded Oats Bite Size	1¼ cups	220	5 g	12 g
Shredded Wheat	2 biscuits	140	5 g	0 g
Shredded Spoonfuls	¾ cup	120	4 g	5 g
Weetabix Organic	2 biscuits	120	4 g	2 g
Weetabix Organic Crispy Flakes	¾ cup	110	4 g	4 g
GENERAL MILLS	**SERVING SIZE**	**CALORIES**	**FIBER**	**SUGAR**
Fiber One	½ cup	60	14 g	0 g

GENERAL MILLS	SERVING SIZE	CALORIES	FIBER	SUGAR
Fiber One with Honey Clusters	1¼ cups	170	14 g	5 g
Fiber One Raisin Bran Clusters	1 cup	170	11 g	13 g
Cascadian Farm—Great Measure	1 cup	190	9 g	12 g
Cascadian Farm—Hearty Morning	¾ cup	200	8 g	11 g
Multi Bran Chex	1 cup	190	7 g	11 g
Raisin Nut Bran	¾ cup	180	5 g	13 g
Total Raisin Bran	1 cup	170	5 g	19 g
Wheat Chex (100% Whole Grain)	¾ cup	160	5 g	5 g
KASHI	SERVING SIZE	CALORIES	FIBER	SUGAR
Good Friends	1 cup	170	12 g	9 g
Vive	1¼ cups	170	12 g	10 g
GoLean	1 cup	140	10 g	6 g
GoLean Crunch	1 cup	190	8 g	13 g
7 Whole Grain—Nuggets	½ cup	210	7 g	3 g
Organic Promise—Autumn Wheat	1 cup	190	6 g	7 g
7 Whole Grain Flakes	1 cup	180	6 g	5 g
Heart to Heart	¾ cup	110	5 g	5 g
Organic Promise—Cinnamon Harvest	1 cup	190	5 g	9 g
KELLOGG'S	SERVING SIZE	CALORIES	FIBER	SUGAR
All Bran—Bran Buds	⅓ cup	70	13 g	8 g
All Bran—Extra Fiber	½ cup	50	13 g	0 g
All Bran—Original	½ cup	80	10 g	6 g
All Bran—Yogurt Bites	1¼ cups	190	10 g	7 g
All Bran—Complete Wheat Flakes	¾ cup	90	5 g	5 g
NATURE'S PATH	SERVING SIZE	CALORIES	FIBER	SUGAR
Flax Plus—Raisin Bran	¾ cup	180	11 g	16 g
Optimum Slim	1 cup	180	11 g	7 g
Optimum Power	1 cup	190	10 g	16 g
Flax Plus Pumpkin Raisin Crunch	¾ cup	200	9 g	12 g
Flax Plus—Multibran	¾ cup	100	7 g	6 g
Multigrain Flakes—Oatbran and Raisins	¾ cup	190	7 g	6 g
Heritage	¾ cup	110	6 g	4 g
Heritage Bites	¾ cup	100	6 g	5 g
Multigrain Oatbran	¾ cup	110	5 g	4 g
Synergy	¾ cup	100	5 g	4 g

(continued)

COLD CEREALS (CONT.)

POST (KRAFT FOODS)	SERVING SIZE	CALORIES	FIBER	SUGAR
100% Bran	⅓ cup	80	9 g	7 g
Shredded Wheat 'n Bran, Spoon Size	1¼ cups	200	8 g	1 g
Grape Nuts	½ cup	200	6 g	5 g
Shredded Wheat, Spoon Size	1 cup	170	6 g	0 g
Bran Flakes	¾ cup	100	5 g	5 g
US MILLS	**SERVING SIZE**	**CALORIES**	**FIBER**	**SUGAR**
Uncle Sam Cereal	¾ cup	190	10 g	<1 g
Uncle Sam Cereal with Real Mixed Berries	1 cup	190	10 g	2 g
Skinner's Raisin Bran	1 cup	170	7 g	13 g
Erewhon Raisin Bran	1 cup	170	6 g	10 g
Erewhon Kamut Flakes	⅔ cup	110	4 g	1 g

HOT CEREALS

ARROWHEAD MILLS	SERVING SIZE	CALORIES	FIBER	SUGAR
4 Grain Plus Flax	¼ cup dry	140	9 g	0 g
Organic Steel Cut Oats	¼ cup dry	160	8 g	0 g
7 Grain Hot Cereal	⅓ cup	140	6 g	0 g
Bulgur Wheat	¼ cup dry	150	4 g	0 g
Oat Flakes Hot Cereal	⅓ cup	130	4 g	<1 g
Organic Old Fashioned Oatmeal Hot Cereal	⅓ cup dry	130	4 g	<1 g
BOB'S RED MILL	**SERVING SIZE**	**CALORIES**	**FIBER**	**SUGAR**
8-Grain Wheatless	¼ cup	150	6 g	0 g
7-Grain	¼ cup	140	6 g	1 g
5-Grain Rolled Cereal	⅓ cup	120	5 g	1 g
10-Grain	¼ cup	140	5 g	0 g
Kamut Cereal, Organic	¼ cup	120	4 g	0 g
Spice 'n Nice Cereal	½ cup	190	4 g	3 g
HODGSON MILL	**SERVING SIZE**	**CALORIES**	**FIBER**	**SUGAR**
Multi Grain Hot Cereal with Milled Flaxseed and Soy	⅓ cup	160	6 g	1 g
Oat Bran Hot Cereal	¼ cup dry	120	6 g	3 g
Cracked Wheat Premium Steel Cut Oats	¼ cup dry	110	5 g	0 g

HOMESTAT FARM WHEATENA	SERVING SIZE	CALORIES	FIBER	SUGAR
Maltex	⅓ cup	170	5 g	1 g
Wheatena	⅓ cup	160	5 g	0 g
MCCANN'S	SERVING SIZE	CALORIES	FIBER	SUGAR
Irish Oatmeal Steel Cut Oats	¼ cup	150	4 g	0 g
NATURE'S PATH	SERVING SIZE	CALORIES	FIBER	SUGAR
Optimum Power Hot Oatmeal	1 packet	150	4 g	9 g
Original Hot Oatmeal	1 packet	190	4 g	0 g
QUAKER OATS	SERVING SIZE	CALORIES	FIBER	SUGAR
Instant—Weight Control (All flavors: Banana Bread, Cinnamon, Maple and Brown Sugar)	1 packet	160	6 g	1 g
Oat Bran Hot Cereal	½ cup	150	6 g	1 g
Quaker Oats—Old Fashioned	½ cup dry	150	4 g	1 g
Quick Quaker Oats	½ cup dry	150	4 g	1 g
Sun and Country Iron-Fortified Quick Oats	½ cup dry	150	4 g	1 g
STONE-BUHR	SERVING SIZE	CALORIES	FIBER	SUGAR
4 Grain Cereal Mates	⅓ cup dry	140	5 g	0 g

FROZEN WAFFLES			
KASHI	SERVING SIZE	CALORIES	FIBER
GoLean Waffles—Blueberry	2 waffles	170	6 g
GoLean Waffles—Original	2 waffles	170	6 g
NATURE'S PATH	SERVING SIZE	CALORIES	FIBER
Lifestream Organic—Fig + Flax	2 waffles	210	6 g
Lifestream Organic—Flax Plus	2 waffles	200	6 g
Lifestream Organic—Hemp Plus	2 waffles	210	5 g
Lifestream Organic—Optimum Power Flax-Soy-Blueberry	2 waffles	160	5 g
Lifestream Organic—Pomegran Plus with Oatbran	2 waffles	190	5 g
Lifestream Organic—Soy Plus	2 waffles	220	5 g
Lifestream Organic—Synergy	2 waffles	200	5 g
Lifestream Organic—MapleCinn	2 waffles	200	4 g

(continued)

FROZEN WAFFLES (CONT.)			
VAN'S	**SERVING SIZE**	**CALORIES**	**FIBER**
Hearty Oats—Berry Boost	2 waffles	200	4 g
Hearty Oats—Maple Fusion	2 waffles	210	4 g
Hearty Oats—Oats N' Honey	2 waffles	200	4 g
Gourmet—Flax	2 waffles	260	6 g
Gourmet—Multigrain	2 waffles	190	5 g
Gourmet—97% Fat Free	2 waffles	180	5 g
Belgian—7 Grain	2 waffles	230	7 g
Organic—Original	2 waffles	190	6 g
Organic—Soy-Flax	2 waffles	230	6 g
Organic—Blueberry	2 waffles	240	4 g

RECOMMENDED BREAD, PITAS, ROLLS, AND WRAPS

ALPHA BAKING CO.	SERVING SIZE	CALORIES	FIBER
S. Rosen's Healthy Multigrain	1 slice	110	3 g
S. Rosen's 100% Whole Wheat	1 slice	90	2 g
ALVARADO STREET BAKERY	**SERVING SIZE**	**CALORIES**	**FIBER**
Sprouted Whole Wheat	1 slice	90	3 g
Sprouted Whole Wheat Bagel	1 bagel	250	3 g
No Salt! Sprouted Wheat Multigrain	1 slice	90	2 g
Sprouted Barley Bread	1 slice	70	2 g
ARNOLD	**SERVING SIZE**	**CALORIES**	**FIBER**
Whole Grain Classics—Double Fiber 100% Whole Wheat	1 slice	90	5 g
Natural Hearty—Bakery Light 100% Whole Wheat	2 slices	80	5 g
Natural Hearty—Oat	1 slice	100	3 g
Natural Hearty—100% Whole Wheat	1 slice	100	3 g
AUNT MILLIE'S	**SERVING SIZE**	**CALORIES**	**FIBER**
Healthy Goodness—Whole Grain Light Fiber for Life	2 slices	70	6 g
Hearth—Fiber for Life Healthy Whole Grain	1 slice	100	6 g
Hearth—Fiber for Life 12 Whole Grain	1 slice	100	6 g
Hearth—Organic Flax Seed	1 slice	100	3 g

AUNT MILLIE'S	SERVING SIZE	CALORIES	FIBER
Hearth—Organic Indian Grain	1 slice	100	3 g
Hearth—Organic Whole Wheat	1 slice	95	3 g
Homestyle—100% Whole Wheat English Muffin	1 muffin	100	3 g
Homestyle—Whole Grain Dinner Rolls	1 roll	130	3 g
Homestyle—100% Whole Wheat	1 slice	100	2 g
BAKER'S INN	**SERVING SIZE**	**CALORIES**	**FIBER**
100% Whole Wheat	1 slice	110	3 g
Harvest Multigrain	1 slice	100	2 g
Honey Whole Wheat	1 slice	100	2 g
9 Grain	1 slice	100	2 g
BREADSMITH	**SERVING SIZE**	**CALORIES**	**FIBER**
Australian Pumpernickel	1 slice	90	4 g
Honey Sunflower Whole Wheat	1 slice	110	3 g
100% Whole Wheat	1 slice	100	3 g
Pecan Sourdough Whole Grain	1 slice	100	3 g
Raisin Cinnamon Whole Wheat	1 slice	110	3 g
Sourdough Whole Grain	1 slice	90	3 g
Frontier	1 slice	90	2 g
Honey Whole Wheat	1 slice	100	2 g
Multigrain Whole Wheat	1 slice	110	2 g
FOOD FOR LIFE	**SERVING SIZE**	**CALORIES**	**FIBER**
Ezekiel 4:9—Organic Sprouted 100% Whole Grain Flourless Tortilla	1 tortilla	150	5 g
Ezekiel 4:9—7-Organic Sprouted 100% Whole Grain Flourless Bread	1 slice	80	3 g
Genesis 1:29—Organic Sprouted 100% Whole Grain and Seed	1 slice	80	3 g
Genesis 1:29—Organic Sprouted 100% Whole Grain and Seed English Muffin	½ muffin	90	3 g
HEALTHY LIFE	**SERVING SIZE**	**CALORIES**	**FIBER**
Original—100% Whole Grain Sugar Free Rye	1 slice	40	4 g
Original—Oatbran Whole Grain	1 slice	40	3 g
Original—100% Whole Wheat Whole Grain	1 slice	35	3 g

(continued)

RECOMMENDED BREAD, PITAS, ROLLS, AND WRAPS (CONT.)

HEALTHY LIFE	SERVING SIZE	CALORIES	FIBER
Original—100% Whole Wheat Whole Grain Flaxseed	1 slice	40	3 g
Southern Country Style—100% Whole Wheat Hot Dog Bun	1 bun	110	3 g
Southern Country Style—100% Whole Wheat Sandwich Bun	1 bun	110	3 g
Southern Country Style—Farmers 12 Grain	1 slice	90	2 g
Southern Country Style—Flaxseed	1 slice	90	2 g
Southern Country Style—Multi-Grain'ola	1 slice	60	2 g
Southern Country Style—Natural All Whole Grain 100% Whole Wheat	1 slice	90	2 g
Southern Country Style—100% Whole Wheat	1 slice	60	2 g
Southern Country Style—100% Whole Wheat Dinner Rolls	1 roll	70	2 g

MISSION FOODS	SERVING SIZE	CALORIES	FIBER
Multi Grain Wrap	1 tortilla	210	7 g
8" Soft Taco Multigrain Flour Tortilla	1 tortilla	140	5 g
6" Fajita Multigrain Flour Tortilla	1 tortilla	110	4 g

NATURAL OVENS	SERVING SIZE	CALORIES	FIBER
100% Whole Grain	1 slice	90	4 g
Golden Grain	1 slice	100	3 g

NATURE'S OWN	SERVING SIZE	CALORIES	FIBER
Double Fiber Wheat	1 slice	50	5 g
Sugar Free 100% Whole Grain Wheat Sandwich Bun	1 bun	110	4 g
Hearty Oatmeal Specialty	1 slice	100	3 g
Honey Wheat Berry Specialty	1 slice	110	3 g
Honey Wheat Specialty with Organic Flour	1 slice	100	3 g
100% Whole Wheat Specialty	1 slice	100	3 g
100% Whole Wheat Specialty with Organic Flour	1 slice	100	3 g
12 Grain Specialty	1 slice	90	3 g
100% Whole Wheat	1 slice	50	2 g
100% Whole Wheat Sugar Free	1 slice	50	2 g
Wheat n'Fiber	1 slice	60	2 g

PEPPERIDGE FARM	SERVING SIZE	CALORIES	FIBER
Whole Grain Multi Grain	1 bagel	250	7 g
100% Whole Wheat Bagel	1 bagel	250	6 g
Whole Grain Golden Harvest Grains	1 slice	110	4 g
15 Grain Whole Grain Bread	1 slice	120	3 g
100% Whole Wheat English Muffin	1 muffin	140	3 g
100% Whole Wheat Mini Bagels	1 bagel	100	3 g
Whole Grain Oatmeal	1 slice	110	3 g
Whole Grain 100% Whole Wheat	1 slice	110	3 g
Natural Whole Grain—Multi Grain	1 slice	120	3 g
Natural Whole Grain—9 Grain	1 slice	110	3 g
Natural Whole Grain—100% Whole Wheat	1 slice	110	3 g
Natural Whole Grain—Soft 100% Whole Wheat Kaiser Rolls	1 roll	200	3 g
RUDI'S ORGANIC BAKERY	SERVING SIZE	CALORIES	FIBER
Whole Grains and Fiber—Apple n Spice	1 slice	110	5 g
Whole Grains and Fiber—14 Grain	1 slice	90	4 g
Whole Grains and Fiber—7 Grain with Flax	1 slice	100	4 g
Whole Grains and Fiber—Wheat and Oat	1 slice	90	4 g
Sandwich—100% Whole Wheat Bun	1 bun	160	5 g
Sandwich—Honey Sweet Whole Wheat	1 slice	110	3 g
Sandwich—100% Whole Wheat	1 slice	100	3 g
Sandwich—Whole Grain Wheat English Muffin	1 muffin	120	3 g
Sandwich—Whole Spelt Tortilla	1 tortilla	150	3 g
Sandwich—Spelt English Muffin	1 muffin	120	2 g
SARA LEE	SERVING SIZE	CALORIES	FIBER
Hearty Delicious—100% Multigrain	1 slice	120	3 g
Hearty Delicious—100% Whole Wheat with Honey	1 slice	110	3 g
THOMAS'	SERVING SIZE	CALORIES	FIBER
Hearty Grains Bagel—100% Whole Wheat	1 bagel	270	8 g
Hearty Grains Bagel—Sahara Pita Bread 100% Whole Wheat	1 pita	140	4 g
Hearty Grains—100% Whole Wheat	1 muffin	130	3 g
Hearty Grains—12 Grain	1 muffin	140	2 g
WRAPITZ	SERVING SIZE	CALORIES	FIBER
Tam-x-ico's! 100% Whole Wheat	1 tortilla	106	3 g

(continued)

RECOMMENDED PASTAS

BARILLA PLUS	SERVING SIZE	CALORIES	FIBER
All styles: Penne, Rotini, Elbows, Spaghetti, Thin Spaghetti, Angel Hair	2 oz	210	4 g
BIONATURAE	SERVING SIZE	CALORIES	FIBER
All styles are made with 100% whole durum wheat: Spaghettini, Spaghetti, Fettuccine, Gobbetti, Elbows, Rigatoni, Penne, Fusilli, Chicciole	2 oz	190	5 g
DA VINCI	SERVING SIZE	CALORIES	FIBER
Whole Wheat Angel Hair, Whole Wheat Lasagna, Whole Wheat Spaghetti	2 oz	170	5 g
WHOLE WHEAT ELBOWS	SERVING SIZE	CALORIES	FIBER
Whole Wheat Fusilli, Whole Wheat Penne	¾ cup	170	5 g
DE BOLES	SERVING SIZE	CALORIES	FIBER
All styles: Organic Whole Wheat Spaghetti, Organic Whole Wheat Angel Hair, Organic Whole Wheat Fusilli, Organic Whole Wheat Penne, Organic Whole Wheat Rigatoni	2 oz	210	5 g
DE CECCO	SERVING SIZE	CALORIES	FIBER
All styles: Whole Wheat Fusilli, Whole Wheat Linguine, Whole Wheat Penne, Whole Wheat Spaghetti	2 oz	180	7 g
EDEN	SERVING SIZE	CALORIES	FIBER
All styles 100% Whole Grain			
Rye Spirals	½ cup	200	8 g
Kamut Ditalini, Kamut Elbows, Kamut Spaghetti, Kamut Spirals, Kamut Vegetable Spirals	½ cup	210	6 g
Kamut and Buckwheat Rigatoni, Kamut and Quinoa Twisted Pair	½ cup	210	5 g
Spelt Ribbons, Spelt Spaghetti, Spelt Ziti Rigati	½ cup	210	5 g
Spelt and Buckwheat Gemelli	½ cup	210	4 g
Whole Grain Spaghetti	2 oz	210	4 g
HODGSON MILL	SERVING SIZE	CALORIES	FIBER
All styles: Whole Wheat Veggie Radiators, Whole Wheat Veggie Rotini Spirals, Whole Wheat Veggie Wagon Wheels, Whole Wheat Veggie Bows	2 oz	210 (except for Wagon Wheels—190)	6 g
All styles Whole Wheat Whole Grain: Spaghetti, Spirals, Fettuccini, Elbows, Lasagna, Angel Hair, Medium Shells, Penne, Thin Spaghetti, Bow Tie, Radiatores	2 oz	190	6 g
Whole Wheat Spinach Spaghetti	2 oz	190	5 g

HODGSON MILL	SERVING SIZE	CALORIES	FIBER
Whole Wheat Yolkless Pasta Ribbons	2 oz	210	5 g
Whole Wheat Egg Noodles	2 oz	190	4 g
RONZONI HEALTHY HARVEST	SERVING SIZE	CALORIES	FIBER
Whole Wheat Blend—Spaghetti Style, Thin Spaghetti, Linguine, Rotini, Penne, Wide Noodle Style Yolk Free, Extra Wide Noodle Style Yolk Free	2 oz	180	6 g
Whole Wheat Blend—Multigrain Spaghetti	2 oz	190	5 g
WESTBRAE NATURAL	SERVING SIZE	CALORIES	FIBER
Whole Wheat Spaghetti	2 oz	200	9 g
Spinach Lasagna	2 pieces	180	8 g
Spinach Spaghetti	2 oz	180	8 g
Lasagna	2 oz	180	7 g

RECOMMENDED BREAKFAST AND SNACK BARS

All calorie and fiber information is for one bar.

CLIF BARS	CALORIES	FIBER
Nectar Bar—Cherry Pomegranate	150	7 g
Nectar Bar—Cinnamon Pecan	170	6 g
Nectar Bar—Dark Chocolate and Walnut	160	6 g
Nectar Bar—Lemon, Vanilla, and Cashew	160	6 g
KASHI	CALORIES	FIBER
GoLean Original—Malted Chocolate Crisp	290	6 g
GoLean Original—Oatmeal Raisin Cookie	280	6 g
NATURE'S PATH	CALORIES	FIBER
Optimum Energy Bar—Blueberry, Flax, and Soy	200	5 g
Optimum Energy Bar—Zen	200	5 g
Optimum Energy Bar—Orange Chocolate	220	4 g
Optimum Energy Bar—Peanut Butter	230	4 g
Optimum Energy Bar—Pomegran Cherry	230	4 g
Optimum Energy Bar—Rebound	190	4 g
PEAK BAR	CALORIES	FIBER
Breakfast to Go—Blueberry Muffin	170	7 g
Breakfast to Go—Cinnamon Roll	130	6 g

(continued)

RECOMMENDED BREAKFAST AND SNACK BARS (CONT.)

PEAK BAR	CALORIES	FIBER
Breakfast to Go—Oatmeal Raisin	180	6 g
Adult Wellness—Apple Crisp	190	6 g
Adult Wellness—Oatmeal Raisin	180	6 g
Adult Wellness—Chocolate Chip	180	5 g
POWER BAR	**CALORIES**	**FIBER**
Harvest Whole Grain—Dipped Double Chocolate Crisp	250	5 g
Harvest Whole Grain—Dipped Oatmeal Raisin Cookie	250	5 g
Harvest Whole Grain—Dipped Toffee Chocolate Chip	250	5 g
Harvest Whole Grain—Heart Healthy—Chunky Cherry Crunch	240	5 g
Harvest Whole Grain—Heart Healthy—Peanut Butter Chocolate Chip	240	5 g
Harvest Whole Grain—Heart Healthy—Strawberry Crunch	240	5 g
PRIA	**CALORIES**	**FIBER**
Grain Essentials—Chocolate Almond Bliss	170	5 g
Grain Essentials—Country Honey and Oats	170	5 g
Grain Essentials—Orchard Apple Cinnamon Crisp	160	5 g
ROMAN MEAL	**CALORIES**	**FIBER**
100% Whole Grain Snack Bars—Apple Cinnamon	190	5 g
100% Whole Grain Snack Bars—Cranberry Walnut	200	5 g
100% Whole Grain Snack Bars—Oatmeal Raisin	190	5 g

INDEX

Underscored page references indicate boxed text.
Boldfaced page references indicate photographs.

Conversion Chart

These equivalents have been slightly rounded to make measuring easier.

VOLUME MEASUREMENTS

U.S.	Imperial	Metric
¼ tsp	–	1 ml
½ tsp	–	2 ml
1 tsp	–	5 ml
1 Tbsp	–	15 ml
2 Tbsp (1 oz)	1 fl oz	30 ml
¼ cup (2 oz)	2 fl oz	60 ml
⅓ cup (3 oz)	3 fl oz	80 ml
½ cup (4 oz)	4 fl oz	120 ml
⅔ cup (5 oz)	5 fl oz	160 ml
¾ cup (6 oz)	6 fl oz	180 ml
1 cup (8 oz)	8 fl oz	240 ml

WEIGHT MEASUREMENTS

U.S.	Metric
1 oz	30 g
2 oz	60 g
4 oz (¼ lb)	115 g
5 oz (⅓ lb)	145 g
6 oz	170 g
7 oz	200 g
8 oz (½ lb)	230 g
10 oz	285 g
12 oz (¾ lb)	340 g
14 oz	400 g
16 oz (1 lb)	455 g
2.2 lb	1 kg

LENGTH MEASUREMENTS

U.S.	Metric
¼"	0.6 cm
½"	1.25 cm
1"	2.5 cm
2"	5 cm
4"	11 cm
6"	15 cm
8"	20 cm
10"	25 cm
12" (1')	30 cm

PAN SIZES

U.S.	Metric
8" cake pan	20 × 4 cm sandwich or cake tin
9" cake pan	23 × 3.5 cm sandwich or cake tin
11" × 7" baking pan	28 × 18 cm baking tin
13" × 9" baking pan	32.5 × 23 cm baking tin
15" × 10" baking pan	38 × 25.5 cm baking tin (Swiss roll tin)
1½ qt baking dish	1.5 liter baking dish
2 qt baking dish	2 liter baking dish
2 qt rectangular baking dish	30 × 19 cm baking dish
9" pie plate	22 × 4 or 23 × 4 cm pie plate
7" or 8" springform pan	18 or 20 cm springform or loose-bottom cake tin
9" × 5" loaf pan	23 × 13 cm or 2 lb narrow loaf tin or pâté tin

TEMPERATURES

Fahrenheit	Centigrade	Gas
140°	60°	–
160°	70°	–
180°	80°	–
225°	105°	¼
250°	120°	½
275°	135°	1
300°	150°	2
325°	160°	3
350°	180°	4
375°	190°	5
400°	200°	6
425°	220°	7
450°	230°	8
475°	245°	9
500°	260°	–

Lose up to 11 inches of body fat in 32 days!

INTRODUCING
flatbellydiet.com!

Finally, the editors of *Prevention* have developed a science-based diet that directly targets harmful belly fat! Lose up to 15 pounds while you slash your risk of heart disease, stroke, and type 2 diabetes. Here's just a sampling of what you'll get by signing up for the **FLAT BELLY DIET** online.

- **Easy-to-Use Food Logs and Meal Plans**
- **Access to Expert Help**
- **Daily Video Inspiration and Tips**
- **Community Support**

SIGN UP TODAY FOR YOUR 30-DAY RISK-FREE TRIAL AT:

flatbellydiet.com/trial